D0990054

BOOKS BY MAX EASTMAN

ENJOYMENT OF POETRY (*Scribner's*)
CHILD OF THE AMAZONS AND OTHER POEMS (*Kennerley*)
JOURNALISM VERSUS ART (*Knopf*)
UNDERSTANDING GERMANY (*Kennerley*)
COLORS OF LIFE, Poems (*Knopf*)
THE SENSE OF HUMOR (*Scribner's*)
SINCE LENIN DIED (*Liveright*)
LEON TROTSKY, THE PORTRAIT OF A YOUTH (*Greenberg*)
MARX AND LENIN, THE SCIENCE OF REVOLUTION (*A. & C. Boni*)
VENTURE, A Novel (*A. & C. Boni*)
KINDS OF LOVE, Collected Poems (*Scribner's*)
THE LITERARY MIND, ITS PLACE IN AN AGE OF SCIENCE (*Scribner's*)
ARTISTS IN UNIFORM (*Knopf*)
ART AND THE LIFE OF ACTION (*Knopf*)

TRANSLATIONS

GABRIEL, by Alexander Pushkin (*Covici Friede*)
THE REAL SITUATION IN RUSSIA, by Leon Trotsky (*Harcourt Brace & Co.*)
THE HISTORY OF THE RUSSIAN REVOLUTION, by Leon Trotsky (*Simon and Schuster, Inc.*)

EDITED

CAPITAL AND OTHER WRITINGS, by Karl Marx (*Modern Library*)

E. W. Kemble

Spring, Spring, Gentle Spring

Out of sixty students in psychology, thirty-seven reported a feeling of "superiority" to the animals in this picture; twenty-three had no such feeling. How do you feel?

ENJOYMENT OF LAUGHTER

By
Max Eastman

SIMON AND SCHUSTER • NEW YORK

1936

Published by Simon and Schuster, Inc.
386 Fourth Avenue, New York

Fourth Printing

Manufactured in the United States of America

Acknowledgments

The author and publishers of *Enjoyment of Laughter* gratefully acknowledge permission to use material from the following books:

AMERICAN HUMOR, by Constance Rourke, published by Harcourt, Brace and Company, Incorporated

THANK YOU, JEEVES, by P. G. Wodehouse, published by Little Brown and Company

GIVE YOUR HEART TO THE HAWKS, by Robinson Jeffers, published by Random House, Incorporated

THE GREAT APES, by Robert Yerkes, published by the Yale University Press

THE COMPLETE WORKS OF ARTEMUS WARD, published in England by Chatto and Windus, in the United States by Charles Scribner's Sons

DEATH IN THE AFTERNOON, by Ernest Hemingway, published by Charles Scribner's Sons

THE STORY OF A WONDER MAN, by Ring Lardner, published by Charles Scribner's Sons

FIRST AND LAST, by Ring Lardner, published by Charles Scribner's Sons

HUMOR BY VOTE, by Hewitt H. Howland, published by Robert M. McBride and Company

THE ILLITERATE DIGEST, by Will Rogers, published by Albert and Charles Boni, Incorporated

IN ONE EAR, by Frank Sullivan, published by The Viking Press, Incorporated

FAMOUS FIMMALES, by Milt Gross, published by Doubleday, Doran and Company, Incorporated

COBB'S ANATOMY, by Irvin S. Cobb, published by Doubleday, Doran and Company, Incorporated

NONSENSE NOVELS, by Stephen Leacock, published by Dodd, Mead and Company, Incorporated

THOUGHTS WITHOUT WORDS, by Clarence Day, published by Alfred A. Knopf, Incorporated

THE TREASURER'S REPORT, by Robert Benchley, published by Harper and Brothers

IS SEX NECESSARY? by James Thurber and E. B. White, published by Harper and Brothers

MY LIFE AND HARD TIMES, by James Thurber, published by Harper and Brothers

MARK TWAIN: A BIOGRAPHY, by Albert Bigelow Paine, published by Harper and Brothers

MARK TWAIN'S LETTERS, published by Harper and Brothers

MARK TWAIN'S SPEECHES, published by Harper and Brothers

MARK TWAIN'S AUTOBIOGRAPHY, published by Harper and Brothers

LIFE ON THE MISSISSIPPI, by Mark Twain, published by Harper and Brothers

THE LAUGHING MUSE, by Arthur Guiterman, published by Harper and Brothers

WILDWOOD FABLES, by Arthur Guiterman, published by E. P. Dutton and Company, Incorporated

GENTLEMEN PREFER BLONDES, by Anita Loos, published by Liveright Publishing Corporation

THE PRIMROSE PATH, by Ogden Nash, published by Simon and Schuster, Incorporated

WHY I WILL NOT IMITATE FOUR HAWAIIANS, by Joe Cook, published by Simon and Schuster, Incorporated

The author and publishers also gratefully acknowledge permission to use the following pictures:

PETER ARNO—"Oh, redskin!" from *Hullabaloo,* published by Liveright Publishing Corporation
Singer and accompanist from *Hullabaloo,* published by Liveright Publishing Corporation
"*Rhein*beck! It's Grandmamma!" from *For Members Only,* published by Simon and Schuster, Incorporated

WILLIAM STEIG—"Good heavens, Mother! Why make a mystery of things?" from *The Stag at Eve,* published by Farrar and Rinehart

EDWARD WINDSOR KEMBLE—"Spring, Spring, Gentle Spring," from *Life*

RUBE GOLDBERG—The McNaught Syndicate

JAMES THURBER—"Sorry, partner!" from *The New Yorker*
"All right, have it your way—you heard a seal bark!" from *The New Yorker*
"Touché!" from *The New Yorker*
"The Hound and the Hat" from *The New Yorker*

SID L. HYDEMAN—"I am the Kuhn of Kuhn, Loeb and Co.," from *Caught Short* by Eddie Cantor, published by Simon and Schuster, Incorporated

AL FRUEH—"Cross-section of a bee" from *A Gazelle's Ears* by Corey Ford, published by Doubleday, Doran and Company
"Delicatessen" from *The New Yorker*

N. KOHTS—Photographs of a chimpanzee from *The Great Apes,* published by The Century Company

DENYS WORTMAN—"Mopey Dick and The Duke" from *The New York World-Telegram.* Copyrighted by the United Feature Syndicate, Incorporated

PEGGY BACON—Caricatures of Dorothy Parker and Sinclair Lewis from *Off with Their Heads!,* published by Robert M. McBride & Company

THOMAS NAST—"Let Us Prey" from *Harper's Weekly,* published by Harper and Brothers

H. T. WEBSTER—"He finds a nickel in the cup of a pay telephone." from *The Timid Soul* by H. T. Webster, published by Simon and Schuster, Incorporated

O. SOGLOW—Bird and the worm from *The New Yorker*

GEORGE PRICE—"That's right, stupid—drop 'em all over the lot!" from *The New Yorker*

BOARDMAN ROBINSON—Caricature of Sinclair Lewis. The Dial Press

GELETT BURGESS—The Muse of Nonsense from *Burgess' Nonsense Book,* published by Liveright Publishing Corporation

ART YOUNG—The Squad of Strikebreakers from *The Liberator* and *The Best of Art Young,* published by The Vanguard Press

CORNELIA BARNS—"Poppa, do they allow boids to build nests in trees?" from *The Masses*

THOMAS DERRICK—"Truth Comes To Fleet Street" from *Modern Caricaturists,* published by Lovat Dickson Limited

COVARRUBIAS—Caricature of Sinclair Lewis, from *Meaning No Offense,* published by John Day Company, Incorporated

GEORGE SHANK—"Oop—sorry." from *The New Yorker*

GROPPER—"Aw—Shut up! This is a Free Country!" from *The Liberator*
"You're a Liar!" from *The Liberator*
"An' you mean to tell me that that dog ain't got no fleas?" from *The Liberator*
"Look yourself in the face—are you honest?" from *The Liberator*

Contents

INTRODUCTORY

Part I

FUN AND FUNNY

Part II

BABIES AND GROWN-UPS

I.	A JOKE ON MR. CLANCY	7
II.	TWO KINDS OF DISAPPOINTMENT	8
III.	HOW TO ENTERTAIN A BABY	9
IV.	THE HANDICAP OF BEING GROWN-UP	10

Part III

WHY WE LAUGH LIKE HUMAN BEINGS

I.	THE IMPORTANCE OF NOT BEING EARNEST	15
II.	THE GIFT OF BEING TICKLED	18
III.	INFANT LAUGHTER	25
IV.	DO BABIES FEEL DERISIVE?	30
V.	ADULT LAUGHTER	34
VI.	EDDIE CANTOR ON THE AUCTION BLOCK	41

Part IV

VARIETIES OF HUMOROUS EXPERIENCE

I.	WITTY JOKES AND LUDICROUS PERCEPTIONS	49
II.	THE DEFINITION OF WIT	53
III.	THAT NONSENSE MUST BE PLAUSIBLE	62
IV.	FUNNY THINGS AND PEOPLE	67
V.	FUNNY PICTURES	72
VI.	POETIC HUMOR	76
VII.	COMICAL FIGURES OF SPEECH	81
VIII.	TWO KINDS OF COMIC ACTION	90

IX. A NOTE ON COMIC STYLES 95
X. POETIC AND PICTORIAL HUMOR WITH A POINT: CARTOONS 101
XI. THAT RICH JOKES ARE BOTH WITTY AND LUDICROUS 109

Part V
HAVING FUN WITH LANGUAGE

I. ATROCIOUS PUNS 115
II. WITTY PUNS 120
III. POETIC PUNS 126
IV. THE FUN OF DISTORTED WORDS 132
V. THAT BAD GRAMMAR IS GOOD FUN 138

Part VI
LAUGHING AT TOO-MUCH AND NOT-ENOUGH

I. EXAGGERATION 149
II. EXAGGERATION AS A WEAPON: CARICATURE, BURLESQUE AND PARODY 156
III. THE AMERICAN BLEND OF HUMOR—A DIGRESSION 163
IV. UNDERSTATEMENT 179
V. UNDERSTATEMENT AS A WEAPON: IRONY 192
VI. SARCASM AND THE IRONY OF FATE 202

Part VII
THE PREVAILING TOPICS OF LAUGHTER

I. PLAYTHINGS OF THE MOMENT 213
II. MATRIMONY AND OTHER PAINFUL PLEASURES 222
III. SATIRE AND SYMPATHETIC HUMOR 226
IV. DEGREES OF BITING 236
V. SLAPSTICK AND AGGRESSIVE HUMOR 245
VI. RISQUÉ AND RIBALD JOKES: FREUD'S THEORY 248
VII. ABOUT NONSENSE AND ABOUT CHILDREN: FREUD'S THEORY SOME MORE 254
VIII. THAT COMICALITY IS NOT RELEASE: FREUD'S THEORY STILL 260
IX. THE FURTIVE SNICKER AND THE RABELAISIAN LAUGH 266
X. WHY TRUTH IS HUMOROUS 270

Part VIII

HOW TO TELL GOOD JOKES FROM BAD

I. TO DIAGRAM A JOKE 279

II. THE TEN COMMANDMENTS OF THE COMIC ARTS 290

1. Be Interesting 291
2. Be Unimpassioned 294
3. Be Effortless 298
4. Remember the Difference Between Cracking Practical Jokes and Conveying Ludicrous Impressions 303
5. Be Plausible 307
6. Be Sudden 309
7. Be Neat 313
8. Be Right with Your Timing 317
9. Give Good Measure of Serious Satisfaction 319
10. Redeem All Serious Disappointments 323

SUPPLEMENTARY

SOME HUMORISTS ON HUMOR 329

NOTES 345

Introductory

I MUST WARN YOU, reader, that it is not the purpose of this book to make you laugh. As you know, nothing kills the laugh quicker than to explain a joke. I intend to explain all jokes, and the proper and logical outcome will be, not only that you will not laugh now, but that you will never laugh again. So prepare for the descending gloom.

It has seemed to me since school days that all textbooks are wrongly written. All courses of instruction are conducted in a way which ignores the natural operation of the mind. As a result the opinion is universal, and it is under the circumstances a fact, that in order to learn anything you have to study. Since this introduction to humor is probably as near as I shall come to writing a textbook, I want to make it illustrate the manner in which I think textbooks should be written and this unfortunate necessity for study eliminated.

The mind should approach a body of knowledge as the eyes approach an object, seeing it in gross outline first, and then by gradual steps, without losing the outline, discovering the details. A book on American history, for instance—I mean a textbook, for I am not talking about literature, thought, argument, or education in the full sense, but only instruction—should begin by telling in a few sentences the author's conception of the significant form of that history as a whole. America was inhabited by Indians, Europe discovered it, certain phases of development were passed through, and we arrived at the Great Depression—not more than a page. Then should follow a chapter giving the history of America from the Indians to the Depression, and laying in the fundamental explanatory factors, historical, racial, geographical, and economic. Then should follow three or four chapters giving the history of America from the Indians to the Depression, and elaborating these factors. Then should come six or eight chapters giving still further fundamental factors, but some glimpse also of the more subtle elements that developed between the Indians and the Depression. Then should follow eight or ten chapters in which race, economics and geography retire toward the fringe of consciousness, and the web of the story becomes visible—but still the full story from the Indians to the Depression. Then perhaps a book of twelve or fifteen chapters could be written, similar to those we now have, giving the history of America from the Indians to the Great Depression. This book could be read by the pupil, as it would by a well-filled mind, not only without tedium, but with active thought and understanding.

Those who find such a prospect monotonous are not thinking about the joy of learning, but the pleasure of hearing a story told. To one interested in furnishing the mind, the monotonous thing is to drop in one fact after another until it fills up from the bottom like a barrel of potatoes. To fit new items into a growing *pattern of knowledge* is an exciting occupation. Every scholar knows that the main charm of reading lies not in learning something, but in learning more where much is known. Pupils could taste this charm almost from the beginning, if information were presented to the mind in the manner in which the mind will naturally receive it.

Not only does the understanding of a child in its own free growth advance from general ideas to particular investigations, but the mind of the race has so developed. Only the pedagogues have invented this unnatural habit of beginning at the beginning and plodding through to the end. I think it is the main reason why so few even of the lively minded ever enjoy anything they hear in school except the recess bell. In school they are always laboring through new subjects for the first time, or "going over" them in the same old form. It is only the second time, and with new details, that the proper joy of learning begins.

A study and classification of the kinds of humorous experience upon the basis of a theory as to its nature, is a science, however immature and imperfect it may be. It offers a fair chance to illustrate my method of instruction. It is not, to be sure, a vitally important science. For even if I manage to make clear the distinction between a good joke and a bad, a thing no other writer on this subject has attempted, that will not prevent you from making bad jokes nor enable you to make good ones. It will polish up your successes, and I hope forestall some of your most awful perpetrations. But that is about all. No art can be taught to the inartistic, and the playful art the least of all. For this reason, and also because my motive has not been purely pedagogical—I am trying to inculcate pleasure as well as information—I have not pushed too far my view of the manner in which textbooks should be written. I have presented a total view of the science of laughter only six times.

Whether under the influence of the humorists, or because this book is a grown-up lecture, I have found it natural to write largely in the first person, and allude to my own experiences in considerable disregard of the ego taboo. I have also quoted conversations with the great and the near-great in a rather scandalous manner. After I wrote the paragraph on page 90 describing James Thurber's art of humor, it occurred to me that I might learn something by consulting Thurber, who was only a few blocks away, and finding out what he thought about it. I learned so much in a brief conversation, not only about him and his colleagues, but about humor in general as it looks from the inside of the creator's brain, that I decided to confer with other popular humorists and comedians and get the low-down, so to speak, on this art of being funny. I have had a rare good time doing that, and as a result my scientific treatise is peppered with such gossipy interpolations as "Charlie Chaplin tells me," "Groucho Marx maintains," "Walt Disney seems to think" . . . I hope the reader will forgive these sins in view of the light-heartedness of the subject.

Humor at its best is a somewhat fluid and transitory element, but most books about it are illustrated with hardened old jokes from the comic papers, or classic witticisms jerked out of their context and tacked up for inspection like a dried fish on a boathouse door. I have tried to avoid this catastrophe by quoting mainly from contemporary American humor, and quoting at some length. For permission to do this I have to thank the humorists one and all, and also their publishers—or they have to thank me. My book, however, is not an anthology. The selections have been made with a view to illustrating the argument rather than covering the field. If you do not find your favorite humorist here, it is pure luck. I did not happen to be reading in him the right passage at the right moment. Also my book is not criticism. If you do not find your pet aversion properly denounced, that also may be luck. This is a textbook in the science of humor and the art of enjoying it—

a book which I invite you to read without mental concentration and in the laziest and most self-indulgent manner of which you are capable. . . .

In return for which gracious benevolence on my part, you do solemnly swear that, in whatsoever objurgations, execrations, hoots, catcalls and traducements you see fit to disport yourself after reading my book, you will never, in public or in private, in speech or in writing, in fair weather or foul, condemn me as a "repetitious" writer. Repetition from a closer view is the essence of my system of instruction.

Part One

FUN AND FUNNY

PART ONE

Fun and Funny

THE FIRST LAW of humor is that things can be funny only when we are in fun. There may be a serious thought or motive lurking underneath our humor. We may be only "half in fun" and still funny. But when we are not in fun at all, when we are "in dead earnest," humor is the thing that is dead.

The second law is that when we are in fun, a peculiar shift of values takes place. Pleasant things are still pleasant, but disagreeable things, so long as they are not disagreeable enough to "spoil the fun," tend to acquire a pleasant emotional flavor and provoke a laugh.

The third law is that "being in fun" is a condition most natural to childhood, and that children at play reveal the humorous laugh in its simplest and most omnivorous form. To them every untoward, unprepared for, unmanageable, inauspicious, ugly, disgusting, puzzling, startling, deceiving, shaking, blinding, jolting, deafening, banging, bumping, or otherwise shocking and disturbing thing, unless it be calamitous enough to force them out of the mood of play, is enjoyable as funny.

The fourth law is that grown-up people retain in varying degrees this aptitude for being in fun, and thus enjoying unpleasant things as funny. But those not richly endowed with humor manage to feel a very comic feeling only when within, or behind, or beyond, or suggested by, the playfully unpleasant thing, there is a pleasant one. Only then do they laugh uproariously like playing children. And they call this complicated thing or combination of things at which they laugh, a joke.

That is about all there is to the science of humor as seen from a distance. That is Part One of our textbook.

Part Two

BABIES AND GROWN-UPS

PART TWO

Babies and Grown-Ups

I. A Joke on Mr. Clancy

PERHAPS A GOOD WAY to bring you closer to this science will be to tell how I myself approached it.

A long time ago when Woodrow Wilson was running for president the first time, I was invited up to the annual banquet of the Chamber of Commerce of Syracuse, New York. Wilson was the guest of honor, and I for some reason was invited to give "A Humorous Talk." I remember that Mr. Clancy, the president of the Chamber, one of those jolly, generous, big-hearted, big-around presidents of Chambers of Commerce, took me aside before the banquet, and told me that he would pay me a dollar a minute in addition to my regular fee as long as I would keep Wilson laughing. When I got up to speak, I saw Mr. Clancy pull out his watch and set it down significantly on the table. I began my speech by telling Wilson about this little arrangement, and saying that if he didn't enjoy hearing me talk, I was sure he would enjoy watching Mr. Clancy lose money. It occurred to me that the best way to entertain Woodrow Wilson would be to produce an idea. And the idea I produced was one I had jotted down on a slip of paper and stuck away in my desk while in college—namely, that humorous laughter is caused by disappointment. Humor *is*, I said, a kind of disappointment. If you expect to drive a tack in the carpet and drive your thumb in instead, that is funny. You may not be able to see the point, but it is there, and if someone is looking on, he will see it and perhaps hope to show it to you, and if he too is disappointed, that will not make the situation any less intrinsically amusing.

I explained in that speech why so many jokes are jokes *on* somebody—because, human nature being what it is, that is the easiest kind of joke to crack—and how appropriate it is and quite providential to have someone on hand like Mr. Clancy, whom the joke can be on all the time, and moreover keep getting funnier in a mathematical ratio the more it is laughed at. And I took out my own watch once or twice, and asked Mr. Wilson please to allow the joke on Mr. Clancy to grow and flourish for a couple of minutes. I made forty dollars out of that joke on Mr. Clancy, and one or two others which I can not remember.

II. Two Kinds of Disappointment

I do remember that I spoke of Queen Victoria, and of how she was considered the most blue-blooded aristocrat of all the crowned heads of Europe, and the proof of it was that when she wanted to sit down, whenever and wherever it was, she simply sat down, trusting to God and the chivalry of the Court of St. James that there would be a chair between her and the floor by the time she arrived. The old lady was never, so far as history records, disappointed. But it might have been even funnier if she had been.

It would not, however, have been funny to her. And that brought me to the second principle of my science of humor—namely, that not all disappointments are funny. It depends upon how your feelings are involved. Humor arises when your feelings are not seriously involved. Humor is playful disappointment—or it is disappointment arising when your brain and nervous system, and your whole organic being, are in a state of *free play*. . . .

That was the origin of my science of humor. Unfortunately, in that speech I got the two first principles turned around. As you saw in the preceding section, a proper presentation demands that the play principle, or the principle of "being in fun," should come first.

Moreover it was a loose way of speaking to identify humor with "disappointment." That was merely the road by which I got into the subject. When I got in, I soon realized that disappointment is only one form of the *unpleasant* or *disagreeable*. And it is the unpleasant in general which, when taken playfully, is enjoyed as funny.

III. How to Entertain a Baby

It was not only by analyzing jokes that I arrived at this more general definition, but by observing the laughter of a good-natured baby. I am convinced that a majority of the learned philosophers who have written treatises on laughter and the comic never saw a baby. And by seeing a baby I mean having an opportunity to look one over calmly and deliberately and without being afraid that somebody is going to ask you to hold it. The next time you are called upon to entertain a baby, I will tell you what to do. Laugh, and then make a perfectly terrible face. If the baby is old enough to perceive faces, and properly equipped for the calamities of the life that lies before him, he will laugh too. But if you make a perfectly terrible face all of a sudden, without laughing, he is more likely to scream with fright. In order to laugh at a frightful thing he has to be in a mood of play.

If that perceptual effort is beyond him, try a practical joke. Offer him something that he wants a little and will reach out to get, and when he is about to grasp it, jerk it smilingly away. Again he may set up a yell of indignation, or he may emit a rollicking and extreme cackle, a kind of kicking scream, as though at the most ingenious joke ever perpetrated since Adam lost a rib.

Those are the two orthodox ways of entertaining a baby. And they correspond to two of the most famous definitions of the comic ever given. Aristotle defined the comic as "some defect or ugliness which is not painful or destructive," and added: "For example, the comic mask is ugly and distorted, but does not cause pain." In other words, it is *making terrible faces playfully.*

Another famous philosopher, Immanuel Kant, defined the cause of laughter as "The sudden transformation of a strained expectation into nothing"—or in other words, as *reaching after something and finding that it is not there.* Kant did not notice what Aristotle saw, that the feelings involved must not be of grave moment, but only because that is too obvious. Otherwise these philosophers defined the comic exactly as you would after performing those simple domestic experiments I have described. It is a pleasurable emotion accompanied by laughter, and arising in play at the very point where one would feel an unpleasantness if seriously concerned.

These two seemingly so different definitions of the comic are not different. They merely describe the two ways in which things can be unpleasant. They can be unpleasant because they offend our sensibilities (Aristotle), or because they frustrate our impulses (Kant). They can be funny for the same two simple reasons.

IV. The Handicap of Being Grown-up

What complicates the problem of humor, and makes us slow to understand it, is that we are not babies. We are not, at least, young children. We have forgotten how to play. We can not go round making faces at each other and laughing our heads off, and we do not become hilarious upon having a dish passed to us across the table and suddenly yanked back. There is "no point," we think, in such behavior. And by this we mean that there is no serious satisfaction lying behind, or implied by, the playful offense or frustration, which might endorse and justify a dignified and seemly person's laughter. The thing is not a joke, but a mere "foolishness."

All jokes are mere foolishness. All jokes are, in their comic essence, offenses and frustrations. They are mere monkey faces, or mere comings-to-nothing of a hopeful expectation. They often contain other values, but in this and this only lies the cause of comic laughter.

When Groucho Marx says, "I would horsewhip you if I had a horse," that is pretty obviously a mere foolishness. It is the holding out of a meaning and then snatching it away. There is a certain complete, and perhaps almost exquisite, plausibility with which the meaning is held out, and an uncouth suddenness with which it is snatched away, which gives this foolishness an aesthetic value appreciable to those who are expert in laughter. Instead of a mere foolishness, they would perhaps call it a "delightful absurdity." But there is no other redeeming feature. The thing is not witty. It is not, properly speaking, a joke. It is elemental, childish humor.

Somewhere in the same comedy Groucho says: "When I came to this country I hadn't a nickel in my pocket—now I have a nickel in my pocket." That is a "joke." That has "some point," as we say, and may be described as witty. But that too is, or at least contains, a mere foolishness. It contains the holding out of a meaning, and snatching it away. "When I came to this country I hadn't a nickel in my pocket—now I am a millionaire," is the meaning held out, and it is held out as the other was, with plausibility. But here there is something peculiar about the snatching away, something almost sleight of hand, or sleight of mind, about it. Neither words nor logic fail, and yet the expected meaning is not there. Moreover, something else *is* there. That is the "point!" That is what makes it a witty joke and not a mere humorous frustration. Our expectation of a banal boast about this glorious country is brought to nothing with a suddenness like magic, and then, still more like magic, in its very place we find a better thing, or one more suited to the temper of the moment, a cool perception that this country is not much more glorious than any other.

Most grown-up jokes have this twofold character—this character of depriving or offending, and yet in the same stroke indemnifying, us. And that mature regard for serious and real values which makes us demand the indemnification is the very thing which prevents our seeing, or believing, that the comic in its essence *is* the deprivation or offense.

Another fact that clouds this from us is that we often smile or laugh at things which are not comic. We smile at those same serious and real values. A smile, indeed, is our natural expression of welcome to anything we like, and a happy laugh is only a more thoroughgoing smile. It is necessary to distinguish this laugh of positive pleasure from the laugh that greets as comical a playful shock. It is necessary to distinguish them and yet observe that they are closely related. They are so closely related that when the playful shock is combined with a serious satisfaction, the two responses also merge together. The satisfaction wears a comic color. The joke, which is in reality composed of two things, seems but one.

Part Three

WHY WE LAUGH LIKE HUMAN BEINGS

CHAPTER I

The Importance of Not Being Earnest

ALL ATTEMPTS to explain humor have failed, and they all look pretty foolish to hilarious people, because they take humor seriously. They try to explain it, I mean, and show what its value is, as a part of serious life. Humor is play. Humor is being in fun. It has no general value except the values possessed by play.

Our words have more sense about this than we have. *Comic* comes from a Greek word describing a village revel, an all-day annual jamboree, when everybody laid off and climbed down into the street with a view to painting the town red. *Ludicrous* comes from the Latin word for pastime or diversion. *Funny* is fun with a tail to it. Even the word *joke,* if you trace it to its source, has to do with high spirits rather than humor.

Every practicing humorist understands how necessary it is to feel playful. That is his main problem when he sits down to his desk. Every enjoyer of humor knows that the most ridiculous of jokes—even the one about the parrot who laid square eggs *—can fall as flat as a wet pancake if it falls into a solemn, anxious, or impassioned mind. Therefore no definition of humor, no theory of wit, no explanation of comic laughter, will ever stand up, which is not based upon the distinction between *playful* and *serious.*

In social life we all realize how important this distinction is, and how sharp. It was emphasized with a six-shooter by Owen Wister's hero, the Virginian. "When you call me that, *smile!*" he said. And the

* "Can she talk?"
"Not very much—she only says 'Ouch!'"

words became proverbial because they fit human nature so well. It is dreadful to think how many lolling or light-tongued persons may have been dropped into eternity because they failed to put across the fact that they were "only fooling." A more concise, clear-cut, explicit, universally perceived and heeded state of being than that called "only fooling," or "in fun," does not exist.

Perhaps the best way to convince yourself of this is to observe the play of animals—or better still, play with them. When you go into a rough-and-tumble with a young and untrained fighting dog, you rely absolutely upon his sensing and responding to the mood of play. You stake your life upon it. You seize him by the ears or throat, you thrust your hand between his teeth, you fling him this way and that, and backward clear across the sidewalk, and he barks and snarls, intense and seemingly ferocious, crouching for a leap—and yet you have no fear. You do not cry out, "When you bark that way, smile!" or, "Remember now, it is all in fun, we're only fooling!" You know without the smile that he is fooling. You know it by the movement of his tail. It is a fact of nature, not an acquired idea, that he is fooling.

Psychologists, although they have been trying to of late, will never get away from that fact of nature. Play is not merely, as some now think it sophisticated to say, "a name for the activities of children." * Didn't you ever hear a child say, "All right, then I won't play!"? And didn't he know what he was saying? Play is a socio-physiological state or posture of instinctive life. It is not only something that we do, but something that we are while we do it. If the above facts have not proven it, the facts about comic laughter will.

I must add that this is no original or peculiar idea of mine. William McDougall in his *Social Psychology* ** insisted that there is "some special differentiation of the instincts which find expression in playful activity," and I suppose you could get about half of the professors of psychology to agree with him. If you can get half of those pro-

* C. T. W. Patrick, for instance, in the *Pedagogical Seminary,* Vol. XXI, No. 13, p. 469.

** In his more recent *Outline of Psychology,* Professor McDougall seems disposed to retract this statement, although he does not explicitly do so, and he gives a description of play which strongly supports it.

fessors to agree about anything, you have what we call a Fundamental Law of Psychology. So let us stand firm in the opinion that being in fun is a definite thing which can be talked about in science just as it can and must in everyday life.

CHAPTER II

The Gift of Being Tickled

A FACULTY for being in fun, for doing things energetically and intensely, and yet not seriously, is of obvious importance to young animals. Its importance is particularly obvious in the matter of fighting. In play fighting they learn without danger to use all the muscles they will later use in real fighting. They learn to defend the same vital points. And they defend these points as violently as though they were in earnest largely because they are ticklish. Did you ever notice that you will fight off being tickled just as hard as though tickling were a terrible pain? And yet when all your frantic efforts fail and you are tickled, you find that it is not a pain at all, but a funny feeling. To be tickled is comical, and makes you laugh. And anyone who pretends to explain humor must begin by explaining that elementary "gag."

There are two peculiar things about that gag. One is that it is not funny at all unless you are "in the mood for it." The other is that when not funny, it is unpleasant. It is unpleasant to be tickled by a stranger, and it is unpleasant to be tickled by a friend when you are "feeling serious." It vexes you, and if continued makes you mad.*

This shift of feeling-quality is often abrupt and automatic as an eyewink. It has been remarked by every grown-up person who ever discussed tickling, and it has recently been testified to by fifteen babies. These babies were introduced into a laboratory in Yale University with a view to finding out what makes them laugh and smile.

* In sexual passion tickling is sometimes seriously pleasant, but when the passion is satisfied it becomes again vexatious to the point of acute pain. A problem here whose solution may some day throw light upon ours.

It was found that their mothers could tickle them into laughter fifteen times as often as a stranger could. And it was found that when they did not laugh or smile on being tickled, they gave a "negative reaction"—which means "withdrawing, whining, 'fussing' or crying." The same tickle that made one laugh, made another so grumpy that his mother laughed.*

As these babies were all under one year of age, it appears that the question whether you can "take a joke" or not, and from whom, is an elementary one. The babies could take the joke from their mothers, you would say, but not from a stranger. And yet upon reflection it is fantastic to attribute such elaborate ideas as "mother" and "stranger" to a baby under one year. Put yourself in the baby's place—with a little practice this can be accomplished—and consider what your perceptions are. They lack the meaningful elaboration of ours, but they must be all the more succinctly marked with *pro* or *con,* pleasant or unpleasant, acceptance or rejection. If something unfamiliar suddenly crawls over your skin, rejection will be about all there is of you. You will be a little bundle of withdrawing, whining, fussing and crying. If, however, the touch is not unfamiliar, and if by a process of "social stimulation"—which is the scientific name for saying "peekaboo," and making "choo-choo" noises through the teeth—you have been brought into the mood for it, this identical crawling sensation will make you laugh and crow. Until some grown-up succeeds actually in getting into the skin of a baby, I do not know any better way to describe this fact than to say that a tickle as an object of serious concern is disagreeable, but a tickle taken in a state of nascent social play is laughingly enjoyed.

Unfortunately these experiments were not conducted with a view to testing any particular theory of laughter. The experimenter had no guiding idea. Just of their own accord the babies testified to the two essentials of my theory—the importance of not being earnest, and the close connection between funny and disagreeable.

Turn back now to Owen Wister's story, and see how much the Virginian resembles those babies in his behavior. If a strange voice

* *A Study of the Smiling and Laughing of Infants in the First Year of Life,* by R. W. Washburn. (Genetic Psychology Monographs, No. VI.)

suddenly calls the Virginian a son-of-a-bitch in earnest, you might as well pull down the blinds and send for the undertaker. But if the voice is not a strange one, and the shock is led up to with a proper kind of social stimulation—it is not necessary to say "peekaboo," but something equally explicit is strongly recommended—the Virginian will take that shock with a chuckle and the game go on. He will, in fact, if you do it skillfully and your luck is good, be "tickled" by it.

There is no fundamental difference between this mental tickle and that physical tickle which helps a baby to enjoy being rolled and kneaded by his mother, and which enables a dog to play-fight intensely without fighting. The physical tickle is a specialized reaction to a particular kind of stimulus, a nervous apparatus like a toy designed especially for play. The mental tickle is like an accessory mechanism which can be attached to our activities in general, ungearing them from life's drivewheels and deep organic passions, so that we are able to employ our whole being playfully. They both

George Price

"That's right, stupid—drop 'em all over the lot!"

depend upon the same conditions, however, and obey the same two laws. All comic experiences obey these laws—seen by us at a distance, you remember, in Part One.

First: It is necessary to be, or become, playful in order to perceive anything whatever as funny.

Second: In everything that we do perceive as funny there is an element which, if we were serious and sufficiently sensitive, and *sufficiently concerned,* would be unpleasant.

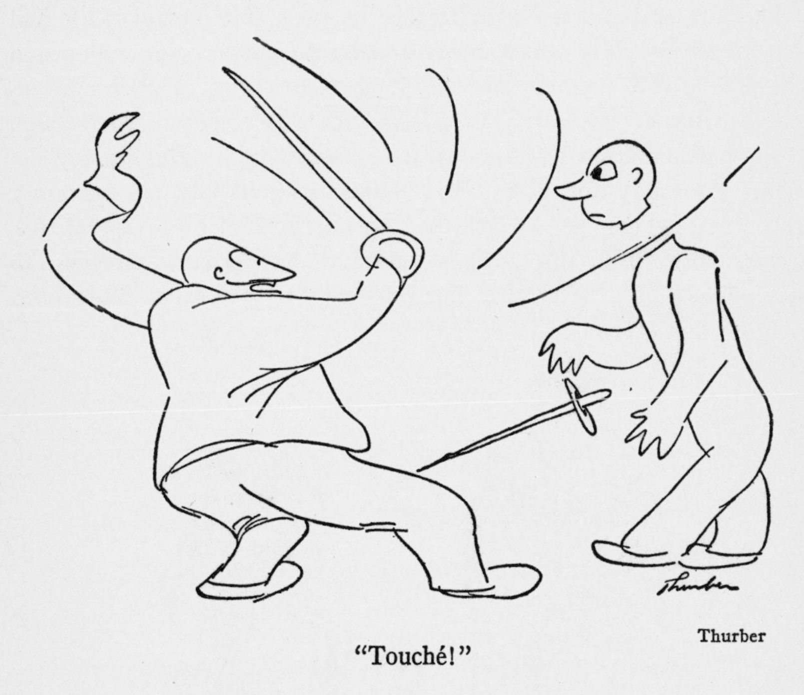

Thurber

"Touché!"

These laws are absolute, and anybody who can disprove them may throw my book out of the window forthwith. Furthermore, in every unpleasantness there is an element which, if we *were* playful, and *not* sensitive, or *not concerned,* might be funny. That also is absolute, and my science stands or falls with its truth.

Mark Twain will show you how easy it is, when you are not concerned—nor he either, any longer—to jump from horrible to funny. Speaking of the lastingness in memory of "repulsive things," he writes:

> I remember yet how I ran off from school once when I was a boy, and then, pretty late at night, concluded to climb into the window of my father's office and sleep on a lounge, because I had a delicacy about going home and getting thrashed. As I lay on the lounge and my eyes grew accustomed to the darkness, I fancied I could see a long, dusky, shapeless thing stretched upon the floor. A cold shiver went through me. I turned my face to the wall. That did not answer. I was afraid that the thing would creep over and seize me in the dark. I turned back and stared at it for minutes and minutes—they seemed hours. It appeared to me that the lagging moonlight never, never would get to it. I turned to the wall and counted twenty, to pass the feverish time away. I looked—the pale square was nearer. I turned again and counted fifty—it was almost touching it. With desperate will I turned again and counted one hundred, and faced about, all in a tremble. A white human hand lay in the moonlight! Such an awful sinking at the heart—such a sudden gasp for breath. I felt—I cannot tell *what* I felt. When I recovered strength enough, I faced the wall again. But no boy could have remained so, with that mysterious hand behind him. I counted again, and looked—the most of a naked arm was exposed. I put my hands over my eyes and counted until I could stand it no longer, and then—the pallid face of a man was there, with the corners of the mouth drawn down, and the eyes fixed and glassy in death! I raised to a sitting posture and glowered on the corpse till the light crept down the bare breast,—line by line—inch by inch—past the nipple,—and then it disclosed a ghastly stab!
>
> I went away from there. I do not say that I went away in any sort of a hurry, but I simply went—that is sufficient. I went out at the window, and I carried the sash along with me. I did not need the sash, but it was handier to take it than it was to leave it, and so I took it . . .

We are too familiar with the heart of humor, and with Mark Twain's genius, to realize what a change takes place between those paragraphs. In the first we have the "creeps" in no diluted form; in the second we are in a bath of unalloyed and laughing mirth. It is not that we have withdrawn from the story, or that Mark Twain has. We are still participating in the boy's terror; his terror is the center and circumference of our experience. But we are not taking it seriously any longer. It has *become* funny.

An endless amount of scaffolding can be, and has been, and will be, erected around this central fact by lugubrious philosophers with their "theories of laughter," which are apologies for laughter and attempts to excuse it by giving it the name of some other act or state of feeling. But the central fact will remain and in the end, I think, be recognized: A painful memory can become a funny memory as directly as an unpleasant tickle becomes comical when we adopt the attitude of play.

In the present state of science there is no explaining *how* this feeling-shift is accomplished in our brains and nerves. In that direction our own science must throw up its hands. We have not "explained comic laughter," and we can not. We have only, as some careful critic will no doubt remark, observed that comic laughter is playful, and then left play to be explained. But that, if the critic will forgive our answering before he speaks, is the very evidence of our good sense. That is the way a scientific understanding in this region will develop —by identifying the subject matter and defining the problem in the terms of our existing speech and knowledge, not by pretending to solve it with some vague mechanics or hydraulics of the brain especially imagined for this purpose.*

We have not the means to understand the physiology of comic

* I refer to theories like that of Herbert Spencer with his idea that laughter occurs only when our nervous energy is prepared to perceive a big thing, and a little one follows; the "psychic damming" theory which the Austrian psychologist Lipps built upon Spencer's foundation; and Freud's idea, derived from Lipps, that comic pleasure is due to an "economy of psychic expenditure." It may be that all pleasure is due to something describable as economy of psychic expenditure. It may be that playfulness, and thus also comic laughter, will ultimately be understood in terms of nervous energy. Until it is so actually understood, and that on a basis of real physiology, the sole reason for inventing these legendary systems for the special benefit of laughter, is that the comic pleasure occurs when to a serious mind pain seems the natural thing to expect. If instead of inventing the legends, psychologists had spent a little time examining this fact, and defining its varieties, they would never have believed that all jokes are "descending incongruities" or cases of little-following-big, or of less energy being employed than had been prepared—it is the easiest thing in the world to disprove—and we should have been spared all the trouble of their wholly speculative mechanics. In short, in insisting that the concept of playfulness or being-in-fun is, in the present state of brain physiology, ultimate, and thus not pretending to know more than I do about comic laughter, although I may not seem very wonderfully ingenious, I believe I am, from the standpoint of scientific method, right.

Of Dr. George W. Crile and his idea of laughter as a substitute for motor activity, and Mr. J. C. Gregory, who has tried to replace my concept of playfulness with the concept of "relief," I have said something in a note on pages 346-50.

laughter, but we can understand the biology of it. We can see *why* creatures who need play in order to develop, should need this inward shock absorber to prevent play from becoming at every tiny balk or bump a serious engagement. Laughter is a protection, so to speak, that children put on when they go out for exercise. Moreover, laughter is itself, as Dr. Walsh has recently made clear, an exercise or jouncing and massaging of the vital organs, a very stirring of the dough of which a man is made.* The elementary usefulness to life of such an apparatus is apparent. Insofar as showing the survival value of an hereditary trait may be said to explain it, the funny feeling and the laugh at playful tickling, and at playful shocks, are thus abundantly explained. Their primary function is to make play just like a serious life, except with added inward exercise, and yet keep it gay, harmless and superficial.

* *Laughter and Health,* by J. J. Walsh. His thesis should not be confused with the adage: "Laugh and grow fat." The answer to that is given by Dr. Joslin in a book on the *Treatment of Diabetes Mellitus:* "Grow thin and laugh longer."

CHAPTER III

Infant Laughter

I ONCE EXPLAINED my theory of humor to a ladies' afternoon society in Fort Worth, Texas, and when I finished the lecture, which seemed to me a very successful and indeed quite a delightful one, a stern and superior young woman with a highly intellectual light in her glasses came up and announced that she would be kind enough to drive me down to my train—which she did, and was further kind enough to say when we shook hands at the station: "Now remember, we want you to come back to Fort Worth again some day *just the same!*"

I leaned back on the air behind me for support.

"You must not mind the fact," she went on, "that nobody in that audience understood a thing you were talking about. I, of course, have studied philosophy and psychology and I enjoyed your lecture very much!"

It was some time before I was in a condition to take that shock playfully, and I am still somewhat tossed back and forth between the humor and the pathos of it. Whatever may have been my sins in the lecture, I can not see why an inkling of "philosophy and psychology" should be necessary to convince any inquiring mind of the objective identity of the funny and the unpleasant. What are most jokes about, and what have they been about through the ages? Mothers-in-law, unpaid bills, drunks, taxes, tramps, corpses, excretory functions, politicians, vermin, bad taste, bad breaks, sexual ineptitudes, pomp, egotism, stinginess and stupidity! If there is any good reason why the *unpleasantness* of all these things has not been observed, and an understanding of the subject swiftly arrived at, it is the very fact I insist on—that our sense of humor is instinctive. These unpleasant things are converted into sources of comic emotion, not by a process of reflection, but by a neural mechanism, so that when they arrive in our playful minds they are already pleasant.

Another way to prove this without too much "psychology" is to push a funny thing into the face of some humorless person, and see what he says. What did John Bright, the great and earnest reformer, say about Artemus Ward's lecture on the Mormons: "Its information was meager and presented in a desultory, disconnected manner." Perfectly true! And perfectly typical of the remarks of humorless people about funny things since time began.

The situation is brought home in another way by Ernest Hemingway in his celebration of the joys of bullfighting, or bullfight-watching. Speaking of the disemboweling of the horses, its most unpleasant feature to those who are unable to accept it in the mood of play, he says:

> "There is certainly nothing comic by our standards in seeing an animal emptied of its visceral content, but if this animal instead of doing something tragic, that is, dignified, gallops in a stiff old-maidish fashion around a ring trailing the opposite of clouds of glory it is as comic when what it is trailing is real as when the Fratellinis give a burlesque of it in which the viscera are represented by rolls of bandages, sausages and other things. If one is comic the other is; the humor comes from the same principle. I have seen it, people running, horse emptying, one dignity after another being destroyed in the spattering, and trailing of its innermost values, in a complete burlesque of tragedy. I have seen these, call them disembowelings, that is the worst word, when, due to their timing, they were very funny."

It is quite true that the humor, if it comes at all, "comes from the same principle" when a horse is really disemboweled, and when the Fratellini clowns pretend or "play" he is. But it is not true that "if one is comic the other is." That depends upon whether the beholder is so constituted, or has been so conditioned, as to be able to make a plaything of a horse's real destruction. In both cases the humor is a quality of emotion, and but for that emotion our feeling in both cases, abnormalities aside, would be one of aversion. It is obviously easier, however, for a sympathetic person with no training to the contrary to take the thing playfully, and thus enjoy the humorous emotion, when the horse's bowels are not bloody and no real agony is involved.

Here again play, or playfulness, is the key to the whole problem. Humor is a unique quality of feeling. It belongs with anger, fear, hunger, lust, among the irreducible elements of our affective life. Like them, it is the inner feeling of a specialized bodily response to special situations. These are, however, situations in which our deep life-interests are not engaged. They are play situations. And since play, or this disengaged functioning of our natures, has its special place of usefulness in infancy and early childhood, it is there that we find this response in its simplest and most uncritical form. That is why I mentioned Hemingway on bullfights. That is why I keep coming back to babies.

And I must now come back to those fifteen babies in the Yale laboratory who were experimented upon with the express purpose of finding out what made them laugh. Miss Ruth Washburn, who conducted the experiments, seems to think—and I come within one of agreeing with her—that those Yale babies contributed more to the understanding of laughter, or at least the not misunderstanding of it, than all the "philosophers, psychologists, anthropologists, physicians, physiologists, physiognomists and neurologists," not to mention the despised "writers of the purely literary type," who have ever tackled the subject. All the old theories, she says, "when one tries to explain the smiles and laughter of young infants by means of them . . . break down." I do not mean to say that she is boastful of her own results. She seems, as a conscientious investigator, rather proud of the slimness of them. But she is aware of the fact that in ignoring infants and young children, the philosophers and physiognomists and despised littérateurs alike have neglected laughter not only at its source, but at the place where it flourishes most luxuriantly. Hers is the first careful study of laughter, so to speak, on the home ground; and her conclusion that none of the classical theories has application here is indeed momentous.

There is one theory, however, if I may be so presumptuous as to remind her of it, which, far from breaking down, is supported by the very slimness of her conclusions. It is the one which describes laughter in general as an expression of pleasure, primarily social, and comic laughter as a specific adaptation to playful shocks and frustrations, having a quality of feeling of its own. There was nothing else observable in those infants which could conceivably be identified as the germ of a sense of humor, nothing absolutely, but the fact that, besides smiling and laughing in welcome to a satisfaction, they smiled and laughed—provided a certain mood was induced, which until further analysis can only be described as playful—in such events as bumps, falls, frights, puzzles, tickles, disappointments, etc., which *would be* dissatisfactions but for that mood.

Dr. C. W. Kimmins, one other laugh-doctor who has been at pains to study children, corroborates this view.* "In learning to walk," he says, "the child appears to delight in mishaps, such as sitting down with a thud during an interval of standing, as it gives rise to uproarious merriment." "The jack-in-the-box," he adds, "with its element of surprise, sometimes at the beginning with a slight sense of *fear*—so soon dissipated—is the starting point for a whole series of mirth-provoking games. . . ." "Bumps, if laughed with," "sounds ending in jolt," "kitten (with fear signs also)," "creeping toward object and being pulled back," are among the causes of laughter cited by Mrs. Shinn in her famous *Biography of a Baby.* Every parent can verify these instances and multiply them. It is only necessary to imagine a completely serious child—or produce one if you can—and inquire what satisfaction he may find in falling down when trying to stand up, being pulled back when creeping toward an object, getting "jolted" when trying to enjoy a nice noise, or being slightly frightened or bewildered by a kitten or a jack-in-the-box, in order to see what the comic

* *The Springs of Laughter,* 1928.

instinct in all infants is.* It is an enlargement of their appetite for punishment when in the mood of play.

* The word instinct is somewhat out of favor among psychologists just now, but I think this is largely a matter of fashion. It is due, at least, to what physiologists do not know rather than to anything they know. Physiologically it is hard to find any difference between anger and fear, but a psychologist who can not discuss the difference between anger and fear seems to me about as brilliant as a zoologist who can not tell a cow from a hedgehog. The distinction is real, and of vital concern to everybody, and if physiology can not define it, the solution is to improve physiology, not to deny the identity of anger and fear. (For those technically interested in this question, "Instinct as an Explanatory Concept," by Lester S. King, M.D., *Journal of Abnormal and Social Psychology,* July–September 1934, is well worth reading.)

CHAPTER IV

Do Babies Feel Derisive?

A SPECIAL VIRTUE of this nursery approach to laughter is that it enables us to usher out of our textbook at the very beginning, and with gentle firmness, those unplayful and unobservant philosophers who insist that comic feeling is a feeling of superiority to someone who gets fooled, that all jokes are jokes on somebody, that there is "hostility," to quote Bergson, "in all laughter."* I suspect them not only of never having seen a baby, but of never having been one. Such an experience, if they could have it, or remember it, would suffice to convince them, not only of the error, but of the absolute irrelevance of what they say. Jean Piaget, who has studied children more patiently than any other psychologist, declares that "the whole content of the infant's consciousness is projected into reality (both into

* Bergson asserts that laughter is purely intellectual, that the slightest gleam of feeling kills it, that we never laugh at things, and never even at animals unless they remind us of people. And he asserts that we laugh at people only when they behave like things—when they behave mechanically, that is, and without the flexibility that implies "soul" or intelligence. The function of this highly discriminating laughter of Bergson's is to aid in the process of Creative Evolution by making life uncomfortable for clods (*Laughter, An Essay on the Meaning of the Comic,* by Henri Bergson, 1911).

Laughter can and does, of course, perform this function, and we shall see how well. But that this is not its primary function, and is not what laughter *is,* would be clear to Bergson if he would spend five minutes in contemplation of a laughing baby.

How much personal temperament finds expression in theories of laughter may be seen in the fact that while Bergson makes "hostility" the keynote, J. Y. T. Gregg (*The Psychology of Laughter and the Comic,* 1923) derives all laughter from "the instinct of love."

things and into others) which amounts to a complete absence of the consciousness of self." The child, he says, "confuses his self with the universe," and even when suffering a localized bodily pain, "still regards it as common to all," and "can not spontaneously realize that he alone is able to feel the pain." To impute attitudes of derision, or ridicule, or "superiority over others," to a being in this blissful state of egocentricity, would be fantastic. One need only remark that babies laugh, remembering what babies are, and the derision theory becomes itself a topic for derision. Babies laugh not *at*, but *in* a funny situation.

Every parent knows what Dr. Kimmins says, that a baby who sits down with a bump in the midst of an effort to stand up is apt to find this experience uproariously funny. Every nurse will recognize the joke which Miss Washburn says was most uniformly successful in eliciting laughter from her fifteen babies—"swinging the subject out as if to throw him to his mother and then rapidly withdrawing him again." That joke we have all enjoyed either coming or going. And is it not quite obviously "on" the baby? It is the baby who gets fooled, and it is for the baby's pleasure that the joke is perpetrated.

It begins to be clear, I hope, what I mean by saying that all theories of humor have failed because they took it seriously. The concept of play, of playfulness, is the sole ground of understanding here. It is not the disappointment of *somebody else* that causes comic laughter; it is disappointment *taken as a joke,* and that means taken playfully.

The reason why, when we are a little grown-up and have begun to be conscious of "selves," so many jokes turn out to be jokes on somebody else, is that it is easier to take other people's disappointments playfully than our own. If you catch your toe in the hall carpet when planning to make a gracious entry into a drawing room full of distinguished guests, and slide in on your belly like a man clambering up a surf board, it is not easy for you to take that disappointment playfully. For one thing, you are in too big a hurry to get up. I don't know why it is we are in such a hurry to get up when we fall down. You might think we would lie there and rest a while. We seem to have some inferiority complex about this whole business of standing on our hind legs. We think it is a serious matter. But all the rest of the human race, as many at least as are maintaining in our vicinity the accredited position, will find it very easy indeed to take our disappointment playfully. That is why they laugh when we fall down. That is why they laugh a comic laugh, I mean, and feel a comic feeling.

There may be mingled with that feeling, and lurking underneath the laugh, a feeling of triumphant glee in our discomfiture. That gleeful feeling, being hard and happy, may be more *like* comic pleasure than a melting mood. But pangs of sympathy may also mingle with a comic pleasure, and tears of pity fill the laughing eyes. The comic feeling is distinct from pity; it is equally distinct from joy. It is born in us before the consciousness of self is born, and before any possibility of crowing over so complicated a conception as "another person" could by any stretch of the probabilities be imagined to exist.

The critics of my theory of humor, those at least who defend against it the derision theory, have imputed to me a soft and dawnlike conception of human nature, and even a determination to make the science of laughter a source of still further irradiations of sweetness and light. The facts are opposite to that. I am soft enough myself, and for that very reason have a stony conception of human nature. Men seem to me, by comparison with my pacific and too easy-melting character, mere thugs and Torquemadas for the most part. And as even I in my state of liquescence am almost entirely selfish and egotistical, I am prepared to subscribe to and lie down under any harsh epitaph that may be devised for the tomb of the human race. Humorous laughter is not, unfortunately, the human race, but only a single function of it. What my critics fail to realize is that if they are going to identify humorous laughter with egotistical cruelty, they must prove that there is *more* egotism and *more* cruelty in humorous laughter than in the general behavior of man, and that I confidently challenge them to prove.*

* The derision theory, as recently expounded and decorated by Mr. A. M. Ludovici, rests wholly on the sentimental notion that "the animals" are ferocious as compared to man. Man's laughter, Mr. Ludovici tells us, is a "spiritualized" manifestation of the crude snarl, or "showing of teeth," with which "the animals" express their feelings of superiority and hostility. The fact is that man is among the bloodiest of the carnivores, and as Mark Twain truly said: "Of the entire brood he is the only one—the solitary one—that possesses malice . . . He is the only creature that inflicts pain for sport, knowing it to *be* pain." Moreover man, besides laughing, snarls and shows his teeth with all but the best of them. And he has invented the further accomplishments of thumbing his nose, sticking out

The mechanism of comic laughter may never be explained, but it will certainly not be explained by giving it the name of some other act or state of feeling. That is not scientific explanation, but literary hocus-pocus. All of us, I suppose, have experienced at some time in our lives a feeling of superiority or "sudden glory." Few certainly have never felt a pleasure in the debasement of others. It takes but a moment of honest recollection to establish the difference between these feelings and the feeling that something which has happened is funny.

---

his tongue, and "showing kukish"—any Russian will tell you how to do it—not to mention cursing, execration and obscene abuse extending to the mother, as supplementary ways of manifesting those feelings of superiority and hostility which he does indeed share, and share abundantly, with the other carnivores. As to the herbivores, they are so much more gentle and charming that I think we had better leave them out of the picture altogether. A cow has a hard time showing her teeth even to the dentist. Mr. Nesbitt, the African explorer, tells us "there is something lovable about the hippopotamus, as about all vegetarian animals," and I can well believe him. The simple truth is that Mr. Ludovici's alleged "biology" is myth, and has about as much to do with the real attributes of man and animals as Mother Goose. (A further note on Mr. Ludovici's book, *The Secret of Laughter*, and on the advocates of the derision theory, will be found on pages 350-53.)

CHAPTER V

Adult Laughter

I HAVE TALKED a good deal about animals and babies so far, because I want to establish a basis for the art of humor in our biological inheritance. Man has been defined as the laughing animal, but that is not strictly accurate. Dogs laugh, but they laugh with their tails. And a tail is an awkward thing to laugh with, as you can see by the way they bend themselves half double in extreme hilarity trying to get that rear-end exuberance forward into the main scene of action. What puts man on a higher stage of evolution is that he has got his laugh on the right end.

As to whether any of the apes laugh and smile as we do, there remains a question. In Mrs. Kohts' pictures of a chimpanzee, reproduced herewith, the one entitled "laughter" is more convincing to my emotions than any of the rest. There is, however, a touch of the Irish about it that may explain that. Robert M. Yerkes, in his classic work on *The Great Apes,* sums up the views of science, so far as concerns the orang-outan, thus:

> Although smiles and laughter are mentioned by several observers of orang-outan behavior, no one has critically discussed the legitimacy of the terms. If they imply a sense of humor one might hesitate to apply them. Yet the abundant evidence of tricks, jokes, and intent to surprise, tease, or otherwise disconcert their ape or human companions would suggest even humor. Possibly it would be as much like quibbling to object to the use of the term laughter as of feeling. Probably most open-minded observers would unhesitatingly say either: I believe that the animals smile or

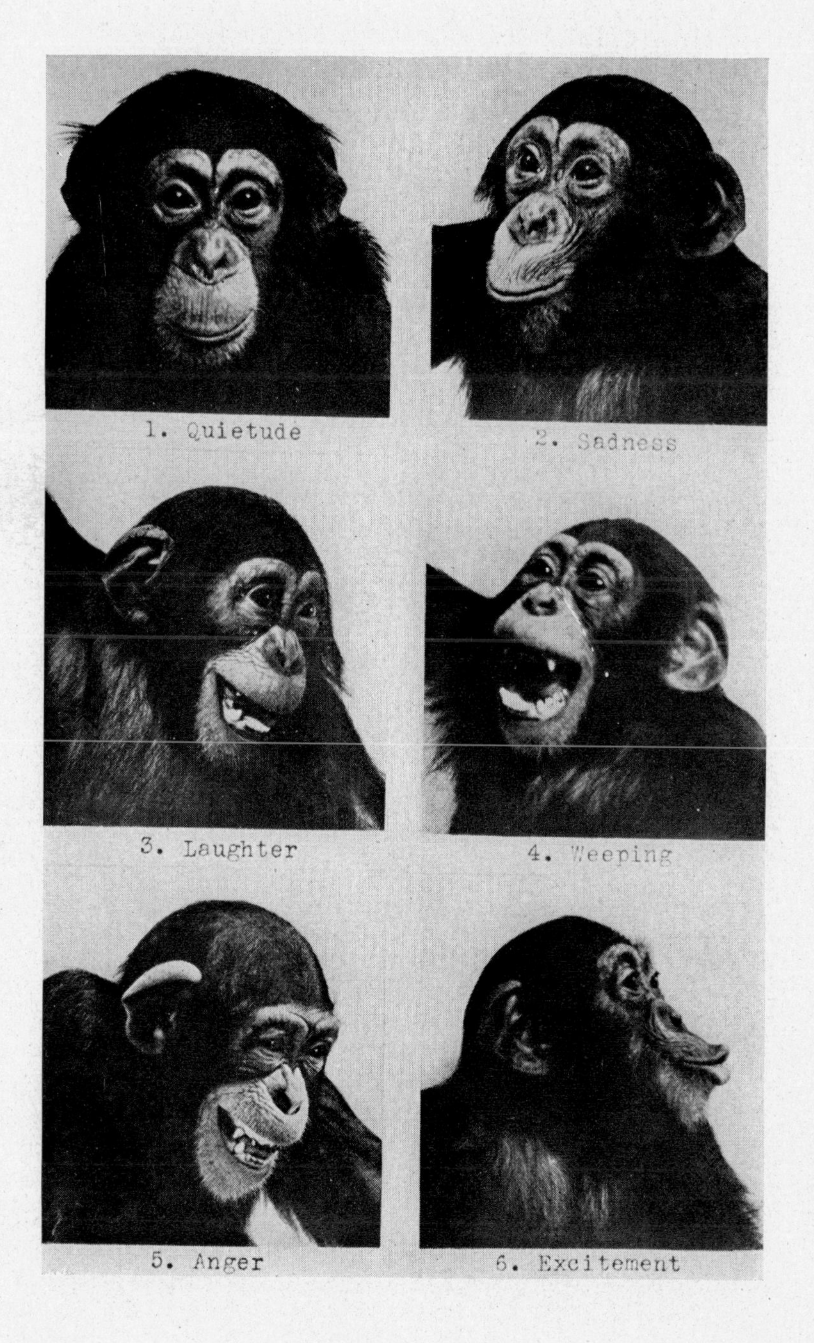

1. Quietude

2. Sadness

3. Laughter

4. Weeping

5. Anger

6. Excitement

Peter Arno

"Oh, redskin!"

> laugh because I have seen them do so, or, I do not believe it because I have not seen it.

He quotes Alexander Sokolovsky's observations of a young gorilla:

> He showed an unmistakable tendency towards humor, since he would gladly make harmless jokes. On such occasions the open mouth and drawn lips gave the appearance of laughter.

If I may intrude with an amateur opinion here, in the absence of any expert one, it seems more certain to me that apes have a rudimentary sense of humor, than that they express it with facial laughter.* If they devise tricks, and surprise and tease each other in fun, they probably find some specialized pleasure in the collapse of a pattern of action or emotional perception. They must be as egocentric as rather young children, and are probably amusing *themselves* with *their* world in these exploits far more than we assume when we watch them. Moreover, even if you attribute to them an explicit self-and-other teasing motive, the thing that needs explaining is not the pleasure of the teaser—that can be understood on grounds of serious feeling—but the fact that the teasee takes it often in good part. He has at least enough feeling for a playful trick to understand that he has been

* William McDougall in accepting—rather grudgingly, it seems to me—my suggestion that comic laughter belongs in his list of emotional instincts, remarks: "Man is the only animal that laughs. And if laughter may properly be called an instinctive reaction, the instinct of laughter is the only one peculiar to the human species." This, as we see above, is an extreme, or at least a premature, statement, even if one insist that in animals the instinct express itself exactly as in us. I must, however, seriously draw Professor McDougall's attention to the movements of a dog's tail. No social psychologist can afford to ignore them. See him lying with his muzzle flat on the floor looking up at you; he catches your eye, and one thump of his tail attests it. That is the smile of friendly recognition, mainly a wrinkling of the eyes with us. You whisper "Hello there," and three thumps are your answer. That is a whole smile. Then you speak his name, and he leaps to his feet with his tail wagging steadily. That is the laughter of social joy. Seize him and tickle him and buffet him about, and that tail-wagging grows so violent that his whole body wiggles, and literally the tail seems to wag the dog. It is a highly instructive process, and incidentally a persuasive answer to McDougall's contention that a smile is sharply different from a laugh.

teased and not attacked. It is the ability to take a joke, not make one, that proves you have a sense of humor.

Another amateur opinion of mine is that bears and seals are not without a comic sense. Seals seem to me the most playful of all animals. They are the only ones at the circus, besides a few dogs, who do all their tricks not only without reluctance, but with impetuous delight.

A strange thing, and significant of the literary mores prevailing in this science, is that while comparative psychologists are disposed to attribute "jokes" and "humor" to the great apes, a man like Sigmund Freud comes out with the announcement that even the human child "lacks all feeling for the comic." * Freud, to be sure, adduces no facts to prove this stark assertion. It is an inference from his theory that the comic is all a matter of release from adult inhibitions.

I asked Walt Disney what he thought of Freud's dictum—he seemed an appropriate commentator—and he said:

"I don't see how that can be. My daughter not only laughs when I do funny things, but does funny things to make me laugh—imitates dogs and owls and everything. She's good too. She does make me laugh."

"How old is she?" I asked.

"Just barely two."

It seemed to me a far more "scientific" approach to the problem than that of the great psychologist. Everybody who has gone to the circus knows that the clowns play up mainly to the children. Many of their rigs and antics are too crude to seem very funny to an experienced adult. Margaret Floy Washburn, one of our leading empirical psychologists, reports that in some experiments conducted by her and M. A. Walker "the intensity of the reaction to the comic . . . [was] greatest in the fourth grade children, less in the seventh grade children, and least in adults." ** And I think almost anybody who observes children without feeling the need to prove a theory, would be inclined to generalize that result. The comic sense in children is more quick and

* Freud also denies "wit" and "humor" to children; his opinion is as sweeping as it sounds.

** *American Journal of Psychology,* 1919, Vol. 30, pp. 304-7.

active than in us, and less discriminating. It is performing its elementary biological function, and is therefore loaded, primed and cocked, and will go off at the drop of a hat or a feather.* Romping children laugh, and laugh beyond all bounds, at any silly monkey face, or little empty jerk or gesture, peep or squeak, that lets on to be something and turns out to be nothing at all. They laugh at nothing. And that, remember, is what we say when we reprove them. We say: "Oh, don't laugh at nothing!"—forgetting the pious and mature philosopher, Immanuel Kant, who maintained that nothing is what we all laugh at, "the sudden transformation of a strained expectation into nothing."

Kant was right too. We do laugh often, adults as well as children, at a mere nothing dexterously presented. We shall see the proof of this. But it is also true that the more sedate and serious adults, including most of those who become philosophers of the comic, have a certain reluctance about laughing at nothing. It is not only that they are inhibited by the ideal of rationality, as Freud thinks. Their nature too is somewhat changed. That mad genius for play, that romping and gamboling and shaking-up of our viscera until they ache, which is needful to our sturdy growth, is no longer needed when we are grown. That is why Balzac could say: "As children only do we laugh, and as we travel onward laughter sinks down and dies out like the light of the oil-lit lamp." It dies down with many people to such a degree that they rarely laugh at all at a mere nothing, or a mere monkey face, unless it is reinforced and sanctioned by some meaning, or some serious emotional attitude, that peers around behind it. They demand, in short, that jokes should have a point. And when they try to explain a joke, or tell you why it made them laugh, it is this point, this serious attitude or meaning, that they dwell upon.

"As to capital punishment: If it was good enough for my father, it's good enough for me."**

Repeat that line to your very grown-up friends and ask them why they laughed. Some will tell you it is because they are against capital

* F. H. Allport says, in his *Social Psychology:* "Children are the greatest laughers. In later years their free and boisterous humor becomes refined and 'intellectualized . . .' "

** A line spoken by Victor Moore in *Anything Goes.*

punishment and like to see its advocates confuted. Others will say that they are progressive, and like to see the cut-and-dried reactionary caught in the teeth of his own formula. Others will mention their feeling of superiority to the stupidity of the speaker. Still others will confess to a blood-lust which rejoices in the suggestion of two pleasant executions. But these satisfactions are all serious, and by themselves would not be funny in the least. The funny thing, in all four cases, is that a plausible movement of the mind has come to nothing. Whatever other feelings may join in, that is the cause of comic feeling, and it is the same in grown-ups and in children.

When more is known than now is about pleasure and displeasure, it will no doubt be found that the comic laugh and the glad or gleeful laugh with which we greet a friend or the discomfiture of an enemy, or indeed any strong satisfaction, are closely related. It will do no good to pretend that we know much about them now, except that they are not the same. I do not believe anyone who has had to do with children will disagree with Dr. Kimmins when he says: "The laughter of young children can be clearly shown to be of two kinds, the laughter of pleasure in the well-being of the child, especially at the completion of any experiment successfully performed; and the laughter of amusement at comical incidents. . . ." The German psychologist, Preyer, said that he could distinguish from the next room the laughter of his child at tickling from the laughter that was an expression of pleasure.*

* Although their mutual reinforcement in jokes is ignored, the distinction between these two laughs is generally recognized by competent psychologists who treat the subject. Georges Dumas, in his monumental *Traité de Psychologie* (1923) writes: "What is the origin of the excitation which manifests itself in laughter? One can not answer that question without first making a distinction, too often neglected, between the laugh which expresses the general excitation of pleasure and the laugh which expresses the pleasure of the comic." Oswald Külpe in his *Grundlagen der Aesthetik* makes a similar distinction. A. Gregg in a *Study of Laughter in Three Year Olds* (an unpublished master's essay at Columbia University) observed that laughter far outruns the perception of the comic in children. E. Dupréel ("La Probleme Sociologique du Rire," *Revue Philosophique*, Sept.–Oct. 1928) bases his whole attempt to explain laughter on social as against biological grounds, upon the existence of two laughs—"the laugh of acceptance" and the comic laugh. Under the influence of Bergson, however, he imagines that the latter can be described as a "laugh of exclusion," and all laughter thus reduced to a matter of preserving one's social group.

The verification and definition of this difference might have provided those experiments of Ruth Washburn's with the guiding idea which they lacked. As things stand now we can only say that these two kinds of act and feeling although kindred are distinct, and that in high spirits they tend to run together into a fluid feeling called hilarity.

It is this fluid called hilarity which explains the peculiar and acute emotional delight of grown-up people in what they call a "good joke." For a good joke gives us the two kinds of laughter concentrated in a single point. It gives us a babylike "exuberant merriment" in the funny experience of falling down when we are trying to stand up—or trying, at least, to make a meaning stand up in our minds—and it gives us also, in the very act of falling down, the exciting pleasure of finding ourselves upon our feet in a new and happy posture. Or, to change the analogy but not the argument, it gives us the pleasure of "creeping toward object and being pulled back," and in the very same instant the pleasure of arriving at some *other* object equally, or perhaps more, to be desired.

If we hear, or hear about, a housewife who throws up her window and calls out to the iceman: "Have you the time?" we are already on our way toward an object—the answer namely, "It is ten o'clock," or "eleven-thirty," or "twelve." And if the iceman replies: "Yes, if I can find somebody to hold the horses," we have been "pulled back" from that object abruptly and hopelessly. We will never get there, never in this world. And that is *funny*. But we have got somewhere else, and somewhere that we find it *fun* to be.

It is only necessary to ignore the feelings of the housewife and the iceman—who do not exist anyway—and remember that we who hear the story are the ones who laugh, and the exact nature of the joke is obvious. It is a trick played upon our minds—a playful disappointment of their momentary expectation, and a pleasure offered to their underlying trends. It is funny reinforced with fun.

In that joke the funny is rather swamped and swallowed by the fun. It seems hardly possible in the excitement of the thought finally arrived at, that the failure to arrive at so pale a prospect as the time of day could be what makes it funny. You must remember, however, that you were giving your attention to the story. And giving attention means that your active mind was engaged in organizing its elements into a structural whole. Your total conscious being at the moment consisted of that enterprise of organization. Its collapse was a collapse of your pattern of experience. Such a thing is not trivial, no matter what the content of the pattern.

CHAPTER VI

Eddie Cantor on the Auction Block

A JOKE, you see, is not a thing, but a process. And the process, although it comes so natural to playful minds, is not simple. I can analyze any joke you bring me, if you will leave it overnight—for the task requires reflection—and give you in the morning the chemical formula upon which it is composed. And it will always be composed of unpleasant experiences playfully enjoyed, combining in various orders, degrees and proportions with pleasant experiences. That is all that a joke is or can be. But that is a great deal. *Anything whatever* that might be unpleasant if taken seriously, combined with anything that might *for any reason* be accepted as pleasant, may turn out to constitute the point of a joke.

What deters me from taking up jocular analysis as a profession is not the difficulty inherent in the job, but the fact that when the job is well done, nobody gets any fun out of it. The correct explanation of a joke not only does not sound funny, but it does not sound like a correct explanation. It consists of imagining ourselves totally humorless and most anxiously and minutely concerned with the matter in question, and in realizing that under those queer and uninteresting circumstances a disagreeable feeling *would* arise exactly where in our mirthful receptivity we experience a comic emotion. That is not funny, and except to the pure love of understanding, it is not fun. You can no more find humor in the proper dissection of a joke than you can fly into a rage over the physiology of anger, or get drunk on a formula for synthetic gin.

There is not even the pleasure of vivisection to be enjoyed in this field. For the moment anyone approaches a joke with intent to dissect, the joke is dead. It dies while he is picking up the knife. There is no conflict in nature more implacable than that between a joke and the explanation of it. And the cause is simple. In order to explain a thing you have to take it seriously; in order to feel humor you have to *be* playful. You can not enjoy an explained joke for the same reason that you do not laugh when tickled by an ant—namely, that the ant is serious and so are you.

That is why all disquisitions on laughter and the comic taste so flat. They taste as though they had nothing to do with their subject. It will be so here, if you try to enjoy my illustrations while I am explaining them. Enjoy them when you can, and when you can not, enjoy if possible the explanation, but do not try to accomplish these feats at the same time. Do not, in fact, try to do anything. Remember that you are reading a modern streamline textbook, and this science is going into your brain without friction from the headwinds and whether you want it there or not.

Here is a joke from one of Eddie Cantor's movie comedies, which will illustrate what we have said so far. Eddie has been forcibly ejected from an American village for getting into an ingenious amount and variety of trouble, and while tramping the road, footsore and forsaken, suddenly finds himself on one of the causeways of imperial Rome. Here he gets into trouble again with the usual dexterity, and is dragged to the auction block and offered for sale as a slave. He cuts such a sorry figure, such an undersized, limp, knock-kneed, small-town, American figure there among the imperial Romans that nobody will make any bids. Sad, worried and humiliated, he pleads with the crowd: "I can work, I can wash dishes, I can mop the floors, I can take care of the children—if there aren't any children, I can take care of that."

Those are not his exact words; I am quoting from memory; but the last two phrases are sufficiently exact.

Let us carry that joke back to our laboratory now, and having put on a square white suit and a serious face, run a knife up its middle and lay it open, and see if we can not enumerate every one of its interior parts, and show how and in what order they were combined to produce a laugh.

In the first place a situation was presented which is funny: a man of our acquaintance being offered as a slave and cutting such a poor, sad figure that he does not even get a bid. Taken seriously that situation is painful enough, but it is so remote from our own lives and so fantastically led up to, that we can not take it so. If we did, it would be tragic—or it would be mean, pathetic, contemptible, disgusting, pitiful, according to our temperament. It would be an object of aversion. It is a thing, then, like the comic mask or ugly faces made by children—funny because put on in fun.

But now while we are laughing at this playfully painful situation, the hero begins to speak, and his words set our minds moving in a certain direction. They are an abject plea for help, and their natural or non-jocular progress will be toward the more and more abject, or at least from one item of abjection to another. "I can mop, wash dishes, take care of the children—if there aren't any children, I can take care of the chickens, take care of the pigs, take care of the meanest thing you've got. . . ." That is the way the speech will continue if left to its own momentum. That is the tendency of our thought as we follow it. And the tendency continues clear up to the end of the phrase "take care of" when repeated for the last time. At that point this tendency is brought to nothing. Here the words "take care of" are not humble, but boastful, and the function proposed is not abject, but insolently bold. *A trick has been played upon us.* We have been led on and fooled. We have been playfully deprived of what we were on the point of grasping. But also, and in the very place of it, we have been presented with a gift—with two gifts, in fact, the opportunity to rejoice in a man bold enough when on the auction block to make the most insolent suggestion imaginable, and the opportunity to think about an illicit and exciting pleasure.

Is there anything else in the inner constitution of this joke which has importance? There is, it seems to me, only one thing, or state of things. That is the *suddenness* of our disappointment and the *immediacy* of our reward—or in other words the dexterity with which the trick was played. The fact that those words "take care of," while habitually used to describe menial functions, are also habitual upon the tongues of cocky managers and efficiency experts of the "Leave it to George" type, is what makes the joke possible, and what makes it a joke. It enables the comedian to lead our minds with entire plausibility right up to the point where they are left staring at nothing, and then allow them to discover within that nothing an interesting something else.*

I do not want to dwell too long upon this joke now that we have killed it with our explanation and it lies here, so to speak, decaying in our hands. But I would like to draw attention in departing to the general aspect of the corpse:

> An abject young man in ancient Rome was put upon the auction block for sale, and when nobody made any bids, he pleaded his own cause, saying that he could mop, wash dishes, or perform any kind of menial labor; he also boasted jestingly that he was potent and could be employed in childless families for the purposes of propagation.

It is still, you see, an interesting anecdote. The affirmative values are all there. You have the abjection, the insolent suggestion, the illicit thought, and you have a comparatively rapid shift from one to the other. Nevertheless it is no longer a joke. The humorous feeling has fled from it. The humorous feeling has fled from the situation because, although still painful, it is not presented playfully. And it has fled from the man's words because, although playful, they are no longer disappointing. They play no trick upon our minds. The humor, then, inhered, not in the affirmative elements, the insolence or illicit suggestion, but in the negative, the painfulness when taken playfully and the getting fooled in fun. It inhered in them, or rose out of them, for a very simple reason—the reason, namely, that we come into the

* The "suddenness" is of the essence of the process, and this has been agreed upon by widely differing thinkers—by Hobbes with his "sudden glory," Kant with his sudden coming to nothing, Dr. Johnson with his "something sudden and unexpected." A young Harvard psychologist, Richard N. Sears, has proven statistically that anything which "eases in" the disappointment will decrease the humor-value of a joke. To him as to his predecessors this necessity for suddenness remains a mystery. But what does it mean except that a successful trick has been played? To have an expectation gradually fade, and our attention turned tranquilly to a new object, is not unpleasant; therefore it is not a trick. It is not a mean trick when seriously engineered, and it is not funny when performed in fun.

world endowed with an instinctive tendency to laugh and have this feeling in response to pains presented playfully. No other explanation of the quality of feeling which we call comic has ever been offered. No other theory has ever even pretended to explain that quality of feeling, which is after all the major thing to be explained.

Part Four

VARIETIES OF HUMOROUS EXPERIENCE

CHAPTER I

Witty Jokes and Ludicrous Perceptions

IF YOU LOOK over all the names for laughable things, I think you will find that the two farthest apart are the word *ludicrous,* and the word *witty. Ludicrous* describes something that "looks funny." *Witty* describes something that happens to your mind and makes you laugh.

Abe Martin says that "ther's few funnier sights than a full set o' whiskers in bed." And those not accustomed to putting a full set of whiskers to bed will probably agree with him. That is what we mean by ludicrous.

Abe Martin's remark that "the only sure way to double your money is to fold it and put it in your hip pocket," will serve as an example of what we mean by wit.

These two extremely different things both give rise to the feeling that we call comic, and both tend to provoke laughter. One of them is a perception and the other a thought-process. The fundamental problem, if you want to classify the forms of humor, is to distinguish these two species and then show that they belong to the same genus.

In order to do that, I must again bring forward that small but important baby from Part Two. We caused him to crow and gurgle in two ways, you remember: by making terrible faces playfully, and by playfully snatching something from his grasping hand. And we found that these two ways of amusing a baby correspond to Aristotle's and Kant's widely differing definitions of the comic: *something ugly or distorted but not painful,* and *an expectation that comes suddenly to nothing.* They also correspond to the above two citations from Abe Martin. That whiskers in bed are of the same nature as making funny faces, and that while they look terrible they really won't hurt you, is fairly obvious. But a recipe for doubling your money which does not actually, or in quite the way you hoped for, double it, is also like snatching something from a grasping hand. The sole difference is that a mind, instead of a hand, now does the grasping, and that the thing grasped for is a meaning. And that difference is not large. It is not fundamental. The motions of a mind are only motions of the body in a cut-off or incipient form. Thought is of the same nature as action. It is action confined within the limits of the body. To disappoint a movement of thought will naturally, therefore, have the same effect as to disappoint an overt movement.

Perception, on the other hand, is different from action. In perception our energies are occupied on the receiving, not the transmitting, side of that central switchboard which we call the brain. The brain has, you might say, two functions—becoming clearly conscious of an environment and responding to it. And these two functions are not only distinct, but in a deep degree opposed. When you decide what to do about something, you cease to be vividly aware of it. The moment of indecision, the moment when your active life is stalled, is the moment of vivid awareness.

And so it is quite natural that the word *ludicrous,* which has to do with perception, should seem so far removed from *witty,* which has to do with mental action. It is natural that the title of the Marx Brothers' moving picture, *Horse Feathers,* should have so different a quality from the title of Eddie Cantor's autobiography, *My Life Is in Your Hands.* The one tempts us to form a pattern of perception, or remember one, and we fail; it baffles our receptors. The other starts us off upon a line of thought, and trips us up by meaning something else from what it always has; it frustrates our responses.

In the clown at the circus you can see these two kinds of humor combined. He puts on a queer costume so that he will "look funny" as soon as he comes in, and then he amuses us by getting ready to jump over four elephants, or lift a two-thousand-pound weight, and of a sudden *not doing it.* The costume is funny, and so is the not-doing-it. Their funniness is profoundly different; the costume disreputable, disgusting, unseemly, outrageous, or perhaps pitiful and heart-breaking, if taken seriously; the not-doing-it a mere distressing failure, loss, or absence, of what we had awaited and were reaching toward. But their funniness is also, still more profoundly, the same—it is the flavor of unpleasantnesses given and received in fun. That is why we naturally expect to find the two together, and hardly ever note the difference.

Not only the chasm between Kant and Aristotle, but almost all the famous disagreements among the philosophers of laughter, arise from a failure to note this difference. Those who make everything hinge on words like "incongruity," or "contrast," or the "strange," the "unfamiliar," the "distorted," the "ugly," the "degraded," etc., are thinking about funny perceptions.* Those who speak of "disappointment," or "relief," or "economy of psychic expenditure," "sudden liberty," "suddenly released energy," or anything with the word *sudden*, or the word *surprise*, in it, are thinking about funny events happening in a course of thought or action. Our own theory is not so much a new idea to place beside these, as a more adequate generalization to include them.**

It might be summed up, in this closer view, as follows: There are two kinds of unpleasantnesses: one is failing to get what you want; the other is getting what you don't want. There are, accordingly, two kinds of humor: taking a frustrated (thought or) action playfully, and taking an unpleasant presentation playfully.

I call the first kind practical jokes, and the second—for want of any

* William McDougall, with his idea that comic laughter has been developed as an "antidote to sympathy," is viewing only the perceptual half of humor. The laughter at ludicrous perceptions might conceivably be interpreted as a corrective of too much sympathy, if you can find it plausible that our species has too much. But the laughter at witty jokes is not subject to this interpretation.

After my book, *The Sense of Humor,* was published, Professor McDougall drew my attention to the fact that, in a lecture summarized in *Nature,* Vol. 67, 1903, he had anticipated me in remarking that there is an element in comic experiences which "would annoy us if we did not laugh." In criticizing his development of the idea, it seems suitable to acknowledge this fact.

** It is because of the need for such a generalization that judicious people so often use the term "incongruity" to identify the cause of comic laughter. Both practical and perceptual humor can be described loosely as incongruous, the one disrupting a temporal, the other a spatial pattern or congruity.

single term—perceptual and poetic humor. I am going to write two chapters about practical jokes, and then seven short ones about perceptual and poetic humor. And then I will show how they combine in most rich jokes.

CHAPTER II

The Definition of Wit

MOST GROWN-UP PEOPLE regard an inveterate practical joker as an affliction. They call him a "wag," by which they mean, I think, that he behaves like a dog's tail, endeavoring to keep up a laughing-process in the wrong place, and all the time, and without any dimples. They are quite right about this. A practical joke in the accepted sense of the term, an elaborate playful perpetration at the expense of some-one not in the game, is a laborious kind of humor. It takes too long; it is too self-conscious, too *other*-conscious; it requires serious effort; it lacks the catching ease and spontaneity of genuine play. It is not so much a jest as an enterprise. Moreover when the playfulness is a pre-tense and serious cruelty the real preoccupation, it is, as Mark Twain said it was, a puerile or decadent pursuit.

Nevertheless all famous wits, Mark Twain included, have in early years been prone to pranks. Mark Twain confessed his joy in accu-rately capping his brother from a second story window with a water-melon rind. Josh Billings is still famous at Hamilton College—and so is the college chapel—for climbing its waterspout and removing a too wakeful clapper from the bell. Artemus Ward once donned a complete suit of armor and walked down Broadway compelling oaths of fealty from the passers with a sword. Eugene Field's drive through Denver impersonating Oscar Wilde, whose highly publicized arrival had been delayed by snow, belongs to literary history. Walt Disney tells me that as a boy he was a great hand at stringing up people's backhouses on the tops of telegraph poles on Halloween night. Joe Cook has a whole system of practical jokes through which he puts the visitor at his

Hopatcong residence, and he played a new one on my publisher and me when we went down there expecting to go through it, by receiving us with complete sobriety. Sidney Smith, the famous British wit, remarked that he had lived his life like a razor, always in hot water or a scrape—and that puts wit in its natural relation to the roguish life. For wit is nothing but a practical joke played quickly, spontaneously, without too much self- and other-consciousness, and played upon the mind.

A word or series of words which seems and pretends to be heading toward a certain meaning, and which "leads us on" in the direction of that meaning, fails abruptly and with playful intent to get us there at all. It lets us down. It leaves us flat. It April-fools us. And like Ruth Washburn's baby sailing toward its mother's arms, we find in failing of our goal a comic pleasure.

In mature and pointed wit, besides failing to arrive where we seemed to be going, we do arrive somewhere else. And we find that somewhere else an interesting place to be. But that, as we have seen—and we shall see some more—is incidental. Wit in its comic essence, in so far as it is distinguished from presenting ludicrous images to the imagination, consists of springing practical jokes upon the mind of the person who is expected to laugh.

As this is a novel proposition, I am going to prove it by exhibiting a series of practical jokes, starting with a gross physical prank, and gradually moving in and speeding up, until we arrive at those instantaneous tricks with pure meaning which are commonly described as wit.

One. A man is sent down to the hardware store to buy a left-handed monkey wrench. He goes a long way, taking his mind, brain, body, clothes, and perhaps even his rubbers and umbrella, with him, and he comes back empty-handed, a wiser and a better man—but not greatly amused. The thing has cost him too much trouble, and he was not feeling frivolous. Nor was he in the first place gifted with an agile taste for play.

Two. A purse with a string attached is left on the sidewalk. A passer-by makes a lunge for it, only to see it skip across the lawn and hear loud laughter from behind the hydrangea bush.

That moves more quickly, and perhaps the victim laughs a little too, if he is not too sedate, or was not too eager—or if it is April Fools' Day. But he does not enjoy the joke, because it was thrust upon him when he was not playful, and because it makes him "look foolish."

One of the chief superiorities of thought over action is that we do not look foolish when it goes wrong. And that is one of the chief reasons why we enjoy getting fooled mentally as babies enjoy it physically. Our picture of ourselves is not involved.

Three. Joe Cook wrote a little book called *Why I Will Not Imitate Four Hawaiians,* which exemplifies humor in its most spontaneous and childlike form. He *talked* the book, he tells me, as rapidly as a typist could take it down. And I believe him, for I have heard him talk as brilliant a mixture of fun, fancy, and foolishness more rapidly than a typist could take it down. Two of his favorite "gags" in that book are a note reading "See frontispiece" and another "See page 226," the frontispiece being totally irrelevant to the matter in question, and the book having only 64 pages. Josh Billings had a similar gag. At the bottom of the card advertising his lecture on milk—in which, moreover, the subject of milk was never mentioned—he printed the word *over* in large type, and the other side was blank.

These are still, you see, crude practical jokes involving physical action on the part of the victim. But they happen quickly, and do not make the victim look foolish, if only because there is no one watching him, and they therefore seem a little more *like* wit.

Four. Someone says: "Let me take your hands and I will show you something funny." He crosses your arms with the thumbs toward you, places the palms together, interlocks the fingers, and then rotates the wrists inward, bringing the two hands thus locked together up under your chin with the thumbs out. Then he points to a finger *without touching it,* and asks you to move it. You try to, but it is the opposite finger which moves; and you burst out laughing. (This is guaranteed.) And yet that too is a practical joke, and the joke is on you. It is not only on you now, however, but in you. It is a fooling of your most self-like expectation, the expectation that your members will obey your mind.

Five. One of Artemus Ward's lovingly remembered drolleries was to stop in the middle of a lecture and say: "Owing to a slight indisposition, I am now going to declare a brief intermission," and then in the astonished silence add, "but to pass the time away I shall continue talking."

Here there is no movement of the members. The whole process takes place within the mind of the audience—or what we call the mind, although muscular attitudes are of course involved. But still it is, in the most obvious sense, a joke on those who laugh.

Six. In his *Story of a Wonder Man*—to pass now into the region of "pure intellect"—Ring Lardner mentions a "famous murder case," and writes of it as follows:

> For the benefit of half-witted readers, I will recount the Helsh case in brief. Wallace Helsh was a wealthy barn tearer in Pennsylvania. He went all over the state tearing down barns so horses could get more air. Mrs. Helsh was the former Minnie Blaggy, prominent in Philadelphia society and the daughter of Blotho Blaggy, who was in charge of one of the switches in the Broad Street railroad yards. Young Helsh and Miss Blaggy became acquainted on one of the former's barn-storming tours and were married two weeks after their first meeting. At the time of the murder, they had been married three years and Mrs. Helsh (née Blaggy) was expecting a baby, the child of one of her sisters. The baby was supposed to arrive on the 12:09 (midnight) train and the police first believed that the murder had grown out of a quarrel between the Helshes over which of them should sit up and meet it.

Does not that sentence about "expecting a baby" play as deliberate a trick upon the reader's mind as Artemus Ward did upon the minds of his audience? Does anybody get fooled by that phrase except the one who laughs?

Seven. Mark Twain—to be still more intellectual—propounds the following aphorism:

> Let us not be too particular. It is better to have old secondhand diamonds than none at all.

There, too, is it not the reader who gets fooled? Is he not, within his mind, or within the pages of a book, as much the butt of Mark Twain's mischief as though he had been sent across town to get a left-handed monkey wrench? He has been sent across the page looking for an illustration of the idea that one should not be too particular, and when he gets back *without the illustration,* there is Mark Twain laughing at him, or with him, and saying: "April fool! Diamonds don't wear out!" Mark Twain is laughing, but so is the reader—and not because either one of them was the victor, but because it is comic to get neatly fooled in fun.

At this point in our series two objections will be made. One objector will say: "You are right, that is a practical joke, but it is mere jesting and not wit, because it has no secondary meaning." The other objector will say: "Oh, but you do not see that Mark Twain had a secondary meaning there—he meant that it is always better to take what you can get!" Which perfectly illustrates and makes plain the adventitious character, from the standpoint of comic emotion, of the secondary, or substituted, meaning. Both to those who see it and to those who do not, the jest is funny. It is funny because the subject is interesting and the trick it plays upon the mind is neat.

Another way to prove that this substituted meaning is not what makes a joke funny, is to show how trivial it can be, even when quite obvious to all.

Eight. Speaking of his marriage to his Eskimo bride, Hugga Much, Ring Lardner said:

> "I wanted the ceremony held at Old Trinity; Hugga said it was below her station—she usually got off at Columbus Circle."

There you do arrive at a meaning, but how much is it worth? How funny would it be to learn that Hugga usually got off at a certain subway station, if you had not been led away on the thought of a very different kind of station?

Nine. Josh Billings said:

> There iz two things in this world for which we are never fully prepared, and them iz—twins.

Here the meaning at which we arrive has a little more dignity. It is at least a sensible and true remark. Twins, moreover, if you can get just the right attitude to them, are a trifle ludicrous to the imagination. Yet no one will contend that the meaning of this remark when it is finished—the truth, namely, that we are never prepared for twins—is what makes us laugh. We laugh because when we heard the words "two things," we expected the two to come separately, although we had no very good reason for it, and we got fooled. We laugh because our uncle Josh Billings has played a good joke on us, and we like it.

Ten. During the depth of the Great Depression a story went round about a young man who had a nervous breakdown. The doctor recommended to his parents that they put him somewhere where he would not be disturbed, and so they put him in business.

That is the kind of joke we are more accustomed to call witty. We call it so because the positive meaning is important. The remark that business is so dull it would not disturb a nervous invalid is worth making. It is more than worth making; it is more than a remark; it is a cry to heaven pent in every breast. But it is not comic. What makes the young man's story comic is that it leads the listener's mind in a direction remote from this cry to heaven, and yet gives it vent.

Freud makes much of the distinction between jokes which just barely make sense, and those whose main value lies in the sense they make. He calls the first kind "jests," and thinks them radically distinct from wit. In jests our motive is the mere pleasure that children have in talking nonsense, a pleasure that he thinks is not of itself comic. The fact that our nonsense does just barely, in another view, make sense, serves only to appease our critical judgment and release us from our adult task of inhibiting these childish proclivities. The energy which we had been employing in this task, however, being thus liberated, not only greatly increases our pleasure in the nonsense, but, in some manner which Freud does not even try to explain, makes it a comic pleasure. When, however, besides barely making sense, a piece of nonsense actually "says a mouthful" on some subject of current interest, or taps our deeper reservoirs of sexual and aggressive passion, then the pleasure is still greater—and still more comic, I suppose—and the jest is properly called wit.

Freud makes, in short, three sharp divisions in our series. Mere pranks like those of Joe Cook and Artemus Ward which do not really "make sense" at all, he would class as childish and not funny pleasures. A joke like that of Ring Lardner about Hugga Much, or Josh Billings about twins, he would class as a jest, an inferior kind of joke since it taps but two sources of pleasure. But a joke like the one about the sick young man in the depression he would call wit, because it taps three.

Now I maintain that from the standpoint of *comic feeling*—which Freud in his preoccupation with pleasure sources totally ignores—our series is homogeneous. Moreover, I think Artemus Ward's nonsensical remark about the intermission is just as comical as Ring Lardner's sense-making "jest" about Hugga Much. And I think Josh Billings' remark about the twins, whose serious meaning is certainly not worth more than two cents, is the funniest of them all—funnier than most witty jokes. It does not matter whether you agree with me about these particular jokes, for instead of three I could insert three hundred, and show that for every laughing mind the comic quality varies independently of the number of Freud's "pleasure sources" that are tapped.

It is well known that people often laugh, and laugh as we say "in spite of themselves," at jokes whose secondary or serious meaning is not a source of pleasure, but of keen and personal pain. This shows again the inadequacy and irrelevance to comic feeling of Freud's pleasure-source mechanics. It shows, indeed, the inadequacy of any theory of humor which does not give to purely playful laughter the character of an emotional instinct. Laughter explodes like anger, and a laughing fit—the last thing it ever occurs to the philosophers of the comic to explain—is of the same fundamental nature as a panic or a fit of wrath.*

* Some recent investigations have shown that people laugh less boisterously at jokes whose serious import lies against them, or against those they favor, and that they give a lower estimate of the comic quality of such jokes. ("The Psychology of Humor" by H. A. Wolff and C. E. Smith, *Journal of Abnormal and Social Psychology,* No. 4, 1934.) Men, for instance, "enjoyed more fully" the jokes on women, and women on men. Here again experimental psychology merely turns an obvious fact into a statistic. The important thing for the psychology of humor is that men do laugh at jokes on men, and women at jokes on women, and find them funny even when there is no serious pleasure in them.

Eleven. To illustrate that "technique of wit" which he calls "condensation with modification and substitution," Freud cites the following example:

> A nobleman, because of an interest in farming, had been appointed Minister of Agriculture, where he proved a total loss. When he retired, they said of him: "Like Cincinnatus of old he has returned to his place before the plow."

Is it not fantastic to talk about "condensation" when men have gone so far out of their way as that to call a man a dumb beast? "The retiring Minister of Agriculture is an ass," would be a condensation of what was said there. But it would not be witty. What makes the remark witty, no matter how much space or time it absorbs, how much or how little "modification" or "substitution" it requires, or how large a wave of "psychic energy" it lets go, is the fact that it leads all educated minds in the direction of an encomium, and by the mischievous shifting of a single word *lands them* in the assertion that the man is an ass.

To be witty is to spring a neat practical joke upon a playful mind. That is the whole story. The function of your real meaning may be merely to make the sentence plausible, and the trick a success; your real meaning may be the weightiest in the world; or you may have no meaning at all. From the standpoint of producing comic emotion, it does not matter. The trick is what produces the emotion. For all Freud's abstruse labors on the various techniques of wit, we can substitute the single statement that wit employs every conceivable device by which a mind can be led on and then fooled.

Josh Billings printed the word *over* on his lecture program and left the other side blank. Joe Cook prints at the top of a page: "Below you will find a list of New York night clubs where a marvelous time can be had for little or nothing," and leaves the rest of the page blank. The jocular technique is the same. The only difference is that Joe Cook's joke means something. What it means, however, is no joke!

Twelve. Mark Twain says in Puddinhead Wilson's Calendar:

> October. This is one of the peculiarly dangerous months to speculate in stocks in. The others are July, January, September,

April, November, May, March, June, December, August, and February.

It is not a very good joke, but useful to show how remote from real fact Freud is—and his teacher, Lipps, before him—in trying to explain the pleasure in wit as due to an "economy of psychic expenditure." The amount of labor expended here in apprehending the simple idea contained in the word *always* would build a boat.

Thirteen. Remember the poor—it costs nothing.

In that swift flash from the pen of Josh Billings an economy of psychic expenditure is indeed plausible, if you know at once exactly what it means to say. But that is not why it is funny. It is funny for the same reason that Mark Twain's uneconomical proverb is—namely, that it starts us off toward an idea and lands us as far from where we were going as the nature of ideas, and of the universe, permit. What happens to those who enjoy it could be accurately paralleled in Ruth Washburn's baby-laboratory, if after tossing out a "subject" toward his mother's arms, she had, instead of "rapidly withdrawing him again," managed with the same abrupt change of direction to land him in the arms of his nurse, or sister, or his father (supposing he was not yet on to his father). That would be a joke with a point. And that is all there is in the most delightful wit.

This explanation of wit accords, as no other does, with the fundamental assumption of psychology that thought is basically the same as action. It identifies wit with the causes of laughter in infants, and with the roguish tricks of apes. It seems to me worthy to be called scientific.

CHAPTER III

That Nonsense Must Be Plausible

THE TROUBLE WITH FREUD—or one trouble with him, for I shall have to gird up my complexes and take a fall out of the astute doctor every once in a while in these pages—the trouble with Freud is that he does not distinguish between nonsense in the abstract, or mere gibberish, and nonsense as the failure of some specific claim to sense. The latter alone is comical, and is comical in the same essential way to grown-ups and to children.

Burgess Johnson, compiler of the *Little Book of Necessary Nonsense,* makes the same mistake. "Nonsense," he says, in a preface, "is something which does not make sense," and he gives an example which is supposed to provoke a laugh:

> She went into the garden to cut a cabbage leaf to make an apple pie, and at the same time a great she-bear coming up the street, pops its head into the shop. "What, no soap?" so he died. She imprudently married the barber, and there were present the Pickaninnies, the Joblillies, the Gayrulies, and the Grand Panjandrum himself with the little round button on top, and they all fell to playing catch-as-catch-can till the gunpowder ran out at the heels of their boots.

This may be funny, as anything may, if you are in a laughing mood, though even then its humor will depend upon the plausibility with which it is uttered. But it is not funny in the way that it is to speak of an oyster that was so large it took two men to swallow it, or of a mathematician who was so absent-minded he put his pants to bed and hung himself over the chair and froze to death. That also is nonsense.

But it is nonsense happening to us as an event, a play-accident, a tripping of our thought when on its way along a track of meaning. "It would have been ten dollars in Jeff Davis's pocket," said Artemus Ward, "if he had never been born." It not only sounds plausible when earnestly spoken, but it *is* plausible.

> "Didn't I meet you in Buffalo?"
> "No. I never was in Buffalo."
> "Neither was I. It must have been two other fellows."

It may not be so in Vienna, but in the Anglo-Saxon world that kind of joke—formerly known by the name of "Irish bull"—is always greeted with a laugh. It is the one kind of joke which is as sure fire as a witty insult or a risqué quip. And it does not matter whether it comes in the form of a jesting remark, or is dressed up with the attributes of a "funny story." Here is a funny story that traveled about New York in the winter of 1934:

> Two of our most eminent intellects were leaning against the bar at the Players' Club. One of them, emerging from a momentary coma, remarked:
> "When I was born I weighed only 2½ pounds."
> The other gazed at him in vague amazement.
> "Is that so? Did you live?"
> "You ought to see me now."

It was not necessary to specify that these were two of our eminent intellects at the Players' Club. That merely helped along by warming up your interest, suspending criticism on the ground of news-value, and permitting you to feel a sudden glory in your superiority to these eminent intellects if you happen to cherish that particular conception of glory. To a humorous mind all that was merely setting for the jest. The cream of the jest—or the meat, rather, for a jest is more like a nut than a pan of milk—lay in two things only: the plausibility with which the words held out a meaning, the abruptness with which they failed to deliver it.

It was the same jest when it turned up six months later in Eddie Cantor's *Kid Millions,* and was spoken by an Egyptian princess and an American millionaire while riding the waves on the back of an imperial camel. The pleasure derived from it was still a pleasure in pure nonsense—a childish pleasure, exactly of the sort you find so frequently in *Alice In Wonderland.*

> "Which reminds me—" the White Queen said, looking down and nervously clasping and unclasping her hands, "we had *such* a thunderstorm last Tuesday—I mean one of the last set of Tuesdays, you know."
>
> Alice was puzzled. "In *our* country," she remarked, "there's only one day at a time."
>
> The Red Queen said, "That's a poor thin way of doing things. Now *here,* we mostly have days and nights two or three at a time, and sometimes in the winter we take as many as five nights together—for warmth, you know."
>
> "Are five nights warmer than one night, then?" Alice ventured to ask.
>
> "Five times as warm, of course."
>
> "But they should be five times as *cold,* by the same rule—"
>
> "Just so!" cried the Red Queen. "Five times as warm, *and* five times as cold. . . ."

That too is pure nonsense dressed in the perfect appearance of sense.

> 'Twas brillig, and the slithy toves
> Did gyre and gimble in the wabe:
> All mimsy were the borogoves,
> And the mome raths outgrabe.

Those verses are superior to most nonsense rhymes, not only because of their musical perfection, but because they combine a completer nonsense with a more meticulous plausibility. Every meaningless word is designed with inimitable skill to suggest those words most rich in meaning which the poets choose.

Compare with them this cruder verse from Edgar Lear, and you will see what I mean:

> The Pobble who has no toes
> Had once as many as we;
> When they said, "Some day you may lose them all,"
> He replied, "Fish fiddle de-dee!"
> And his aunt Jobiska made him drink
> Lavender water tinged with pink;
> For she said, "The World in general knows
> There's nothing so good for a Pobble's toes!"

To me a very charming atom of nonsense is the tail of this paragraph from Artemus Ward's essay on *Forts:*

> Old George Washington's Fort was to not hev eny public man of the present day resemble him to eny alarmin extent. Whare bowts can George's ekal be fownd? I ask, & boldly answer no whares, or eny whares else.

There too, when I seek the source of my pleasure, I find it not only in the logically perfect want of meaning, but in the compelling swing, both logical and emotional, of the pretense or claim to meaning.

Thus even when jests have no point, they still have two distinguishable elements: the plausibility, or suggestion of some approaching sense, and the frustration or failure of the sense to arrive. And both these elements must be well managed if a pointless jest is to prosper. The listening mind must be genuinely moved to form a pattern of apprehension, and the pattern must abruptly fail of "closure." It is but another way of saying that a neat trick must be played upon the listening mind.

Perhaps a good way to convince the Freudians that pure nonsense can be funny, would be to assert that it can be funnier, when delicately engineered, than nonsense which makes sense. I think most humor-loving people would be sympathetic to such an assertion. There is more humor, for instance, in the story about the man who went to a baker and asked him to bake a cake in the form of the letter S, than there would be if the man had got away without paying the baker, or provided some other "release," or refuge from complete absurdity.

The baker said, you remember, that he had never baked a cake in the form of the letter S, but he thought he could manage it, if the customer would give him a week to prepare the necessary tins. The customer agreed, the tins were prepared, the cake baked, and proudly passed out to the customer when he returned a week later. "Oh, but you misunderstood me," the customer said. "I am sorry. You have made it in a block letter, but I wanted script." "Oh well, that's all right," the baker said, "if you have the time to wait, I can make one in script. It will take me another week, however, as the tins will have to be made all over again." The customer agreed, and again the tins were prepared and the cake baked. When the customer returned a week later and saw the cake, he was delighted. "That is exactly what I wanted," he said. "I am very glad," said the baker, preparing to wrap up the cake. "Now would you like to take it with you, or shall I send it round to your house?" "Oh no, don't bother," the customer said. "If you'll just give me a knife and fork I'll eat it right here."

It is jests like that which test your sensitivity to humor—the absurd and not the witty ones. Bergson quotes a whole page of such jests from Mark Twain—a page that to a humorous perception perfectly refutes his thesis that "there is an animus in all laughter."

> *Question.* "Isn't that a brother of yours?"
>
> *Answer.* "Oh! yes, yes, yes! Now you remind me of it, that *was* a brother of mine. That's William—*Bill* we called him. Poor old Bill!"
>
> *Q.* "Why? Is he dead, then?"
>
> *A.* "Ah! well, I suppose so. We never could tell. There was a great mystery about it."
>
> *Q.* "That is sad, very sad. He disappeared then?"
>
> *A.* "Well, yes, in a sort of general way. We buried him."
>
> *Q.* "*Buried* him! *Buried* him, without knowing whether he was dead or not?"
>
> *A.* "Oh no! Not that. He was dead enough."
>
> *Q.* "Well, I confess that I can't understand this. If you buried him, and you knew he was dead—"
>
> *A.* "No! No! We only thought he was."
>
> *Q.* "Oh, I see! He came to life again?"
>
> *A.* "I bet he didn't."
>
> *Q.* "Well, I never heard anything like this. *Somebody* was dead. *Somebody* was buried. Now, where was the mystery?"
>
> *A.* "Ah! that's just it! That's it exactly. You see, we were twins,—defunct and I,—and we got mixed in the bathtub when we were only two weeks old, and one of us was drowned. But we didn't know which. Some think it was Bill. Some think it was me."
>
> *Q.* "Well, that is remarkable. What do you think?"
>
> *A.* "Goodness knows! I would give whole worlds to know. This solemn, this awful tragedy has cast a gloom over my whole life. But I will tell you a secret now, which I have never revealed to any creature before. One of us had a peculiar mark,—a large mole on the back of his left hand; that was *me. That child was the one that was drowned! . . .*"

CHAPTER IV

Funny Things and People

NOW THAT WE UNDERSTAND WIT in its simple essence, let us return to the subject of perceptual humor. We shall find that just as it was possible to arrange a graduated series of practical jokes, starting with a raw physical prank and ending with the inward flash of wit, so it is possible to pass by gradual steps from the external perception of funny things toward the imagination of them. And we shall see how the imagination of funny things combines with wit, enriching it, and making it seem more complicated than it is.

Artemus Ward, who seems to have possessed the most unalloyed humorousness of all the laughter-loving immortals, described an old unevenly worn grindstone wobbling round on its unsteady axis as the type and symbol of all funny things. "There," he said, waving an arm in imitation of its motion, "is wit personified or thingified." And he proceeded to define the comic, better than it has been done by most philosophers, as "the eccentric" in contrast to "the well-rounded." He was thinking perhaps of his own unsteady sentences—such for instance as the one herein about the pea-green ox:

> "Dr Sir,—Yrs, into which you ask me to send you sum leadin incidents in my life so you can write my Bogfry for the papers, cum dooly to hand. I hav no doubt that a article onto my life, grammattycally jerked and properly punktooated, would be a addition to the chois literatoor of the day.
>
> "To the yooth of Ameriky it would be vallyble as showin how high a pinnykle of fame a man can reach who commenst his career with a small canvas tent and a pea-green ox, which he rubbed it off while scratchin hisself agin the center pole, causin in Rahway,

N. J., a discriminatin mob to say humbugs would not go down in their village. The ox resoom'd agricultooral pursoots shortly afterwards."

As an attempt at grammar that is ludicrous much as the attempts of a tired-out grindstone to describe a circle might be. It is a funny huddle of words and images, rather than a joke.

Artemus Ward, laughing at the purely geometric eccentricity of a grindstone, and laughing so hard he declared it typical of all comic things, is pretty high authority against the view of Bergson that we never laugh at "things." Expert testimony against his assertion that we never laugh at animals is provided by another American humorist, E. B. White, who, when you raise the topic of essential humor, begins at once to speak of kittens and puppies. White's answer, in fact, when I quoted him Bergson's assertion that "there is an animus in all laughter," was to say: "I have seen puppies that were comical *per se,* and you certainly feel no animus against a funny-looking puppy." Another expert witness to the error of Bergson—the limitations, rather, of his playfulness—is Irvin S. Cobb:

> "A ham is funny, a sausage is positively uproarious, and fishballs are sort of laughable; but a veal stew is regarded as possessing few, if any, of the true elements of humor. Soup is still funny, but not as funny as it was a few years back. Hash is immensely humorous, but a croquette is not. Yet, what is a croquette but hash that has come to a head?"

I do not see that laughter is any more exclusively directed toward persons than wrath is. We laugh at things and animals when in a jocund mood, just as we frown and swear at them when we are serious. Like all of our emotional life, however, humor is deeply, and is indeed primarily, social. It flourishes best among the genially gregarious, the man and dog and apelike animals. A cat will wave her tail, but never wag it. You cannot tickle yourself—except unpleasantly. We find things funnier, too, when we are in company than when alone.* And

*R. E. Perl (*American Journal of Psychology,* 1933, Vol. 45, pp. 308-12) proved that people consistently rate jokes higher when they read them from a screen together, than when they take them home and mark them privately.

so naturally the best example of a funny thing—if we may have in one more Irish bull—is a person who is funny.

As an example of such a person, take Ed Wynn. Take him seriously, and what have you? A man who is unusually clumsy, and lisps, and has a bad speaking voice, and cannot sing, and yet insists upon appearing in public. I was talking to David Freedman the other day about our popular comedians, and he remarked: "Ed Wynn has made a brilliant career out of his defects." In a recent article in *The New Yorker,* Alva Johnson makes a similar remark about Charles Butterworth: "His physical handicap created his comic style." These seem to be particular remarks about particular comedians, but you will find that they are true, although not always obvious, about every intrinsically comic person. Every such person has something the matter with him.

That Jimmy Durante and W. C. Fields have something the matter with them is evident, so to speak, on the face of it. But the same thing is true in a less protrusive way of Groucho Marx. He is, without his make-up, a handsome and sensitive-featured young man with an exquisite profile—a man who might well in serious drama play the part of Heinrich Heine. But when he stands or moves about, he bends in the middle in a highly impractical manner, as though he were working himself not very successfully on a pair of ill-adjusted hinges. And when he says something, his eyes drop off into the corners of their sockets like those of a doll that you have moved into a horizontal position by accident in the midst of a polite conversation. These traits are comic, if you feel like laughing, even when he does not mean them to be. And they are, from the standpoint of the normal operation of the human mechanism, defects.

I do not mean to slur the problems of personality here, or pretend that we know more than we do about how it works. I merely say that a comic person is a person who is somehow "off" or "out-of-true," and yet possesses the magnetism necessary to attract you to this, and make you like it playfully. Even Beatrice Lillie's elusive comic charm can only be defined by saying that, although there is something very subtly and delicately the matter with her—a too slick, angular, almost mannish, awkwardness might part-way describe it, if you were seriously repelled—nevertheless, her lovely dimple and high poise and intelligence shine through and make you know that it is to be fastidiously loved with laughter, instead of rejected with a hypersensitive distress. And so it is of every intrinsically comic character, of every person about whom we say: "I don't know why, but it just makes me laugh to look at him."

Charlie Chaplin is not an intrinsically comic character. He conveys, on the contrary, when you meet him, the impression of a being that, although slight and almost miniature, possesses a kind of perfection—a grace, poise and agility both of body and speech, that you are not moved to improve upon. I once heard an enamored woman sum up the impression—in words that Charlie will not like too well: "He is so exquisite that you feel like wrapping him up carefully and taking him home and setting him on the mantelpiece." Moreover, Chaplin is an extremely serious person, so serious that he will talk your very head off—he will lecture you into a sound sleep—if you get him on one of his favorite topics, like Social Credits or the fluctuations of the gold standard. Instead of a funny man, he is a man of humorous imagination, the most original, perhaps, since Mark Twain, and also a consummate actor. He can imagine and act like a funny man—like almost any funny man, for the little tramp that has become identified with his person in the public mind is but one of an endless repertory of such roles that he has at his command, if he were bold enough to show them. But in his own person he is impressive rather than funny. And it is this fact that sets him apart, and makes the word comedian seem a little inadequate to describe him. He is a poet of humor.

In Chaplin's comedies then, more than in others, we enjoy the representation, and not the actuality, of a comic person. In them we take one step toward the purely imaginative enjoyment of the ludicrous, and we see all the more clearly what the ludicrous is. The little tramp's shoes are too big; he can not manage his feet; his pants do not fit; he has a habit of getting in wrong wherever he goes. So much so, that at moments we feel more like crying than laughing. His humor, as we say, comes close to pathos. Or in the words of Milt Gross: "He's sotch a dolink, wot one minute he makes you you could rur from leffing und gredually in de naxt minute it becomes so sed, wot it could make you you should cry—is werry appilling to de emulsions."

This particular way of appealing to the "emulsions" is, of course, a very object-lesson in our theory of humor. If the same character and situation which were provoking us to comic laughter can by a mere movement of the wrist, the flexing of an eyebrow or a muscle round the lips, be made a cause for tears, it is clear that objectively the comic and the painful are the same. The character and situation remain unchanged, but we of a sudden have become serious. The opposite shift of feeling, described in the phrase "laugh it off," is equally good evidence of the correctness of our view.

CHAPTER V

Funny Pictures

A FURTHER STEP toward purely imaginative humor is taken by the comic artists. I mean the intrinsically comic artists, and not the good artists who draw illustrations of jokes. George Bellows was a good and perhaps a great artist, and he used to enjoy illustrating jokes for the old *Masses.* He had a jovial sense of humor, too, and his jokes were good. Nevertheless his drawings never seemed to me intrinsically comic. They were dramatic, but there was no laugh in them. The laugh was in the caption.

By contrast, the drawings of Art Young and Cornelia Barns and William Gropper were of their own intrinsic nature comic. Captions here were unnecessary, or were at least a supplemental element—often, in fact, supplied by the editors in the office.

It was one of the brightest mornings in that office when a youth with large blue eyes and the manner of a just-about-to-be-startled fawn stepped in softly with a little sheaf of drawings in ink on tiny squares of paper. They were signed with the funny name of Gropper, and they were funny. Some of them had no captions; others had captions not of themselves jocular, like "You're a Liar!" or, "An' you mean to tell me that that dog ain't got no fleas!" But they were all funny. They were his first drawings to be offered for publication, and I never felt more definitely in the presence of what is called a budding genius.

Gropper has gone in for political-party-regulated cartoon wit rather more than is good for him, but I think he still has more humor in his actual drawing than any other American artist since Art Young. At least I would place him side by side in that respect with James Thur-

Peter Arno

"*Rhein*beck! It's Grandmamma!"

Peter Arno

ber. A sort of liquid humor unhinges the very muscles of these men when they draw. The drawing is funny as well as the things drawn. There may be a witty caption, but its wit is not so much illustrated as enriched by the picture.

Peter Arno, another man who has humor in his wrist motions, frequently publishes a full-page drawing without a title, presenting it as a pure act of humorous perception. The first drawing reproduced herewith would be intruded upon by any form of words. And in the second it is certainly not until you *see* "grandmamma," that the laughter floods your soul.

Al Frueh's line is not so hilarious perhaps, but what he sees is funny and fantastically so. He sees it sometimes in his sleep and draws it when he wakes up. Or he will be heard chuckling to himself while hoeing in the garden, and before long the hoe will lie forgotten, and he will have sneaked indoors to put some most outlandish scene or situation down on paper. I mention him here—among so many that I might be talking about—because we are traveling from perceptual toward imaginative humor, and Al Frueh's inventions go farther away from anything that could actually be perceived than most others. A silent elfish sort of person, who lives a smiling life almost wholly inside his own head, he forms a natural transition from pictorial humor to the humor of the imagination.

A gradual realization that there is pictorial humor, and that the comic artist is not a mere illustrator of jokes, has been one element in that maturing and varicolored blooming of the comic arts which has taken place in America in the last twenty-five years. For those in the current of it, therefore, the distinction between such humor and the humor of a trick upon the action of the mind ought to seem a natural one. It is not only natural, but absolutely fundamental.

* * *

As to that maturing and blooming of American humor, I want to make a small excursus here in honor of the artists of the old *Masses* staff. Robert Benchley says, in a preface to the *Fourth New Yorker Album:*

"*The New Yorker* revolutionized the illustrated joke and made it a fresh and exciting thing just as it was about to die of He-and-She."

"With the advent of *The New Yorker*," he says elsewhere, "and with *The New Yorker* Peter Arno, the entire technique of picturized jokes underwent a sudden and complete change. The old feeble two-line joke practically disappeared, and, in its place, came a fresh and infinitely more civilized form—the illustrated single remark."

Changes hardly ever come "sudden and complete" like that unless somebody intrudes with forceps. They mature slowly in the womb of time or thereabouts, and you can almost always find that they were present before many people were aware of them. There were no He-and-She jokes in the old *Masses*, which flourished ten years before *The New Yorker* was born, and I find by actual count in the first volume I take down that the one-line caption prevails almost six to one.

> "My dear, I'll be economically independent if I have to borrow every cent!"
>
> "Oh papa, that poor little birdie hasn't got any cage!"
>
> "Your Honor, this woman gave birth to a naked child!"
>
> "Why a fella says to me only yistidday, he says, 'This ain't war, it's murder!' "
>
> "Gee, Mag, think of us bein' on a magazine cover!"

That was the prevailing style of the pictorial humor in the old *Masses*, and I attribute it largely to the fact that painters and artists not primarily engaged in journalism published their work there. The magazine belonged to them, and was issued by them with no idea of profit and therefore no regard for the accepted standards. It was, in fact, largely a revolt against commercial journalism, and like so many revolts it succeeded in greatly improving the technique of the tyrant. That is no doubt why it is forgotten, too, when you come to tell the story of the change.

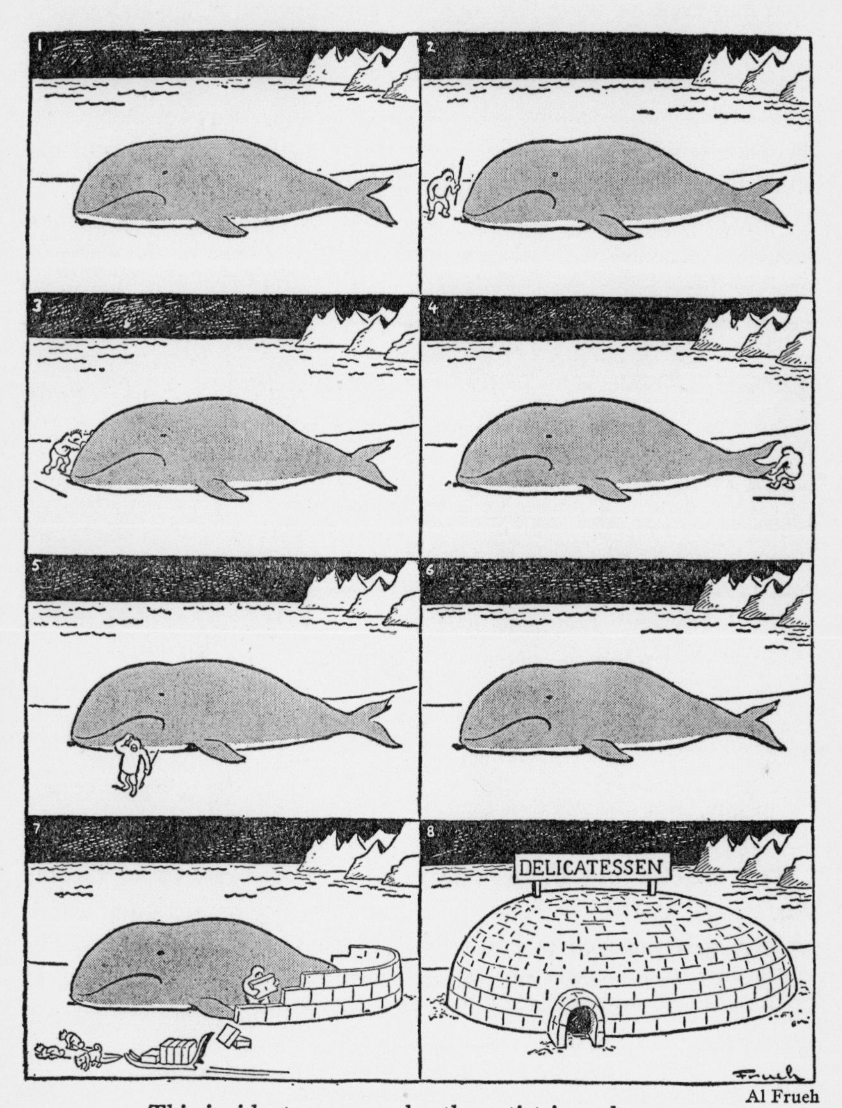

Al Frueh

This incident was seen by the artist in a dream.

CHAPTER VI

Poetic Humor

JUST AS A PETER ARNO picture can be funny without a caption, so a mental image can be funny without wit. Perhaps "mental image" is not quite the right term, for some people assert that they never see actual pictures inside their heads. But all people have the faculty of recalling things and appreciating their qualities when they are not present, and in all people this is different from trying to think, or reason, or arrive at some conclusion. Therefore the distinction between witty jokes and ludicrous perceptions continues substantially unchanged even when the perceptions are only imagined.

> The Shanghai rooster,—Josh Billings said,—is built on piles like a sandy hill crane. . . . They often go to sleep standing, and sometimes pitch over, and when they do they enter the ground like a pickax.

That is not a joke, but a funny picture.

> A strong cyclone that would unroof a courthouse, or tip over a through train, would also upset you, in spite of your broad firm feet, if the wind got behind one of your ears.

That also, from Bill Nye, is to my mind a funny picture.

> A Danbury man imagined himself a hen, and while under the influence of that conceit, sat down on a dozen eggs, and hatched out an Italian sunset and a circus poster. His wife removed the debris with the bald end of a broom. (The Danbury News Man.)

> He had flaxen hair, weak blue eyes, and the general demeanor of a saintly but timid codfish. (Wodehouse.)

> This produced that separation of the physical and the psychic which causes the adult to remain in a state of suspended love, as if he were holding a goldfish bowl and had nowhere to put it. (Thurber and White.)

> He is so stingy he wouldn't pay ten cents to see Christ wrastle a bear. (Arizona colloquialism.)

In all these sentences the humor lies in what is suggested to the imagination, rather than in any trick that is played upon the mind. I call it poetic humor, because it bears substantially the same relation to wit that poetry does to practical or prose speech. Its central preoccupation is with the communication of an experience, not with the manipulation of a thought-process.

I know quite well that a number of my readers most esteemed for their hardness of head are going to desert me when I talk about "poetic humor." They are going to relax, at least, the acuteness of their attention, their inner remark being, "Now he is getting fancy!" If I spoke of the "humor of thought" and the "humor of feeling," instead of saying *practical* and *poetic*, they would imagine they were still on solid ground. Nothing is less solid than the ground they would be on. There is no such thing as thought without feeling; and thought, as we have seen, is nothing else but inward action. The vital and deep distinction is between the whole mood of action, or of "adaptation," or of conscious movement toward an end, and the mood of realization —a mood in which action is suspended, and interest engaged in receiving the qualities of a present experience. It is this state of realization, of artfully suspended enterprise, that aestheticians actually refer to, almost always, when they talk about "feeling" or "emotion." And it is this which I designate with the term poetic. The whole technique of poetry—rhyme, rhythm, epithet, figurative language and all—is a technique for suspending action and causing us to become vividly aware of something.

Here, for instance, is Shelley's effort to make us realize the brevity and emptiness of fame. He is not telling us anything we do not know, but merely impressing our knowledge upon us in the form of an emotional image.

OZYMANDIAS OF EGYPT

I met a traveler from an antique land
Who said: Two vast and trunkless legs of stone
Stand in the desert. Near them on the sand
Half sunk, a shatter'd visage lies, whose frown
And wrinkled lip and sneer of cold command
Tell that its sculptor well those passions read
Which yet survive, stamp'd on these lifeless things,
The hand that mock'd them and the heart that fed;
And on the pedestal these words appear:
"My name is Ozymandias, king of kings;
Look on my works, ye Mighty, and despair!"
Nothing beside remains. Round the decay
Of that colossal wreck, boundless and bare,
The lone and level sands stretch far away.

If you will take that as an example of what serious poetry is, I can show you what poetic humor is by quoting Mark Twain's presentation of the same sad fact.

After browzing among the stately ruins of Rome, of Baiae, of Pompeii, and after glancing down the long marble ranks of battered and nameless imperial heads that stretch down the corridors of the Vatican, one thing strikes me with a force it never had before: the unsubstantial, unlasting character of fame. Men lived long lives, in the olden times, and struggled feverishly through them, toiling like slaves, in oratory, in generalship, or in literature, and then laid them down and died, happy in the possession of an enduring history and a deathless name. Well, twenty little centuries flutter away, and what is left of these things? A crazy inscription on a block of stone, which snuffy antiquaries bother over and tangle up and make nothing out of but a bare name (which they spell wrong)—no history, no tradition, no poetry—nothing that can give it even a passing interest. What may be left of General Grant's great name forty centuries hence? This—in the Encyclopedia for A.D. 5868, possibly.

"Uriah S. (or Z.) Grant—popular poet of ancient times in the Aztec provinces of the United States of British America. Some authors say flourished about A.D. 742; but the learned Ah-ah Foo-foo states that he was a contemporary of Scharkspyre, the English poet, and flourished about A.D. 1328, some three centuries *after* the Trojan war instead of before it. He wrote 'Rock Me to Sleep, Mother.'"

These thoughts sadden me. I will to bed.

Each of these artists is supreme in his field, and their fundamental technique is the same. A general idea is made vivid to our sensibility by presenting a concrete instance. Mark Twain's instance is, if taken seriously, just as sad as Shelley's. But it is so contrived that instead of saddening us, it sends us to bed laughing. It goes too far, it goes off the track; it destroys the very realization it professes to arouse. Being bad poetry, it is good poetic humor.

The same may be said, in a quite different way, of this Salvation Army hymn:

> My soul is like a rusty lock.
> Oh, oil it with Thy grace!
> And rub it, rub it, rub it, Lord,
> Until I see Thy face!

Perhaps I can convince my hard-headed readers, in whom alone I place any faith, that the distinction I am making is not academic by reporting a conversation I had with the leading joke fancier in the United States, Harold Horne. By profession Mr. Horne is the advertising man for United Artists, but by nature and avocation he is a man who has collected, sifted, sorted, codified and filed away in six gigantic filing cases something between a million and two million jokes. These he has installed with a secretary to watch over them within half a block of Broadway, where desperate and breathless comedians can dash in and get one on any subject, and of any necessary style, tint or configuration, with a delay of not more than sixteen seconds. When I saw him, he had just received an order from a five-and-ten-cent chain store for a joke book, and he told me that three stenographers would go to work in the morning, and the book be ready for the printer at four in the afternoon. From these facts it will appear, I hope, that Mr. Horne's attitude to humor, if not hilarious, is at least not "fancy." To him classifying jokes means filing them on cards in a cabinet in such a way that you can find the one you want, and find it quick.

I remarked to Mr. Horne that jokes are complex in their values, and not easy to analyze, and he replied:

"They are the simplest things in the world. They all consist of frustrated expectations. The only difference is that some make a picture and some don't. The ones I like best leave me with a funny picture."

I believe that the reader, before he gets through this book—and still more surely if he never does—will be convinced that jokes are complex in their values and not easy to analyze. But I also think it significant that a man who has oversimplified their forms through sheer excess of acquaintance should find but one deep and real distinction among them, and that our distinction between those which present an experience to the imagination and those which live only in the action of the mind.

Milt Gross, to a question about the kind of thing he laughs at, made an answer which perfectly illustrates what I mean by poetic humor.

"The other day," he said, "a gang of us were discussing insurance agents and other pests, and how they seem to be attracted by guys in our racket. Somebody asked Rube Goldberg how these mugs get a hold of him.

" 'Search me,' he said. 'I'm standing on the corner with my arm out—all of a sudden there's a guy on the end of it and he's my pal.'

"The thing that made this remark extremely funny to me, is the fact, not of somebody rushing up and grabbing Rube by the hand, but that he sort of suggested a mental picture of this thing growing right out on the end of his arm like a bubble is blown out of a pipe."

CHAPTER VII

Comical Figures of Speech

THE MEANS by which words are made to suggest things to the imagination are, if you brush aside minor variations, extremely simple. Sometimes the things themselves are so interesting or unusual that a mere mention of them is enough. "A dog bit a man," is not news, and for that reason is not poetry. It slides through the mind without evoking any vivid realization. But "A man bit a dog," is startling enough to arouse the imagination as it stands. You have to try at least to see *where* he bit him. That is one way that words "paint pictures" in the mind.

> The sexual revolution began with Man's discovery that he was not attractive to Woman, as such. The lion had his mane, the peacock his gorgeous plumage, but Man found himself in a three-button sack suit. (E. B. White.)

That is a picture too—because of the subject, and not because of the words. So was Marshal Foch's remark when he first went to the *Follies:*

> I never saw such sad faces or such gay behinds.

There are two ways, however, in which words themselves can make an experience vivid to our minds. One is by singling out some quality or detail which would, if the experience were present, provide a suitable focus for the attention. Ernest Hemingway describes the ardor of this act, which I call poetic choice, in his *Death in the Afternoon,* where he wants to paint the goring of a matador.

> "For myself, not being a bullfighter . . . the problem was one of depiction and waking in the night. I tried to remember what it was that seemed just out of my remembering and that was the thing that I had really seen and, finally, remembering all around it, I got it. When he stood up, his face white and dirty and the silk of his breeches opened from waist to knee, it was the dirtiness of the rented breeches, the dirtiness of his slit underwear and the clean, clean, unbearably clean whiteness of the thigh bone that I had seen, and it was that which was important."

That is poetic choice in its most serious aspect.

There is a passage in one of Wodehouse's stories where he has got his fatuous hero, the Honorable Bertie Wooster, into a scandalous tangle with the cherished daughter of a ferocious American multi-millionaire. An interview occurs in which the millionaire sits like an armed fortress fixing him with his "cold, gray stare," and the Honorable Bertie, who tells the story, is badly scared. Bertie writes:

> "He flicked the ash from his cigar. I did not need to do it to mine."

This seems to me, on the comic side, as brilliant an act of choice as Ernest Hemingway's so horribly immaculate thigh bone. And that is high praise.

More often, of course, this emphasis of a detail which makes the poet's language vivid is accomplished by a single adjective or adverb keenly chosen, or by letting the actual name of the part stand for the whole. Aristotle remarked that it is proper for a poet to say "white milk," but that in prose this would be "rather bad taste." What he would think about white thigh bones in a Hemingway rhapsody, I find it difficult to imagine. It is, anyway, as proper to the poetic humorist as to the poet to make the colors, shapes and tastes and motions of things stand out by naming them with concrete names. A poetic humorist made "spittin' image" out of the phrase "spirit and image"—he made a lively and a laughing mode of speech. American slang is full of such comic liveliness. Jack Conway's invention, to "high hat," is as brilliant a synecdoche, or naming of the part for the whole, as any to be found in Shakespeare or the Bible.

The other way in which poets make things stand sharp in the dullness of our minds is by finding an appropriate thing to compare them with. Whenever we want to know what the intrinsic quality of an experience *is,* we ask: What is it *like?* And when poets want to convey that quality, they answer this question.

> Lance passed the gate and stood in the open dust
> Like a blind marble pillar-stone . . .
>
> The old man looked up at cloud-flecks
> Like algae breeding on clear deep well-water around the moon . . .
>
> The wind increased. It lay
> Like a quivering steel blade on the necks of the herbless mountains . . .
>
> The old man saw her hair
> Against the wide white breast like a burst of blood
> Deep in the moonlight, then Lance flung her aside
> As white foam flies from the oar . . .
>
> Her thoughts were wailing
> Away on the wind like killdeer . . .
>
> Lance said: "It is horrible to hear the lies from her mouth like bees from a hive hot in the sun."
> (Robinson Jeffers.)

That is the speech of the poet. The words *like* and *as* are more distinctive of his art than rhyme or meter. And it is so of the poetic humorist.

> "Oh, Cuhnel," she said, and her voice seemed like the soft susurrus of a boll weevil and his loved one munching their way through a Georgia cotton patch. (Sullivan.)
>
> You mumble something about being in a hurry and coming back again, and retreat with all the grace and ease that would be shown by a hard shell crab that was trying to back into the mouth of a milk-bottle. (Cobb.)
>
> Sending men to that army is like shoveling fleas across a barnyard—they don't get there. (Lincoln.)
>
> The call of the yellow-billed cuckoo of North America is often mistaken for a Bloodhound drinking a bowl of milk. (Cuppy.)

Often a hen who has only laid an egg will cackle as though she had laid an asteroid. (Mark Twain.)

Sometimes the poet omits to say *as* or *like,* and simply names one of two similar things with the name of another, or talks about it as though it were the other. This the grammarians call "metaphor" as opposed to "simile," but it rests on the same psychological fact—the fact that comparing a thing with some other that is similar in perception but not for purposes of action, is like actually perceiving it.

The wind came down from heaven
And smoked in the fields . . .

She stood with her face high, the great sponge of red hair
Lying on her shoulders . . .

Pale violet, high over the lifted hawk-wings of divided hills . . . (Jeffers.)

And the poetic humorist employs the same device:

He give her a look that you could have poured on a waffle. (Lardner.)

He generally slept with his mouth open so that you could read his inmost thoughts. (Nye.)

There isn't a parallel of latitude but thinks it would have been the equator if it had had its rights. (Mark Twain.)

"One night," Lincoln told General Porter, "I passed through the outskirts of Louisville, when suddenly a man sprang from a dark alley and drew out a bowie knife. It glistened in the moonlight, and for several seconds he seemed to try to see how near he could come to cutting off my nose without doing it. Finally he said, 'Can you lend me five dollars on that?' I never reached in my pockets for money so quick in the whole course of my life. Handing him a bill, I said: 'There's ten dollars, neighbor. Now put up your scythe.' " That word *scythe* is a characteristically American way of letting a ray of playfulness into a somber situation. That too is comic metaphor.

I have shown in other books that the whole essential art of poetry, but for the adventitious aids of rhyme and meter, comes down to these two inward acts of graphic choice and colorful comparison. I think I have explained why this is so. Here I merely want to show that the poetic humorist is doing the same thing playfully that the poet is with serious intent. He is using words in such a way as to give us visions, and even if he can, hallucinations. Vision is, in fact, an inadequate word with which to describe his art, and so is "word-painting" and "mental pictures." For these terms have to do with eyesight only, but poetry and poetic humor appeal to every sense.

> Cherries are good, but they are too mutch like sucking a marble with a handle tew it.
>
> Peaches are good, if you don't git enny ov the pin-feathers into yure lips.
>
> When boblinks sing their mouths git as full ov musik as a man's does of bones who eats fried herring for breakfast.

These remarks from Josh Billings, a poetic humorist of genius, will show that *realization* rather than vision is the word to use. Not only sounds, smells, tastes and tactual sensations, but ideas, characters, emotions, *even actions when contemplated or described,* can form the material of poetry and poetic humor.

We saw how Shelley realized an idea with solemnity, and Mark Twain with humor. Let us see how Wodehouse realizes a character—or rather two of them. It won't hurt us if they turn out to be ourselves.

> In my experience there are two kinds of elderly Americans. One, the stout and horn-rimmed, is mateyness itself. He greets you as if you were a favorite son, starts agitating the cocktail shaker before you know where you are, slips a couple into you with a merry laugh, claps you on the back, tells you a dialect story about two Irishmen named Pat and Mike, and, in a word, makes life one grand, sweet song.
>
> The other, which runs a good deal to the cold, gray stare and the square jaw, seems to view the English cousin with concern. It is not elfin. It broods. It says little. It sucks in its breath in a pained way. And every now and again you catch its eye, and it is like colliding with a raw oyster.

In Chekhov's notebooks they found this sketch of a husband's character:

> A man, married to an actress, during a performance of a play in which his wife was acting, sat in a box, with beaming face, and from time to time got up and bowed to the audience.

Thurber

"All right, have it your way—you heard a seal bark!"

Speaking of the anti-contactual or kiss-declining male, in that learned inquiry, *Is Sex Necessary?* Thurber and White explain:

> In effect, he is a throwback to another period in history, specifically to the Middle Ages. He is a biological sport. (Note: this is very confusing, calling him a "sport," because the ordinary "sport" is not a kiss-decliner at all, anything but. Please keep in mind, then, that when I use the term "sport" I want the strict biological interpretation put upon the word. I want it and I intend to get it. If there are any of you who think you are going to find the use of the word "sport" in this connection so confusing as to make the rest of the chapter unintelligible, I wish you would drop out. Get something else to read, or, better yet, get some exercise.)

The thing that is ludicrous there, if you delve to the heart of it, is an emotion. For an author to become irate to the point of driving a reader out of his book on the grounds offered is funny. It is either funny or a case for the padded cell.

Thurber is a living disproof of Bergson's assertion that laughter is incompatible with emotion. He is as fatally preoccupied with taking painful emotions playfully as the decadent poets were with taking them seriously. He holds, too, the view of humor that Poe, the father of the decadents, held of poetry: it must be brief. Since he has, besides, a fantastic visual imagination, and what is rare among our comic writers, a literary style, we may well regard him as the very type of the poetic humorist. He hardly ever cracks a joke. Even his "Seal in the Bedroom" drawing—greeted by Robert Benchley as "the funniest line and picture ever printed in a magazine"—is not a joke. There is no point, properly and sharply so called, either in the line or picture. It is an act of hilarious imagination. And so is his story of "The Night the Bed Fell," or "The Dog That Bit People," or "The Day the Dam Broke," or any other piece or portion of that immortal book, *My Life and Hard Times.* His account of the end of the old Reo is perhaps the best one with which to illustrate the unadulterated fluid of poetic humor.

> Our poor old Reo came to a horrible end, finally. We had parked it too far from the curb on a street with a car line. It was late at night and the street was dark. The first street car that came along couldn't get by. It picked up the tired old automobile as a terrier

might seize a rabbit and drubbed it unmercifully, losing its hold now and then but catching a new grip a second later. Tires booped and whooshed, the fenders queeled and graked, the steering wheel rose up like a specter and disappeared in the direction of Franklin Avenue with a melancholy whistling sound, bolts and gadgets flew like sparks from a Catherine wheel. It was a splendid spectacle but, of course, saddening to everybody (except the motorman of the street car, who was sore). I think some of us broke down and wept. It must have been the weeping that caused grandfather to take on so terribly. Time was all mixed up in his mind; automobiles and the like he never remembered having seen. He apparently gathered, from the talk and excitement and weeping, that somebody had died. Nor did he let go of this delusion. He insisted, in fact, after almost a week in which we strove mightily to divert him, that it was a sin and a shame and a disgrace on the family to put the funeral off any longer. "Nobody is dead! The automobile is smashed!" shouted my father, trying for the thirtieth time to explain the situation to the old man. "Was he drunk?" demanded grandfather, sternly. "Was who drunk?" asked father. "Zenas," said grandfather. He had a name for the corpse now: it was his brother Zenas, who, as it happened, *was* dead, but not from driving an automobile while intoxicated. Zenas had died in 1866. A sensitive, rather poetical boy of twenty-one when the Civil War broke out, Zenas had gone to South America—"just," as he wrote back, "until it blows over." Returning after the war had blown over, he caught the same disease that was killing off the chestnut trees in those years, and passed away. It was the only case in history where a tree doctor had to be called in to spray a person, and our family had felt it very keenly; nobody else in the United States caught the blight. Some of us have looked upon Zenas' fate as a kind of poetic justice.

Now that grandfather knew, so to speak, who was dead, it became increasingly awkward to go on living in the same house with him as if nothing had happened. He would go into towering rages in which he threatened to write to the Board of Health unless the funeral were held at once. We realized that something had to be done. Eventually, we persuaded a friend of father's, named George Martin, to dress up in the manner and costume of the eighteen-sixties and pretend to be Uncle Zenas, in order to set grandfather's mind at rest. The impostor looked fine and impressive in sideburns and a high beaver hat, and not unlike the daguerreotypes of Zenas in our album. I shall never forget the night, just after dinner, when this Zenas walked into the living room. Grandfather was stomping up and down, tall, hawk-nosed, round-oathed. The newcomer held out both his hands. "Clem!" he cried to grandfather. Grandfather turned slowly, looked at the intruder, and snorted. "Who air *you?*" he demanded in his deep, resonant voice. "I'm

> Zenas!" cried Martin. "Your brother Zenas, fit as a fiddle and sound as a dollar!" "Zenas, my foot!" said grandfather. "Zenas died of the chestnut blight in '66!"

That is surely as far away as you can go from "witty" writing. It is the pure play of the humorous imagination. And if you will reflect a moment what the playthings are, a bad smash-up, a financial loss, an angry motorman, a family in tears, an insane old man, a sensitive young man's untimely death, a decaying corpse—all in one paragraph! —you will concede, perhaps, that unpleasantness and humorous delight are not remote.

CHAPTER VIII

Two Kinds of Comic Action

I SAID THAT even actions when contemplated or imagined can be ludicrous, just as things or situations can. They can partake of the nature of perceptual rather than practical humor. This complicates our science, but I do not know anything to do but face the complication.

When you see Charlie Chaplin trying to carry a roast duck through a crowded restaurant, get into a mix-up which gradually assumes the outlines of a football game, you do not wait for him to make, or fail to make, a touchdown with the duck before you laugh. When you see Harpo Marx leap into a wheeled garbage can and ride away to war as in a chariot, you do not care whether he wins the war or not. You laugh when the act begins and you are still laughing when it ends, and no matter how it ends. You laugh because there is something wrong with the whole thing as an object of perception. Its humor lies not in the failure of an expected result, but in a violation of the patterns in which we contemplate the world.

When Joe Cook goes eagerly to a telephone on the wall, rings the bell, and takes down the receiver, and the whole instrument comes off in his hands, that is funny in a different way. It becomes funny at a certain point in time. It moves toward an appropriate end, and is funny because it fails to get there.

Franklin P. Adams, when I asked him what essential humor is, said that he could not tell me, but he could show me what it is. He went outside and put on his hat and coat, and then walked in, removing them in a perfectly natural manner, and hung them up on the wall where there was no hook. My laughter, and that of his secretary, followed as spontaneously as a conclusion follows its premise. But again they followed at a certain point in time. The action as a whole was not funny. It became funny, just as a witty remark does, when it failed to reach its natural and appointed goal. Such acts as these, although enjoyed by a perceiver, do not belong in our science with perceptual or poetic humor, but with practical jokes.

W. C. Fields had a scene in which he came on the golf course with a caddy and spent eighteen minutes making ready and retired without ever hitting the ball. He tells me this is generally regarded as his most successful act. And it too, although he himself was ludicrous enough to look at, was in its structure practical rather than perceptual humor. To watch somebody make a bodily effort to hit a golf ball and fail, is not substantially different from hearing somebody make a mental effort to arrive at a meaning and fail. It is like an Irish bull. Or still more, it is like one of those intricate and patiently extended efforts of Frank Sullivan to explain something—the Lausanne Pact, for instance, or the ramifications of the Vanderbilt family. If you remember W. C. Fields on the golf course, read Frank Sullivan on "The Vanderbilt Convention" and see how much alike they are. It takes too long to be reproduced here, but there is a sentence or two in his piece on "Ocean Travel" which will recall the quality of it.

> . . . The word deck by the way, reminds me of cards and cards remind me of a feature of ocean travel which, next to falling down open hatchways, constitutes perhaps the greatest menace to the inexperienced ocean traveler. I mean the card sharp.
>
> Every liner has one or more card sharps aboard and experience has taught me that there is only one safe rule for a passenger to follow, i.e., never play with a stranger unless you yourself are a card sharp. If you are a stranger and do play cards with a sharp, then do not scruple to give him a rubber check in payment of your losses. These rubber checks, together with seasoned travelers who want to tell you about their eighty-six crossings, constitute perhaps the greatest menace of ocean travel to the poor card sharp, particularly if he is inexperienced or his faith in human nature is easily shaken. My experience as a card sharp has taught me that the safest rule for a sharp to follow is never to play with strangers unless they are card sharps too, and even then demand cash payment for all losses except your own. Is this clear? Oh, and by the way, never call the captain a card sharp. Call him "scupper."

In our conversation, Fields and I arrived at the formula that "the funniest thing a comedian can do is not to do it." And that is, remember, the opinion arrived at above about spoken jokes—that those which do not "get anywhere," if they are funny at all, are usually funnier than those which do. The same sole thing, moreover, is required to make these two not-gettings-anywhere funny—namely, the plausibility of their setting out to go. Any faltering or faking, any hint to the audience that you are not honestly and truly trying, is as fatal to a comic act as "giving away the point" is to a joke.

From the standpoint of the gifts required, it is of course one thing to make an action move honestly toward an end you are not going to reach, and a very different thing to make words drift plausibly toward a meaning and not get there. The one depends more upon simulation, the other upon ingenuity. That makes comic action seem very different from wit, although they are in final essence the same.

Another thing that makes them seem different is the ease with which people, laughing at the failure of an action, identify their comic pleasure with the pleasure of feeling superior to the actor. Here more than elsewhere the derision theory seems plausible. If a man goes eagerly to the telephone to call a number and the instrument comes off in his hands, the joke is on him, and what can our pleasure be except the hostile one of seeing him get fooled? How else can the facts be explained? If we were sympathetic, we should feel sorry, shouldn't we? So the argument runs.

The facts can be explained very simply, however, if you will stop being so adultly personal. When a man goes to the telephone to get a number, and you make him an object of idle attention, you are, barring special sources of emotion, neither sympathetic nor hostile. You are far more egocentric than either of those words implies. You are concerned with completing his movement as a part of *your* experience. The first thing that happens, therefore, when he fails, is a collapse of *your* plans—a collapse, in fact, of your whole momentary pattern of consciousness. That is the only thing that would happen if you had the perfect egoism of an infant, and that is what makes the action comic. Whether, and in what degree, other feelings enter in, and what these feelings are, will depend on accidental circumstances, your temperament among them. But no matter what they are—hostile and "superior," or pitiful and sympathetic—if they are too strong, they will drown and destroy the humor. That shows that humor is, like these others, a feeling in its own right. J. P. McEvoy, in *Mr. Noodle,* asserts that a feeling of superiority drowns the humor, if there is any, in our comic strips.

> They don't have to be funny. Did you ever watch anyone read a comic page? Did you ever see him laugh? Was there ever a laugh in "Little Orphan Annie," one of the most successful comic strips running? People don't want to laugh so much as they want to feel superior to somebody else. They want to be taller, or richer, or better-looking, than the people they associate with, and the only places most newspaper readers can find such people to gloat over are in comic strips.

There is much truth in those statements—much instruction too for those, if they are still with us, who insist that laughing and feeling superior are the same thing.*

W. C. Fields confronted me with a problem whose solution belongs in this chapter.

"It seems in general," he said, "as though people laugh only at the unexpected, and yet sometimes they laugh still harder exactly because they expect something. For instance, I play the part of a stupid and cocky person who has invented a burglar trap. I explain to the audience how I shall make friends with the burglar, and invite him to sit down and talk things over, and I show how the instant his rear touches the chair bottom, a lever will release a huge iron ball which will hit him on the head and kill him instantly. From then on the audience

* Gilbert Seldes has a like opinion of the comic strips. "According to my records," he says, "the last time a grown man laughed at a comic strip was in February of 1904, but that may be a typographical error. So far as I know, no child, male or female, has ever laughed at the funny page. Something is wrong. Perhaps with the comics. Perhaps with the name."

My own explanation of the popularity of the comic strip and the funny page is that, the dialogue being scrawled into the picture in a rather messy manner, it requires a little brain work to decipher it and see how it applies, and to people who use their brains as little as the average American newspaper reader does, this intellectual effort is an exciting adventure—especially on Sunday mornings when he has had a good long sleep and feels up to it.

knows what's coming. They know that I am going to forget about my invention, and sit down in the chair myself. They begin laughing when I start toward the chair, and their laugh is at its peak *before* the ball hits me. How do you explain that?"

I find the explanation in my feelings. A man who has invented a burglar trap and then goes and sits down in it is funny. Merely to mention him is funny. He does not have to do the sitting down. He does not have to do anything. He would be funny in a still picture—particularly if he happened to be W. C. Fields. The humor therefore, although involving an action, is perceptual rather than practical. But if I saw the act, my rich enjoyment of that ludicrous man and situation would be heightened and made gleeful by the assured prospect of the joy of seeing him—biff!—receive the iron ball on his own skull. It would be further heightened by the exciting question just exactly *when* that joy was coming.

If the laugh was at its peak before, and not after the blow fell, that proves, I think, that my feeling is correct—that this was the humor of a ludicrous situation heightened by suspense, and not the humor of a practical joke. For a practical joke, as we all know, whether enjoyed within the brain or followed with the eyes, does depend upon the abrupt collapse of an expectation, and the laughter at it always follows the collapse.

CHAPTER IX

A Note on Comic Styles

THOSE TO WHOM poetry means nothing but metrical or rhymed language will have a special difficulty in accepting the term *poetic humor*. Metrical and rhymed language, although not the essence of poetry, are deeply appropriate to it because their effect upon sensitive natures is hypnotic. They tend to produce a trance in which we realize the qualities of absent things almost with the sharpness of hallucination. The union of serious poetry, therefore, with versification is both natural and immortal.

This is not true about playful poetry. It is impossible to hypnotize in fun, and there is nothing more remote from playfulness than lyric rapture. Meter and rhyme, therefore, far from being native to poetic humor, are an anti-body, or at best a quite irrelevant adornment.

Rhymed verse, on the other hand, *is* peculiarly fitted to bring out, or back up, or chime in with, the point of a witty joke. This may be seen clearly in the following classic from the pen of Franklin P. Adams, our reigning genius in this field:

THE RICH MAN

The rich man has his motor-car,
His country and his town estate,
He smokes a fifty-cent cigar
And jeers at Fate.

He frivols through the livelong day,
He knows not Poverty her pinch,
His lot seems light, his heart seems gay,
He has a cinch.

Yet though my lamp burns low and dim,
Though I must slave for livelihood—
Think you that I would change with him?
You bet I would!

The unexpected vigor of the bard's honesty is what makes us accept with glee this deliberately mischievous wrecking of a sentimental train of thought. That is the "point" of the joke. But the rhyme also, chiming in so pat and perfect, like a light but timely clash of cymbals, just at the moment when that sudden honesty lands in our laps, adds reinforcement to the laugh.

That is the principal thing that rhyme or metric language does for humor. And so arises the paradoxical fact that practical wits resort to verse more often than poetic humorists. It is not paradoxical really, but another evidence of what we have insisted on, that play is a definite state-of-being in which things are not what they are in serious life. The poetic humorist, sensing this, prefers to lead us on in a calm and often somewhat square-toed style from one preposterous situation to another.

Dickens' sedate and rather green-grocerly oracular prose was an excellent vehicle for poetic humor. "Mr. Winkle, thus instructed, climbed into his saddle, with about as much difficulty as he would have experienced in getting up the side of a first-rate man-of-war," he says. And that is an excellent beginning for the funny story of a runaway. The inadequacy and anxious ineptitude of Mr. Winkle, his small size and the large size of his horse, are realized in one stroke of the poet's brushlike pen; and yet they are not realized as ugly, contemptible, pitiful or alarming—which of course they are. The simile, although true, is sufficiently out-of-true so that the situation can not be taken seriously. It is Dickens at his best—or rather better than his best.

"What makes him go sideways?" said Mr. Snodgrass in the bin to Mr. Winkle in the saddle.

"I can't imagine," replied Mr. Winkle. His horse was drifting up the street in the most mysterious manner—side first, with his head towards one side of the way, and his tail towards the other.

Mr. Pickwick had no leisure to observe either this, or any other particular, the whole of his faculties being concentrated in the management of the animal attached to the chaise, who displayed various peculiarities, highly interesting to a bystander, but by no means equally amusing to anyone seated behind him. Besides constantly jerking his head up, in a very unpleasant and uncomfortable manner, and tugging at the reins to an extent which rendered it a matter of great difficulty for Mr. Pickwick to hold them, he had a singular propensity for darting suddenly every now and then to the side of the road, then stopping short, and then rushing forward for some minutes, at a speed which it was wholly impossible to control.

"What *can* he mean by this?" said Mr. Snodgrass, when the horse had executed this maneuver for the twentieth time.

"I don't know," replied Mr. Tupman; "it *looks* very like shying, don't it?"

Still more amusing are those parts of the story which tell how, after the smash-up, these men were accompanied for some hours, and through a considerable series of life's involvements, by a now totally irrelevant and unnecessary and exceedingly tall horse. Don Marquis chose this chapter when asked to name his favorite piece of literary humor, and I imagine it was the insufferable intrusion of this gigantic horse, dissevered from all usefulness and yet inextricably involved with his unmitigated horsefulness in everything the patient heroes tried so manfully to do, which led him to rate the tale so high.

"It's like a dream,"—ejaculated Mr. Pickwick, "a hideous dream. The idea of a man's walking about, all day, with a dreadful horse that he can't get rid of!" The depressed Pickwickians turned moodily away, with the tall quadruped, for which they all felt the most unmitigated disgust, following slowly at their heels.

Irvin S. Cobb has an old-school, prosy-gaited style not unlike Dickens. And if you want to taste the difference between British and American poetic humor, I know no better way than to compare Mr. Winkle's experience on this "tall quadruped" with that of Irvin S. Cobb on a horse sixteen miles high.

Mind you I have no prejudice against horseback riding as such—Cobb says. Horseback riding is all right for mounted policemen and equestrian statues of generals in the Civil War. But it is not a fit employment for a fat man, and especially for a fat man who insists on trying to ride a hard-trotting horse English style, which really isn't riding at all when you come right down to cases, but an outdoor cure for neurasthenia invented, I take it, by a British subject who was nervous himself and hated to stay long in one place. . . . I have one friend who is addicted to this form of punishment in a violent, not to say a malignant form. He uses for his purpose a tall and self-willed horse of the Tudor period—a horse with those high dormer effects and a sloping mansard . . .

Once I tried it myself. I was induced to scale the heights of a horse that was built somewhat along the general idea of the Andes Mountains, only more rugged and steeper nearing the crest. From the ground he looked to be not more than sixteen hands high, but as soon as I was up on top of him I immediately discerned that it was not sixteen hands—it was sixteen miles. What I had taken for the horse's blaze face was a snow-capped peak . . .

Before I could make any move to descend to the lower and less rarefied altitudes the horse began executing a few fancy steps, and he started traveling sidewise with a kind of slanting bias movement that was extremely disconcerting. . . . I clung there astraddle of his ridgepole, with my fingers twined in his mane, trying to anticipate where he would be next, in order to be there to meet him if possible . . .

At that moment, of all the places in the world that I could think of . . . there were just two where I least desired to be—one was up on top of that horse and the other was down under him. But it seemed to be a choice of the two evils, and so I chose the lesser and got under him. I did this by a simple expedient that occurred to me at the moment, I fell off. I was tramped on considerably, but I lived and breathed—or at least I breathed after a time had elapsed—and I was satisfied. And so, having gone through this experience myself, I am in a position to appreciate what any other man of my general build is going through as I see him bobbing by—the poor martyr, sacrificing himself as a burnt offering, or anyway a blistered one—on the high altar of a Gothic ruin of a horse . . .

I am not trying to say which of these horseback rides is funnier or better, but merely what is the striking difference between them. Cobb's language is more vigorously imaginative than that of Dickens. There is more of the mind's play in it, and the mind is more utterly at play. Dickens, after departing from that man-of-war, only depicts with a discerning pen the actual events, which are themselves funny. Cobb's way of depicting the events is funny. A good part of what Dickens writes could be inserted in a tragic account of the same accident, it being mere graphic realism laughingly presented. Cobb's laughter molds the names he gives to things. It makes his language, as well as his experience, ludicrous.

It is customary to say that American humor is distinguished from British by exaggeration, but that is not the depth of the difference. All vigorously imaginative humorists exaggerate. The play of the imagination is what distinguishes American humor. The fact that this horse is sixteen miles high is secondary, a thing wholly and quite properly incidental to such a procession of equine attributes as a ridge-pole and high dormer effects, a sloping mansard of the Tudor period, snow-capped peaks and the solemnities of sacrifice in a Gothic ruin. . . . Dickens never used his mind that way, nor Charles Lamb either, nor Goldsmith, nor Fielding, nor even Shakespeare, nor any British humorist antedating the American influence—antedating, I mean, that late moment, approximately one hundred and twenty-five years after the surrender of Lord Cornwallis, when Great Britain woke up to the literary existence of the United States of America, a moment which we may for convenience identify with the conferring of a degree upon Mark Twain at Oxford in the year 1907. P. G. Wodehouse uses his mind that way all the time. But Wodehouse belongs conspicuously to the period of Anglo-American reunion through the moving picture and the radio—the period, so to speak, of the hook-up. He is, I believe, the only man living who speaks with equal fluency the American and English languages.

I shall return to this subject of American humor again—in fact, every time I come within jumping distance of it. For I enjoy the belief that America's most vigorously original contribution to the arts in general—with the exception of Walt Whitman's poems, and perhaps Isadora Duncan's dancing—has been her art of humor. Only in the matter of laughing and quizzically smiling and kidding things along did we pioneers feel entirely at home and imperious right from the start. Only here did we feel incomparably superior to the mother country. And without feeling incomparably superior to everybody, especially your mother, what can you accomplish in creative art? That robust and jovial humor, distinguished offhand by its recklessness, its willingness to take things laughingly right up to death's door and the throne of God, and trust for redemption not in some saving delicacy of expression, or some gentlemanly polish, or ultimate reverence for truth or the angels, but in an underlying faith in social laughter—that has been our chief new contribution to the poetry of life.

To return, however, to our textbook: poetic humor is *not* comic verse, and I hope it may be clear by this time what it is. It is the imaginative realization of the ludicrous. Since the ludicrous is some form of pain or unpleasantness playfully enjoyed, and since poets are famous for their *serious* enjoyment of pain, our theory runs here into another complication. It is only, however, a new occasion to stress the sharpness of the distinction between playful and serious. We enjoy the excitement of disgust seriously when Baudelaire tells us how he found on a beautiful morning at a turn of his path—

> A superb cadaver which the sky watched
> Open out like a flower. . . .

Yet how easily we could be led to take that same excitement playfully—to read even those sublime words as a jest.

I think one of the great difficulties about the so-called "modernist" writers—a reason why they seem so humorless—is that in their revolt against formal and philistine niceness they have made almost a cult of solemnly enjoying the unpleasant. Joyce even asks us to take puns and all sorts of linguistic tricks and misadventures seriously and regard them as a fervent literary experience. He has been compared to Rabelais, but he is less like Rabelais in this than any other writer. Other modernists ask us to savor with solemnity the fine edge of the preposterous in metaphor and simile. They are within their rights; to extend the range of experience is a primary function of the poet. But playful people find it a little difficult to stay long in the same book with them. They feel after a while like excusing themselves and saying: "Teacher, may I go out and laugh?"

CHAPTER X

Poetic and Pictorial Humor with a Point: Cartoons

IT REMAINS TO SHOW that ludicrous realizations like practical jokes may mean something to our minds, or suggest some attitude-of-feeling beyond that of comic laughter. They may or may not do this. And moreover the question whether they do or not is often, as in the case of Mark Twain's practical joke about the diamonds, a delicate one.

I will illustrate this with two news items from Abe Martin, whose real name was Kin Hubbard, and who stands high among modern American humorists because instead of insisting on a large salary, he insisted on writing not more than one item a day.

> 1. Druggist Lem Small severed an artery while fillin' a prescription fer a pork sandwich.

To me that was, in practically the same instant, ludicrously funny and a pointed comment on the modern drug store.

> 2. A funeral wuz haled before Squire Marsh Swallow's court and fined eight dollars fer speedin'.

That was ludicrously funny too, but some moments passed before I thought of the implied reflection on the deceased. For that reason my comic amusement and my serious satisfaction—for a reflection on somebody, dead or alive, is always a satisfaction—remained distinct.

These two things, when both present, do not usually remain distinct, but fuse and run together like tin and copper to make brass, or awe and humbleness to make reverence. That makes it natural to imagine that the comic emotion *is* the serious satisfaction, and hard for the true explanation of this emotion to stand up against the instinctive rationalization of it. The situation will be more clear, therefore, if we contrast an atom of poetic humor that has no point with one that has.

To call waffles "non-skid pancakes" is pure poetic humor. At least I think even the zealots of the derision theory would have a hard time finding an "animus" here, or deciding which noble entity, pancakes or automobile tires, is "degraded" by this metaphor.* When Artemus Ward called the American eagle "patriotic poultry," that too, if you can take it, was ludicrous, but it had most certainly a point, an animus, a "meaning." Artemus Ward's eagle could say with George Herriman's Krazy Kat: "It's wot's behind me that I am . . . It is the idea behind me, Ignatz, and that's wot I am." The same thing is true of Lincoln's remark about his difficulties with office-seekers: "The trouble is there are too many pigs for the teats." It is a picture with meaning, a political cartoon flashed on the inside walls of the skull.

Anything, of course, may have a meaning, and will in fact acquire one if you dwell on it with idle energy. Funny things are not different in this respect from solemn ones. Even Gelett Burgess' purple cow, I dare say, means a great deal to some of her admirers. But that is not why the cow is funny.

> I never saw a purple cow,
> I never hope to see one;
> But this I'll tell you, anyhow,
> I'd rather see than be one.

* Any such metaphor, of which one could find a million, is sufficient to disprove the assertion of Ralph Piddington (*The Psychology of Laughter,* 1933) that "every ludicrous situation involves two conflicting evaluations in the social order." Mr. Piddington most assuredly never saw a baby. I wonder if he ever enjoyed a farce or got into a laughing fit? The very existence of laughing fits disproves most effectively these recent efforts to find a "social" as opposed to a biological explanation of the comic feeling.

Cows seem to be inherently funny if you state them with accuracy, as Ogden Nash does:

> The cow is of the bovine ilk;
> One end is moo, the other milk.

And Arthur Guiterman:

> The cautious, collapsible cow
> Gives milk by the sweat of her brow;
> Then under the trees
> She folds her front knees
> And sinks fore and aft with a bow.

These droll and innocent cows occupy the same position in poetic humor that pure absurdities do in wit. They belong in the same category—I beg your pardon, but it is true!—with Irish bulls. And if you want to convince yourself that they too are usually more comical when innocent of meaning, a good way to do it is to turn back the leaves of your daily paper until you find one pictured in a political cartoon. She will be more important there, and more ingenious, and perhaps in other ways more admirable to an adult, but she will not be quite so droll.

A political cartoon, or indeed any humor with a serious point, is like a play school—it puts over a certain amount of education on the children, but this is made possible, as well as necessary, by the fact that the children are interested in play, not education. J. N. Ding, a genuinely humorous cartoonist, defined the cartoon in a way that makes this clear. "A sort of humor-coated capsule," he called it, "by means of which the sober judgments of editorial minds may be surreptitiously gotten down the throats of an apathetic public. In other words . . . the apple sauce in which political pills are immersed and fed to unwilling children." The children, I fear, are not always unwilling, the editorials being for the most part applesauce. But otherwise the definition is apt.

In Rube Goldberg's burlesques of the machine age, the pill is so distinct from the apple sauce that the children, he thinks, never get

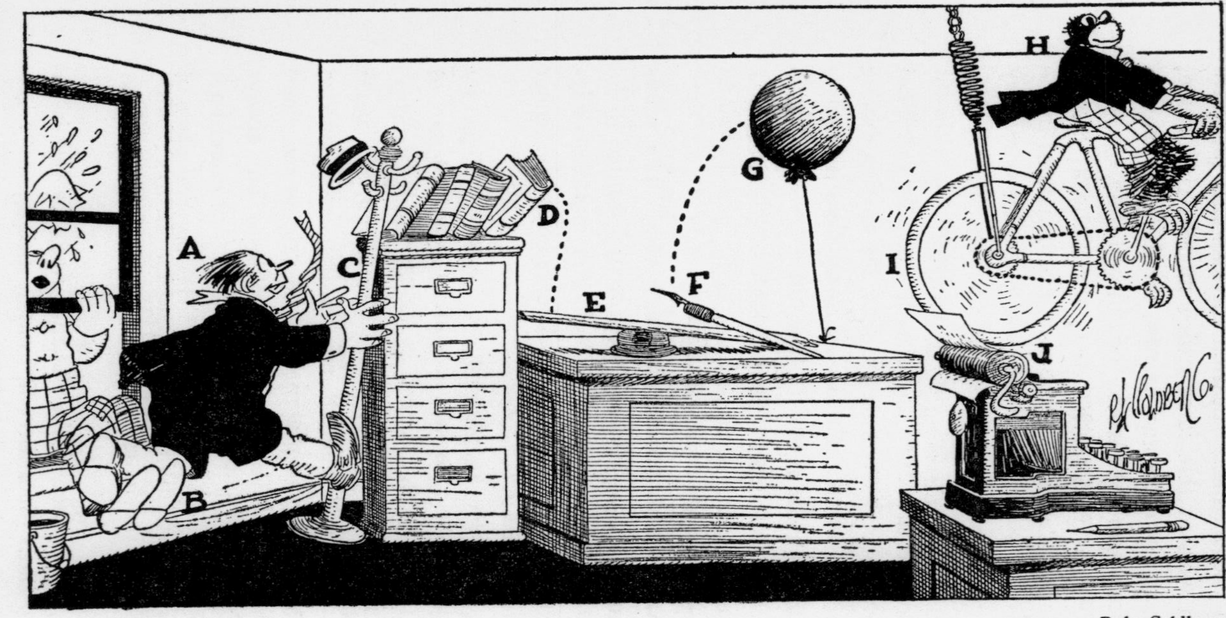

Rube Goldberg

Professor Butts chokes on a prune pit and coughs up an idea for an automatic typewriter eraser. Ring for office boy (A), who comes running in and stumbles over feet of window cleaner (B). He grabs for hat-rack (C) to save himself. Hat-rack falls against books (D) which drop on ruler (E), causing pen (F) to fly up and puncture balloon (G) which explodes with a loud report.

Trained monkey (H) mistakes report for gun that is the signal to begin his vaudeville act and he starts pedalling like mad. The rubber tire (I) passes over paper (J) and erases mistake made by sleepy stenographer who is too tired to do it herself because she had such a long walk home from an automobile ride the night before.

It is advisable to have your office over a garage so you can get quick service in case of a puncture.

it. He will describe to you with some passion the elaborate processes that are gone through with in this farce called modern civilization, beginning with the spade, the plow and harrow, the drill, the mower-and-reaper, the thrashing engine, the truck, the railroad train, etc., etc., in order to get a little flour into the hands of the National Biscuit Company; and then he will describe its intricate manipulations in the hands of that august company; and when he has built this true story up to surpass the wildest fantasies in his mad pictures, he will say: "And after all that, what do you get out of it—Jesus!—a little bit of a cracker!" And he will show you the size of that cracker. That is the "point" of Rube Goldberg's pictures to him. He studied mining engineering as a youth, and one of the tasks set to the class in Analytical Mechanics was to weigh the earth. It took them several months to do this, and when they got it done their answers would be forty to fifty quadrillion tons off, and the earth's specific gravity would have changed in the meantime.

"That gave me the humorous angle," Goldberg says. "The whole thing was a laugh to me, it was so far away from what I wanted to do. And to me that idea is still important, but it doesn't matter to anybody else. I am no satirist. I have no message. People enjoy the humor as they follow the pictures along."

Another way to sense the chasm between the humor of a picture and its serious meaning, is to contemplate the variegated blooms of laughter that spring up out of the inner darkness of James Thurber. Thurber will tell you in a very sweeping way—or would, two years ago—that his humor is "about" one thing, "beaten-down married people." "The American woman is my theme," he said to me, "and how she dominates the male, how he tries to go away but always comes back for more, being romantic and everlastingly nice and having an almost religious feeling about marriage." His favorite piece of humor, he said, is this stanza from Clarence Day, Jr.:

> Who drags the fiery artist down?
> Who will not let the sailor roam?
> Who keeps the pioneer in town?
> It is the wife, it is the home.

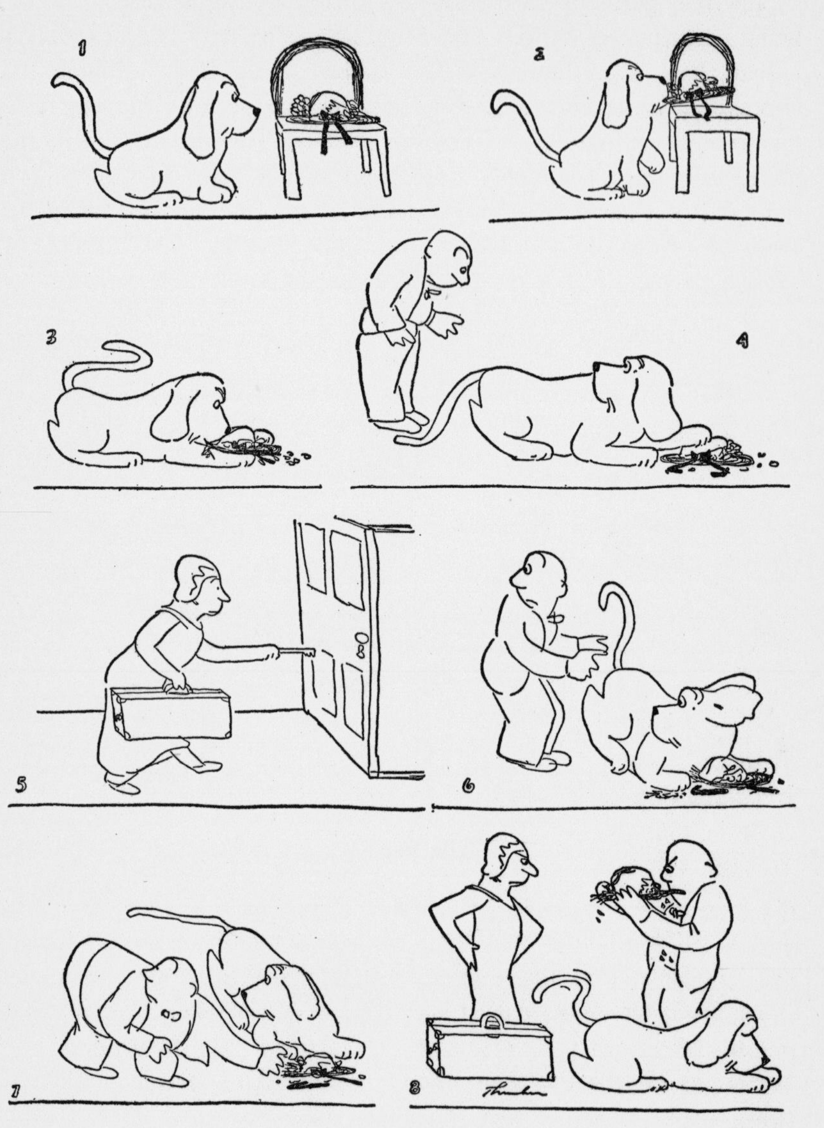

Thurber

The Hound and the Hat

Now it is perfectly clear to me—and to you also, of course, for we, being scientific, are entirely above any battles we may stoop to analyze—that there is no humor in that stanza at all. It is a simple and approximately accurate statement of fact. Thurber's attachment to it, far from being playful, is intensely serious. He recited it with the joyful expression commonly worn by a sexton when tolling his own funeral bell. And this serious concern of his finds expression in his comic drawings—in the Hound and Hat drawing, for instance, or "Sorry, partner!" It gives these drawings a value not possessed by

Thurber

"Sorry, partner!"

the intermittently insane grandfather above, or the young man who died of chestnut blight. It inhabits their humor, and merges with it inseparably, and without making it funnier makes it more acceptable to adult minds—acceptable at least to more adult minds. And it makes it more important.

I found Charlie Chaplin not only conscious of the distinction between pictorial humor and its point, but disposed to take a stand in favor of its having, in America in the future, a little more point.

"It seems to me," he said, "that there are two different kinds of laughter. Superficial laughter is an escape. The waiter comes in and the duck isn't cooked properly, and you pick it up and throw it at him—yes, and by God, he throws it back! That's an escape. It's a break in the monotony of normal conduct. That's superficial humor, slapstick. Subtle humor shows you that what you think is normal, isn't. This little tramp *wants* to get into jail. The audience thinks at first that he's ridiculous. But he isn't. He's right. The conditions are ridiculous. If I make them laugh that way, it's what I call subtle laughter.

"Modern humor frightens me a little. The Marx Brothers are frightening. Thurber, Stewart, Joe Cook, Benchley—yes, all of them. They say, 'All right, this is how we live and we'll live that way.' They go in for being crazy. It's a soul-destroying thing. They say, 'All right, you're insane, we'll appeal to your insanity.' They make insanity the convention. They make humor a premise. Acquiescence in everything disintegrating. Knocking everything down. Annihilating everything. There's no *conduct* in their humor. They haven't any attitude. It's up-to-date, of course—a part of the chaos. I think it's transitional."

CHAPTER XI

That Rich Jokes Are Both Witty and Ludicrous

THIS WORLD IS RUNNY, as Heraclitus said, and none of the square-cornered distinctions that words seek to establish in its elusive fluid will hold good everywhere and always. This is true of the distinction between chemical and physical, plant and animal, drunk and sober, poetry and prose. It is more obviously true of the distinction between poetic and practical jokes. There is no understanding humor until you grasp this distinction. And there is no understanding humor until you also perceive that certain unicellular jests elude it, and that the richest witticisms usually combine the mental trick with the ludicrous presentation. We must therefore devote a chapter to taking back what we said in the last ten. Such is life—or such at least the honest part of it.

For instance, when we were examining this subject from a distance I cited as an atom of practical humor the remark of Groucho Marx: "I would horsewhip you if I had a horse." That seemed a piece of pure nonsense, the holding out of a plausible meaning and snatching it away. Upon a closer view, however, it is not only the plausibility and the nonsense that make that remark funny, but also the horse! We saw in the quotation we made from Dickens how a horse's presence in a series of distinctly human transactions could be ludicrous; this remark of Groucho's, although in procedure a practical joke, borrows a smile from the same funny situation.

It also borrows a smile from the personality of Groucho Marx, who, as we have seen, is funny just as he stands—or walks.* And that is, of course, the simplest way in which a witty joke may be seasoned by an admixture of the ludicrous. It may be told by somebody who is himself ludicrous. That witty jokes when so told are a thousand times funnier than they are when you or I try to repeat them, is a sad fact that I need not dwell upon. But many a poor joke also, and not only poor but dying of old age, has been restored to health and vigor by a comic drawing. And it is a mere continuation inward of this same fact that when a witty remark, besides tricking the mind, suggests some funny perception to the imagination, its wit will seem more rich.

The man who came into a sporting-goods store to buy a pair of rowing pants, and said, "I want the kind with sliding seats," was entertaining you, from the point of view of the thought-process, with a pun, or near pun, on the word *seats*. A similar prank was played by the small Jew at Minsky's who, when denounced as a spoiled child, said: "No, you're wrong—our whole family smells that way." Yet certainly the humor in these two incidents is more than that of a mere play upon words.

Even B. L. Taylor's dinosaur, who had two brains,

> One in his head, the usual place,
> The other at his spinal base,
> And thus could reason *a priori*
> As well as *a posteriori,*

fooled you with a verbal trick, the old trick of starting you off on the figurative, and landing you in the literal signification—or vice versa, it does not matter. But it would be a pitiful science that tried to explain the humor of his lines as inhering wholly in that trick. Their humor is more rich than that. It is the humor of a super-Aris-

* Groucho Marx himself told me that it is one of the rules of his troupe never, if they can help it, to let a spoken joke stand by itself, but always to combine it with some comic "business." His empirical good judgment was confirmed in a "Statistical Analysis of Crowd Laughter" made by F. E. Lange at Columbia University. Lange reported that costumes enhance the funniness by one hundred per cent, business by four hundred per cent, and together they enhance the funniness by six hundred per cent. (Unpublished Master's essay.)

totelian dinosaur caused to rear up in the jungles of your fancy *by means of* such a trick.

In these examples the mixture of wit with poetic humor is fairly obvious, but it is present in many jests that seem at first glance purely witty. Artemus Ward's best joke, in the opinion of Josh Billings, was his remark when talking of Brigham Young and the Mormons that, "the pretty girls in Utah mostly marry Young." And there the wit is so dexterous, and the ludicrousness so everyday—a mere mischievous exaggeration—that you might be content to describe that as a clever pun and nothing more. It would be less than half as funny, however, were it not for the exaggeration. The two kinds of drollery, the pun and the mischievous fancy, fuse into a whole that is more comical than the sum of the comicalities of each.

Another immortal pun is Eugene Field's comment on the actor, Creston Clarke, that "he played the king as though he were in constant fear that somebody else was going to play the ace." The brilliancy of the trick of speech is blinding for an instant, but if you could depict the man's scared kingliness as graphically as that with a straight comic metaphor in the manner of Bugs Baer, it would still be funny. It does not need the trick. The fusion of the two comic kinds in one is what makes the remark not only brilliant but opalescent.

That is what Josh Billings meant when he said that "humor is wit with a rooster's tail feathers stuck in its cap." You might also say that wit is like a straight hand, poetic humor like a flush, and the richest jokes are like a straight or royal flush.

Next to the failure to distinguish practical from perceptual humor, the failure to see that in the richest jokes they are combined, is the chief cause of the inadequacy of all attempts to tell us why we laugh. They oversimplify the source of laughter. They imagine that some one phrase or formula, if they can find it, will convey all there is in a rare work of comic art. The truth is that jokes seem simple because like gunfire, or like polished gems, they flash, but they are in inner structure of all speech-values the most complex. That is why their full flavor will sometimes steal over you and occupy you slowly—far more slowly than the flavor of a phrase of poetry or truth or eloquence.

A school-teacher in Ann Arbor was once discoursing to her class about the romantic lives led by the American Indians.

> "I wonder," she said, "if there is any boy or girl in this class who has Indian blood in his veins?"
> Hubert Skidmore raised his hand.
> "Oh is that so?" she said. "What tribe, I wonder?"
> "Well, it wasn't exactly a tribe," Hubert explained. "It was just a wandering Indian."

It would be ungrateful to analyze an incident so rich in charm as that—one of the few true stories of our generation not to be found in the joke books of the preceding century. Even Mr. Horne will concede, I think, that its charm is not simple. It contains, to say the least, a plausible act of thought which comes to nothing; a schoolboy, dumb and wistful, in scorning or adoring whom, according to your temperament, you can find rest after that accident. It contains a comment on school-teachers, a gibe at the sentimentalizing of the teaching process, at the romanticizing of the American Indian. It contains images for the humorous imagination—not least engaging that of Hubert himself sitting there in such large innocence of the festivities entailed if his father had been a whole tribe of Indians. It contains those festivities of the tribe, the secret adventure of the wandering Indian . . . How foolish to turn from such a treasure with some offhand formula: "degradation," "superiority," "relief of tension," "psychic economy," "descending incongruity," "aggression," "compensation," "sexual release." What a waste of rich experience!

Part Five

HAVING FUN WITH LANGUAGE

CHAPTER I

Atrocious Puns

PUNNING IS A DRY CEREBRAL SPORT very far off, it would seem, from the bodily joy of being tossed through the air toward the arms of a nice plump mother and failing to arrive. And yet a pun too, if successful, is a process. And the process is substantially that same one of starting off hopefully somewhere and not getting there. In this case, however, it is not the meaning of the words which fools you, but the words themselves. The very sounds or letters which compose them have turned out to conceal a trapdoor or a sliding panel, and have cheated you and "let you down."

> The results of the activities of the D.A.R. might not be so minus—
> Says Ogden Nash (in a verse which to interrupt with a "says Ogden Nash" is not very heinous)—
> Were the ladies not troubled by sinus.
> Alas, every time they try to put people who don't agree with them on the stand as defendants
> They find themselves troubled by the sinus of the Declaration of Independence.

That is a good example of what we are talking about because it is so elaborate. It is not a pun but a punitive expedition. It differs from other puns, however, only in the amount of ground traveled. If you could see them in a slow movie, you would find that all puns, or the sentences containing them, set out on a similar journey. They all make ready, at least, for such a journey, and they invite you to go along. You pack up your intellectual baggage and climb aboard. The horn blows, the sentence starts—and then it stops and lies down in the road. It has a false axle, or paper spokes in the wheels. The whole thing, sentence structure, preparation, invitation, horn-blowing and all, was a hoax. This is what you would see if you could take a slow moving picture of any really jocular pun. A pun is a practical joke played upon the mind, not by means of a deceptive meaning, but by means of a flaw in the vehicle of meaning.

* * *

There is a persistent difference of opinion about puns, some finding them cottony in the mouth, and others doting on the taste of them. It is due in part to the fact that there are, corresponding to the three possible ingredients of a practical joke, three different kinds of puns: pointless, witty, and poetic. The pointless pun, known to the trade as *atrocious,* is to any lively sense of humor an affliction. Will Cuppy in his gentle and Lamblike—I mean Charles Lamblike—work on *How to Tell Your Friends from the Apes,* has confined three such puns, to keep them out of his text, in a footnote. Mr. Cuppy, I hasten to explain, is not a punster, but an authority on natural history. He has made a special study of beavers which ought to be in every beaver-loving home in our broad land, and he was writing at the time when these puns happened to him about gnus.

> Gnus—he said—are used chiefly by a certain class of authors for making atrocious puns, such as "No Gnus is good Gnus" and "Happy Gnu Year!" This will go on forever, too, because you can't teach an old Gnu tricks.

Leaving aside the fact that he is taking a crack at punsters, what you have there is three tiny claims or pretenses to mean something, which break down owing to a fault in the verbal vehicle. And the last one, "You can't teach an old Gnu tricks," is a double breakdown, because even if you mend the vehicle, spelling the faulty word n-e-w before you start, it still won't get you anywhere.

Charles Lamb recorded a similarly redoubled accident as one whose "utter and inextricable absurdity" he had enjoyed, but was at a loss to explain.

> An Oxford scholar, meeting a porter who was carrying a hare through the streets, accosted him with this extraordinary question: "Prithee sir, is that thy own hare or a wig?"

Absurdity as such, when presented in a proper-looking vehicle of meaning, just as it may be trying to a serious thinker, may be amusing to a mind at play. Once that is understood, it is no mystery if the amusement doubles when the absurdity does. The sentence tricks you neatly with the word *hare,* and it tricks you again when you try it out with *hair.*

What I meant to call attention to, however, in Will Cuppy's footnoteful of puns, was the peculiar way in which they are introduced. They are not "sprung" or "cracked" without a warning, and their jocularity allowed to emerge artlessly in the mind, as jokes usually are and should be. They are dragged expressly in, preceded indeed by a blare of trumpets announcing that they are going to be jokes, and that moreover they are going to be bad ones. The idea in this procedure seems to be that if you can not enjoy a pun as a good joke, you may at least, regarding jokes for a moment as serious creations, take its very badness playfully and laugh. A bad practical joke thus becomes a ludicrous object of contemplation. This peculiar way of introducing pointless puns doubtless dates back to Thothmes of Egypt, but it was first mentioned in English literature by John Dryden, who coined the aphorism that "the worst puns are the best." Charles Lamb was developing the same theme when he quoted the "utter and inextricable absurdity" we have been discussing. Bill Nye, in his essay on "The Care of House Plants," provides a raw example of it. Speaking of a calla lily, he says:

> One evening we had a free-for-all musicale at my house, and a corpulent friend of mine tried to climb it, and it died. (Tried to climb the plant, not the musicale.) The plant yielded to the severe climb it. This joke now makes its debut for the first time before the world. Anyone who feels offended with this joke may wreak his vengeance on a friend of mine named Sullivan, who is passionately fond of having people wreak their vengeance on him. . . .

If Bill Nye had believed in that pun as a joke, and not merely an atrocity colossal enough to be funny, he would not have told us that the plant died. He would have allowed the pun to tell us that. ". . . a corpulent friend of mine tried to climb it. The plant died of the severe climb it." That would have been a joke with a point, although for plenty of reasons a poor one. But his pun as it stands is not so much a joke, as a caricature of joking—an introverted form of humor that has of recent times become a pest.

> From our conversations with voters we are able to tabulate some trends in popular sentiment and perhaps even make a graph. (O Lord! keep us from making a joke about Graph Zeppelin!)

That is Robert Benchley. And here, still worse, is Dorothy Parker:

> *Appendicitis* is the work of Thew Wright, A.B., M.D., F.A. C.S., who has embellished his pages with fascinatingly anatomical illustrations, and has remarked, in his dedication, that he endeavors through this book to bring an understanding of appendicitis to the laity. And it is really terribly hard to keep from remarking, after studying the pictures, "That was no laity; that's my wife!" It is hard, but I'll do it if it kills me.

Frank Sullivan saves with a flight of fancy both the atrocity and the apology for it.

> He also showed us a place which he called "Mammoth Cave." It is a sort of cave, so called because one day a little girl, passing through, noticed that the cave was a good deal like a cave her father had given her mother for Christmas, so the little girl, who lisped quite badly, exclaimed, "Oh, there'th Mammoth Cave!" Well, sir, everyone laughed heartily at the tot's ready wit, which encouraged her so much that she immediately nicknamed the cave next door "Poppath Cave." The little tot's body was unfortunately never recovered.

This humor of the badness of bad jokes, although a neat corroboration of our theory, does not belong, I fear, to great literature. Ring Lardner put it where it belongs in his story "I Can't Breathe":

> So we got to talking and he is even cuter than he looks, the most original and wittiest person I believe I ever met and I haven't laughed so much in I don't know how long. For one thing he

> asked me if I had heard Rockefeller's song and I said no and he began singing "Oil alone." Then he asked me if I knew the orange juice song and I told him no again and he said it was "Orange juice sorry you made me cry." I was in hysterics before we had been together ten minutes. . . .

On the radio things have gone so far in this direction that our comedians are becoming serious, and leaving to the stooge the lowly task of lugging in jokes bad enough to be ridiculous. It is one of the sad results of making a mass-production business out of what is in its essential nature play.

It proves however—and this is our present business with it—that there is something wrong with a pun in the first place. In the chapter on nonsense, we agreed, or at least I did, that a pointless and absurd mental joke, if it is funny at all, is apt to be funnier than a joke with a point. With puns it is not so. A pointless pun is an affront to the sense of humor. It has to be mocked and ridiculed as a cripple before it will seem funny at all. What is the reason for this?

It is because the trick played upon the mind by a pun is not neat and purely playful. The punster does not lead us to expect one word, and then laughingly slip across another. He can not do that, because it is not our habit or nature to expect words. We expect meanings. Words are only containers of meaning. When one of these containers kicks back therefore, or springs a leak, we do not experience a sudden coming-to-nothing of our expectation. The collapse is not instantaneous. It does not grow out of the very act and posture of our minds. We have to pull up first, and remind ourselves that these pulpy vocables do exist, and only after that can we perceive that one of them has played us false. That momentary serious pause and readjustment of attention spoils the playful humor of the trick.

That is why when puns offer us nothing else but nonsense, no matter how neat and plausible their claim to sense, we call them atrocious, trying with this playful exaggeration to extract the ghost of a pale smile out of them.

CHAPTER II

Witty Puns

WITH THAT MUCH by way of protest against pointless puns, let us pass on to the subject of puns with a point—or rather pass back to it. For Ogden Nash's transcontinental expedition against the Daughters of the American Revolution was a pun with a point. It started us off, you remember, on a trail of sinus trouble in the head bones of some socially but not logically superior grand dames; we got nowhere on that trail because the word *sinus* let us down, not being what it seemed. But we did, as a result of that very let-down, find ourselves at the end of another trail we are not loath to travel—one offering a view of the weak logical position of those same grand dames whose social position, they frequently remind us, is so high. The good ladies are not troubled with sinus—no, that is nonsense—but they *are* troubled with signers, and that is a statement worth making.

There is, moreover, a secondary humor in this pun. It is a very lame pun—ridiculously lame like those we quoted in the preceding chapter—the words *sinus* and *signers* not being identical even in pronunciation. But there is a point in this lameness too, for one of the ways in which these exalted ladies are accustomed to demonstrate their elevation is by pronouncing *signers* as though it were identical with *sinus*. Thus again the joke is on them—the campaign, rather, for it has now assumed the proportions of a First and Second Punic War.

So much for the inner workings of a witty pun slowed down so you can see them. A swifter one will show better how delightful they can be. I once asked James Thurber to tell me the funniest line he remembered hearing on Broadway, and one of the two he remembered was a pun. The first was Fred Allen's remark to a bass-viol player who made strange noises, causing him to pause and gaze down into the orchestra in amazement:

> "How much would you charge to haunt a house?"

The other was the answer of the colored maid in Frank Craven's comedy, *The First Year,* when asked: "Did you seed the grapefruit?"

> "Yes ma'am, I seed 'em."

"For conveying the hopeless situation of a young wife trying to prepare a dinner with an ignorant servant," Thurber said, "I thought that line was about perfect."

When a line like that is spoken by a person conscious of its significance, it is an especially startling form of wit. It seems as though the very verbalness which makes a pun unplayful and uncouth when pointless, makes it a more brilliant achievement when the point is keen and clear. It may not be funnier than other kinds of wit, but it seems more wonderful.

A classic example will be found in the chapter where Mark Twain's Connecticut Yankee examines his assistant, Clarence, about the state of their fortifications against the nobility and the Church:

> "You tested the torpedoes?"
> "Well, I was going to, but—"
> "But what? Why, it's an immense oversight not to apply a—"
> "Test? Yes, I know; but they're all right; I laid a few in the public road beyond our lines and they've been tested."
> "Oh, that alters the case. Who did it?"
> "A Church committee."
> "How kind!"
> "Yes. They came to command us to make submission. You see they didn't really come to test the torpedoes; that was merely an incident."
> "Did the committee make a report?"
> "Yes, they made one. You could have heard it a mile."
> "Unanimous?"
> "That was the nature of it."

In the matter of demanding that puns make good, as in so many other matters, Mark Twain set a high pace for American humor. His reaction against the British habit of pointless punning, inveterate ever since King James made it a court fashion, was important in the development of our humorous style. We are more hilarious than the British, more trustful to the mood of play, and therefore freer with our laughter. But ours is an outdoor, imaginative freedom. Our excessive tolerance is toward fatuous horseplay. Toward fatuous little tricks of tongue and grammar we are less tolerant than the British. We think that kind of pointlessness is "sissy." We did, at least, in the days before mass production had broken down all our standards, and made playful taste an intrusion on the serious business of turning out ten thousand jokes a day for the joke market.

Will Rogers flourished before this change. And if that implies that he failed to flourish after it, I have no correction to make. He represented the decline of American "homely" humor into commercialism, rather than its survival into the age of commercialized jokes. In his heyday, however—on the vaudeville stage with a lasso—Will Rogers was a great humorist. He tells the story of an appearance before President Wilson in Baltimore just before we entered the World War, a dramatic moment in the history of American humor, and there is a witty pun in that story which gives me an excellent excuse to quote it. He himself gave me the permission.

> It was just at the time we were having our little Set Too, with Mexico, and when we were at the height of our Note Exchanging career with Germany and Austria. . . . I was the least known member of the entire Aggregation, doing my little specialty with a Rope and telling Jokes on National affairs, just a very ordinary little Vaudeville act . . .
>
> I was late, and as the show went along I would walk out of the Stage door and out on the Street and try to kill the time and nervousness until it was time to dress and go on. I had never told Jokes even to a President, much less about one, especially to his face. Well, I am not kidding you when I tell you that I was scared to death. I am always nervous. I never saw an Audience that I ever faced with any confidence . . .
>
> The nearer the time come the worse scared I got. George Cohan, and Willie Collier, and others, knowing how I felt, would pat me on the back and tell me, "Why he is just a Human Being; go on

out and do your stuff." Well, if somebody had come through the dressing room and hollered "Train for Claremore Oklahoma leaving at once," I would have been on it . . .

Finally a Warden knocked at my dressing room and said, "You die in 5 more minutes for kidding your Country." They just literally shoved me out on the Stage.

Now, by a stroke of what I call good fortune, (for I will keep them always) I have a copy of the entire Acts that I did for President Wilson in the Five times I worked for him. My first remark in Baltimore was, "I am kinder nervous here tonight." Now that is not an especially bright remark, and I don't hope to go down in History on the strength of it, but it was so apparent to the audience that I was speaking the truth that they laughed heartily at it. After all, we all love honesty . . .

Now Pershing was in Mexico at the time, and there was a lot in the Papers for and against the invasions. I said "I see where they have captured Villa. Yes, they got him in the morning Editions and in the Afternoon ones let him get away." Now everybody in the house before they would laugh looked at the President, to see how he was going to take it. Well, he started laughing and they all followed suit.

"Villa raided Columbus New Mexico. We had a man on guard that night at the Post. But to show you how crooked this Villa is, he sneaked up on the opposite side." "We chased him over the line 5 miles, but run into a lot of Government Red Tape and had to come back." "There is some talk of getting a Machine Gun if we can borrow one. The one we have now they are using to train our Army with in Plattsburg. If we go to war we will just about have to go to the trouble of getting another Gun."

Now, mind you, he was being criticized on all sides for lack of preparedness, yet he sat there and led that entire audience in laughing at the ones on himself.

"See where they got Villa hemmed in between the Atlantic and Pacific. Now all we got to do is to stop up both ends." "Pershing located him at a Town called, Los Quas Ka Jasbo. Now all we have to do is to locate Los Quas Ka Jasbo." "I see by a headline that Villa escapes Net and Flees. We will never catch him then. Any Mexican that can escape Fleas is beyond catching."

Will Rogers was much and very skeptically amused at my disposition to "analyze humor"—also at my inability to do it offhand while he and Irvin Cobb were filling the air with reminiscences of their greatest gags. This one about Villa and the fleas came up, and in reply to his challenge I made him a small bet that, given time, I could distinguish "fourteen points" in which it excelled the common run of puns. His part of the bargain was to read the fourteen points and tell me what he thought about them. I did not find fourteen points, but I found ten, and I sent them to him—but he was off to Alaska . . .

Here are the ten points:

In the first place the subject matter is, or was, intensely interesting; our minds are set moving by the phrase "Villa escapes net and flees," with genuine excitement. Second, the plausibility is perfect; the phrase is honestly quoted from a headline, and we move forward without any forced effort to co-operate along a line of thought dependent upon the word *flees*. Third, we are encouraged by the phrase "We will never catch him then," to keep moving a little time in that same direction—not too long, but long enough to feel well on our way toward an idea. Fourth, the collapse of our verbal vehicle is unforeseen and instantaneous. In the words "Any Mexican who can escape . . ." we are still traveling serenely along on the original argument; the collapse is sudden, therefore—is instantaneous—when we find out that the word we were relying on is not *flees* but *fleas*. Fifth, besides being instantaneous it is unusually comprehensive, the word having not only deceived us in meaning, but in pretending to be a verb when it was really a noun. Sixth, having recovered our balance, we find ourselves traveling the new line of thought as serenely, and with as little forced effort as we were the old. Seventh, this new line of thought, besides being genuine, is interesting, and leads to an idea that we enjoy—the prevalence of fleas in southern countries being to northerners a fixed symbol of their own superiority. Eighth, this idea does really in a formal way complete the original argument, so that the speech not only makes enjoyable sense, but makes the very sense we set out after. It doesn't matter whether Villa escapes net and *flees*, or escapes net and *fleas;* in either case we can't catch him. Ninth, and by no means least in importance, the images evoked by the two readings are totally incongruous; it is impossible to combine the perception of a general and his army escaping a military net with the perception of a man escaping fleas; it is interestingly impossible, and therefore it is ludicrous. Tenth, a man escaping fleas, or trying to, is funny anyway. Being a minor and not in the least sublime affliction, the idea of fleas is and always has been a stock property of comedy, one of the perennial mental playthings of the race. The joke is therefore as rich for the imagination as it is neatly played against the reason.

Those who can add to these ten points of perfection the image of Will Rogers himself standing there chewing gum in a lazy way, performing feats of skill with a lasso as absently as other loafers whittle a stick, and throwing off somewhat accidentally like electrons from a spinning atom these slow gleams of humor and flashes of electric wit, will not need my insistence that a pun can be a brilliant work of art. This Oklahoma cow-puncher, "doing his little specialty with a Rope and telling Jokes on National affairs," before he himself got roped in the juggernaut of American commercial entertainment and induced by payments in gold to water down his infinitely more precious ore, was a high point in our native art of humorous monologue. It never went higher.

"I am the Kuhn of Kuhn, Loeb and Co."

CHAPTER III

Poetic Puns

As we saw in the case of the general and the fleas, a double-meaninged word, besides tricking the mind, may conjure up two images in the imagination which violently refuse to mix. That is the funniest thing a pun can do, the thing it is most fit to do. And when it does that, it has no need of meaning.

Take the frontispiece to Eddie Cantor's book on the panic in Wall Street:

> "I am the Kuhn of Kuhn, Loeb and Co."

That has no point, and the little trick it plays on the mind is not interesting, the word *coon* having no more significant business in the phrase "Kuhn, Loeb and Company" than the word *gnu* in "Happy New Year." But Cantor's pun is funnier than Cuppy's, because the imagery in both directions is specific, and the tones of feeling conflict actively. A gnu merely has no place in a New Year's greeting and no relation to it. But a coon and a Kuhn have enough points in symmetry so that their refusal to coalesce is an event. Instead of a mere nothing with a slight flush, so to speak, of color, we have a definite effort of the imagination baffled in a definite way.*

People with a violent prejudice against "coons" will, I suppose,

* This pun is made more humorous too by the word *the,* which makes it possible to play the whole trick through without altering the spelling of the word *Kuhn.* This strengthens the claim upon the imagination, it seems to me, of the phrase "Kuhn, Loeb and Company," and yet at the same time gives a kind of emphasis or fine edge to the inappropriateness of what is entailed by the other spelling.

imagine that their comic pleasure lies in scorning the Negro in this picture. People whose racial prejudices, abetted by their financial experiences, lie rather against Kuhns, will be equally sure they are deriding the banker. People who possess the gift of humorous laughter will know that what they are doing is enjoying a joke.

Both Frank Sullivan and Ring Lardner make frequent use of nonsensical puns, but their puns have quality because they are not plays upon words only, but upon image and emotional atmosphere. They are not dragged in dead and backwards like conundrums, either, but arrive on their own wings trailing clouds of incongruity.

> When I went to college—says Frank Sullivan—I went out for checkers, and reported for a try-out one night after I had been bowling. So I said to Tad Meriwinkle, the famous coach, "I'm a little stiff from bowling." And he looked at me and roared, "I don't care where you're from, take a couple of those checkers and work out with them five or ten minutes till I see what you can do."

Punch had a custom, like *The New Yorker,* of quoting news items from provincial papers and laughing at them in a brief comment. It once quoted from the Leeds *Courier* the following obituary notice:

> Died April 15th 1895, John, the son of Henry and Rachel Longbottom, at the age of 2½ years.
>
> *Punch's* comment was: *"Vita brevis est, ars longa."*

Perhaps *"Vita brevis est . . ."* is all that *Punch* actually printed, but that served to bring two sufficiently incompatible landscapes into juxtaposition for those who knew their Latin . . . And I will hope my supersensitive readers do not.

Before departing from the subject of puns I want to make them an occasion for another short sermon on the derision theory. It may have surprised some readers when I called Frank Craven's line above about the grapefruit, "I seed 'em," a pun. A pun is generally thought of as a perpetration, rather than a mistake. An unconsciously funny mistake, moreover—called "naïve humor" in the literature of this subject—tastes so different from a witty crack that it seems almost to belong to another order of being. However, the very same verbal accident may appear either as wit or a mistake, and the significant fact is that in both forms, notwithstanding their profound difference, it will evoke laughter and the feeling of the comic.

This indicates again that the comic feeling is elementary, and not to be identified with other emotional reactions. Particularly it indicates that the comic feeling is not to be identified with a feeling of the prestige relation between the laugher and the laughee. For this relation differs to the depth in the two cases. In "naïve humor" we are amused *at* a person's stupidity; in wit we are amused *by* his ingenuity. In the one case our serious feeling might normally be "superior"; in the other it would be envious or admiring. As Josh Billings said:

> When a man laffs at *yu,* he duz it because it makes him feel superior to you, but when yu pleaze him with what yu have uttered, he admits that yu are superior tew him.

That is the simple fact about men's feelings. And it leaves nothing for the derisionists to do but build up rationalizations so elaborate that a moment's contemplation of the simple fact—or a mere memory of the existence of simple facts—ought to be enough to break them down. They say, for instance, that a witty person amuses us by *pretending* to make mistakes, and thus enabling us to *pretend* to be superior to his *pretended* stupidity, and that we derive from these pretenses—by what further process of pretense is not explained—a *real* feeling of glory over him. Or still more fantastically, they assert—in the case of puns, at least—that the word itself appears in an inferior position, and that our feeling is one of "triumph (superior adaptation) over the degradation of a nobler word." I quote this from A. M. Ludovici, who gets it from Alexander Bain. Apply it, if you can, to some of the puns we have been enjoying in this chapter. Or even if you have not enjoyed them—whatever you have been doing—was it remotely similar to looking down from heights of self-complacence upon an unfortunate word that has got caught, so to speak, with its pants down, and congratulating yourself that you are the more "noble" of the two? Is that what you have been doing with your mind? Is there any actual fact in it at all? For my part, I find the idea not only false to my experience, but in my reasoned opinion—to be quite candid—a little bit cuckoo. I am, like Mr. Ludovici and others, quite hard up for self-esteem, but I am not so hard up that I can get a kick out of my superiority to a misused word, and I think few sane people are.

The mistakes of children often take the form of puns, and they have a flavor of their own due to the very remoteness from derision of our delight in them. A child has a right to make mistakes. Moreover the mistakes of children betray their interests as well as their ignorance, and most of us have a lingering sympathy for the interests of childhood. Imagine a person of any gentleness of heart, or wistfulness of memory, being moved to "show his teeth" in a spiritualized snarl

Al Frueh

Diagram showing cross-section of a bee. (The cross-section is located just behind the tail.)

of superiority on finding in his small boy's notebook these carefully remembered lines from a familiar hymn:

Shall a mother's tender care
Fail toward the child she-bear?

There may be people in the world like Mr. Ludovici's portrait of himself, but I doubt it. Sudden affection and not sudden glory would flood most civilized minds in the recoil from the ludicrous humor of that pun. Its point or affirmation, if it has one, is not that children are stupid, but that they are dear.

In Corey Ford's Diagram showing cross-section of a bee, which he has kindly loaned me as a decoration for this chapter, I detect a trace of the same engaging charm—"cross" being a childhood word, especially when applied to the place where he applies it.* But that is

* The drawing is one of Al Frueh's illustrations in Corey Ford's *A Gazelle's Ears*.

an individual reaction, of consequence only as showing the folly of asserting that any particular emotion other than the humorous one must be present when we laugh. So far as other emotions are concerned, the same joke will be felt in different ways by different people.

Stephen Leacock, in discussing what he calls the "secondary effect" of certain puns, reminds us of the schoolboy who defined the equator as "a menagerie lion running around the earth." * He says that for him the secondary value in this schoolboy lay in a "reflection on the mechanical way in which he had been taught." When I made the acquaintance of the same schoolboy, nothing in heaven or earth was more remote from my mind than a reflection upon the way he had been taught. A delight in his vivid and real interests overflowing the rigidities not only of education, but of the outlines of words, was what reinforced for me the ludicrous humor of the pun. My pleasure focused, in reflection, upon those words "running around," their two-way appropriateness, the perfect plausibility with which they sustain the schoolboy in his erroneous but creditable assumption that a circumference is really something interesting and worth talking about.

If Mr. Leacock's introspection is as good as his humor—which upon some other grounds I doubt—it is hardly too much to say that he has "missed the point" of this pun. He has missed, at least, the better half of the treasure that lies under it. Influenced, perhaps, by his belief that "the savage who cracked his enemy over the head with a tomahawk and shouted 'Ha! Ha!' was the first humorist," that giving somebody "the merry ha! ha!" is, in fact, the origin of all laughter, he has tried to perceive as satire what is richer when perceived as sympathetic humor.

That savage who was so harsh and murderous, and from whom we are supposed to have evolved into a race of peace-loving and benevolent Christian gentlemen, has had no scientific standing for the last fifty years. If he did not perish at the hands of the nineteenth-century anthropologists, he certainly died in the World War. And if he did not die then, it will do him no good to learn the news in yesterday's papers, that Jean Charcot, polar explorer for the French Ethnographic Museum, came home with the evidence that Eskimos laugh "1200

* *Humor, Its Theory and Technique,* 1935.

per cent" more than any other people of the earth. For Eskimos are the most peaceful people of the earth, a people to whom war is absolutely incomprehensible, and the whole business of leaving tomahawks in other people's skulls for patriotic reasons is regarded as an unpardonable, if not monstrous, breach of good manners.

CHAPTER IV

The Fun of Distorted Words

IT IS COMMONLY ASSUMED that when we smile at a misused language, what amuses us is the ignorance, or pretended ignorance, of the character using it. The fact is that distortions of our speech patterns are intrinsically funny when plausibly introduced, and the function of the ignorant character is usually to introduce them plausibly. James Russell Lowell attributed substantially the same mispronunciations to Hosea Biglow, whom he offered as a guide and counselor to the nation, and to Birdofreedom Sawin, whom he held up as a prime rapscallion to the nation's contempt. He did so for the same reason in both cases—namely that mispronunciations are funny.

> A man came into a butcher shop and asked for "a pound of kidlies."
> "Kidlies?" the butcher said. "You mean kidneys, don't you?"
> The man looked surprised.
> "I said kidlies, did'l I?"

You may feel scornful; nothing can stop you. I merely find it droll. To my mind the old philosophers of India approached this problem wisely. They approached it, as a laughing infant must, impersonally.

> The comic—they said—in which the permanent condition is mirth . . . may arise from the fun of distorted shapes, words, dresses, gestures, etc.

That is the simple truth. In the permanent condition called mirth, and called by us the play attitude, distorted things are funny—and words sometimes the funniest of all. Everybody who has been a child, or been in a laughing fit, knows this.

Joel Chandler Harris boasted that his Uncle Remus dialect was "phonetically genuine," and attributed to the Negroes themselves the "quaint and homely humor" conveyed by it. Somebody at least, either Mr. Harris or Uncle Remus, was indulging in the conscious fun of word-distortion when Brer Rabbit asked the Tar-Baby:

> "How duz yo' sym'tums seem ter segashuate?"

Mr. Dooley's Irish brogue made no pretense to be phonetically correct; it just went in for being funny. The author himself once described it to me as "a language never heard on land or sea." Certainly that word *jackuse* in "The Dreyfus Case"—to my mind and eye one of the funniest yet invented—belongs to no known tongue.

> Whin th' judge come up on th' bench an' opined th' coort, Zola was settin' down below with th' lawyers. 'Let us pro-ceed,' says th' impartial an' fair-minded judge, 'to th' thrile iv th' haynious monsther Cap Dhryfuss,' he says. Up jumps Zola, an' says he in Frinch: 'Jackuse,' he says, which is a hell of a mane thing to say to anny man. . . .

As to Milt Gross, I hardly know what to say. He seems to combine a marvelously true ear with a recklessly fanciful imagination, and give us a dialect that is at once "phonetically genuine" and utterly preposterous. Those who back the claims of Arthur Kober against him affirm that Kober's dialect is more "exact"—an unsmiling affirmation which leaves the humorous presumptions, so far as I am concerned, entirely with Milt Gross.

> Of cuss, in de beginning when was joost bing esteblished de woild it deedn't was nidder by Ijjipt a seengle pyrameed nodder by Sweetzerland ivvin a Elp—was hall over de woild Hice wot dees was de Hice Hage.
>
> So occurding de system wot is entitled de ceetizens from China, Chinamen, so was entitled de inhebitants from de Hice Hage, Hicemen!!

So dees Glazers from hice wot it was hall over de woild so was a whole time trevelling arond; nutt-bond, witt sout-bond, witt Trenscontinantel, witt Union Paceefic Glazers wot it deedn't nidded in dem days de pipple nidder Sobways nodder trollicozz . . .

So was foist de foist hage den gradually a sacund hize hage, und in cocklussion was a toid witt a futt hize hage witt in bitwinn itch wan a hintermeesion. . . . So in itch hintermeesion it axeested critchures wot it belunged in de following kettegories. Wiz:

Nomber Wan—SEA FOOD—Feesh, clems, hoysters, lobsters, shreemps, scellops.

Nomber Two—RAPTILES—Snakes, woims, ketterpillows, leezards, scuppions, mounsters.

Nomber Tree—MEMMELS—Kemels, &c.

Nomber Furr—PIPPLE—Man, weemen, goils, boyiss, babizz, tweens . . .

What Milt Gross did with pronunciation and represented with spelling, Artemus Ward did with spelling itself. Without much regard for the spoken tongue, he made words look funny to the eye.

Sir,—I'm movin along—slowly along—down tords your place. I want you should rite me a letter, sayin how is the show bizniss in your place. My show at present consists of three moral Bares, a Kangaroo (a amoozin little Raskal—'twould make you larf yerself to deth to see the little cuss jump up and squeal), wax figgers of G. Washington Gen. Tayler John Bunyan Capt. Kidd and Dr. Webster in the act of killin Dr. Parkman, besides several miscellanyus moral wax statoots of celebrated piruts & murderers, &c., ekalled by few & exceld by none. . . . If you say anythin abowt my show say my snaiks is as harmliss as the new born Babe. What a interestin study it is to see a zewological animil like a snaik under perfeck subjecshun!

This invention, appearing in the Cleveland *Plain Dealer* in 1858, was the beginning of a great career—the beginning, you might almost say, of the literary career of a distinctively American humor. As I read it with a playful sympathy—and without that there is no use reading pure humor at all—a smile arises at the word *tords*. That word is funny just as it sits there on the page. The word *zewological* is still funnier, and in the same instantaneous way. I find the whole sentence, "What a interestin study it is to see a zewological animil like a snaik under perfeck subjecshun" a delicate circus—and largely, for some reason, because of the rather mild distortion of the word *snaik.*

To the prigs of modernity the mere fact that this style is past is enough to condemn it. But modernity is a poor thing to feel priggish about; it only makes you a more obvious mark for the prigs of a new modernity to sneer back at. No man can keep up with the times for more than seventy years, and after that his frantic efforts to do so look silly forever. So let us be a little philosophic. Let us remember that in those days "correct" spelling was a comparatively recent invention—spelling having been an adventure for everybody in the seventeenth century—and playful bad spelling was a new and natural delight.

Artemus Ward's readers, among them men as gifted in laughter as Abraham Lincoln, found this new way of distorting words so delightful that it became a humorous convention, and Josh Billings felt compelled against his wish to follow it. His essay on "The Mule" when printed in correct spelling was ignored, but when made over in deliberate imitation of Artemus Ward, opened the way to fame.

> The mule is haf hoss and half Jackass, and then kums tu a full stop, natur diskovering her mistake . . .
>
> Tha are the strongest creeturs on earth, and heaviest akording tu their sise; I herd tell ov one who fell oph from the tow path, on the Eri kanawl, and sunk as soon as he touched bottom, but he kept rite on towing the boat tu the nex stashun, breathing thru his ears, which stuck out ov the water about 2 feet 6 inches; i didn't see this did, but an auctioneer told me ov it, and i never knew an auctioneer tu lie unless it was absolutely convenient.

I hope these examples have proven that distorted words can be funny of themselves when presented in the condition called mirth. The problem is to make that fun accessible to us in our sobriety and sad old age. And this is accomplished for misspellings, as it was for puns, in two ways—the witty and the poetic.

The distorted spelling of one word may turn out to be the natural spelling of another, and the word thus accidentally arrived at may make sense in a new direction. Thus Bill Nye writes: "The story was foundered in fact." And Ring Lardner: "Doctor Gasp had been drinking heavenly"; "As I sit here I am surrounded by a corpse of experts just as ignorant as me . . ."

On the other hand, the imagery or poetic flavors of the words thus accidentally identified may—as in the "three moral Bares" above—amusingly refuse to mix. Not only is the word *bare* a poor imitation of the word *bear,* but the bear himself is not *bare,* which is a more imaginative accident.

> Listen to my tail and be silent that you may here.
> I girded up my Lions & fled the seen.
> Peas to his ashes.
> I paws and address you.

One reason we feel so emancipated from bad spelling is that poetic humor has taken wings among us these last twenty years to an extent that makes the device unnecessary. Our humorists quite arbitrarily, and by divine right of riot, identify one word with another that looks a little like it, and achieve these same effects with no pretext at all. Hear Frank Sullivan, for instance, enjoying a reverie about the Old South.

> Aunt Cindy Mammy. Dear old soul. How many times I had sought consolation in her vast and comfortable bosom for some real or fancied tragedy of childhood, a stubbed toe—or *any* kind of toe. Aunt Cindy Mammy may have been black, but her heart was big enough for any kind of toe, stubbed or unstubbed. We children all used to rush to that capacious bosom for comfort in time of sorrow. Few bosoms were so rushed as hers. (Of course, those were the days, the good old days, when a bosom was a bosom, and vast herds of bosom ranged the western plains. With the advance of civilization the bosom gave way and is now practically extinct.)

With people who spell correctly behaving that way, what is the use of bad spelling! Also what is the use pretending that the writer's ignorance is what makes you laugh?

Of course the point of a misuse of language *may* lie against the user of it. Here, as elsewhere, humor, besides being humorous, can bite. Of that these lines will recall a classic example:

> Paris is devine. I mean Dorothy and I got to Paris yesterday, and it really is devine. Because the French are devine. . . .
>
> And when a girl walks around and reads all of the signs with all of the famous historical names it really makes you hold your breath. Because when Dorothy and I went on a walk, we only walked a few blocks but in only a few blocks we read all of the famous historical names, like Coty and Cartier and I knew we were seeing something educational at last and our whole trip was not a failure. I mean I really try to make Dorothy get educated and have reverance. So when we stood at the corner of a place called the Place Vandome, if you turn your back on a monument they have in the middle and look up, you can see none other than Coty's sign. . . .

A fine humorous taste ought to sense the difference between a satire like *Gentlemen Prefer Blondes,* in which every linguistic misstep is a fresh shaft of laughter against the imagined writer, and a style like that adopted, for instance, by Ring Lardner in his news comments.

> Well it seems that a big bunch of the riff and raff has been horning their way into New York society the last year or two and things has come to such a pass that the elite was libel to find themselves time after time attending partys which people that work for a liveing was also guests at same, with the result that high mucky mucks would half to rush home early and disinfect themself. Some hostesses has forgot their social standing to such a extent that they have included Indiana and Wisconsin born folks in their invitations. It has got so that a person of breeding and refinement don't hardly dast come out of the house for the fear of being spoke to by some scum that they had met the night before by mistake, and it certainly is a terrible thing to be crouped up at home without nobody but your own wife or husband to talk to.

It would be a feat of emotional gymnastics to deride both the author and the objects of his derision in such a passage.

CHAPTER V

That Bad Grammar Is Good Fun

ARTEMUS WARD coined the word "ingrammaticisms" to describe some ways of making language funny not expressly included in the previous chapter. They are co-equal with the ways of making it unsightly to the inner eye. As soon as you have learned that some grammatic form is "wrong," and learned to feel it wrong, you are prepared to enjoy it playfully as funny. You will find, moreover, that that wrongness is most humorous in play which repels you most in serious composition. To me the most unpleasant ingrammaticisms are those which sin against reason—using words, I mean, without a keen sense of their logical relations. As an earnest composer of "English," I am a little old-maidish about these matters. If I write the sentence, "There is nobody in the world who could do what he has done," I miss the word *else* acutely. Correspondingly, I find excessive pleasure in a funny line like this:

> There is probly more promersing and virtuous young men in toledo than there is anywheres.

Tautology, or using two or more words to express the same meaning, is another sin of logical obtuseness that in humor always makes me laugh.

> My kompany consists of myself two boys a forrun Italyun who plays the hand orging, 1 cangaroo, 6 snakes, calerforny bare and other wild beasts two numerous to mention.

That "forrun Italyun" has no point, but I like him beyond measure. I like still better these tautologies which have, I think, a point:

> When a feller once gets it into his head that female women are all after him, you might just as well dispute with the wind as argue with him.
>
> His wife's mother on the female side.

Another ingrammaticism we all learned to abhor is the double negative, and that too is a treasure to the comic writer. Indeed the quadruple negative in Robert J. Burdette's "Romance of the Carpet," is his chief surviving claim to immortality.

> And he turned away with a heart full sore,
> And he never was seen, not none no more.

Ambiguity is funny, and is especially dear to the humorist because, like the pun, it provides a pretext for ludicrous imagery.

> Mrs. S. was the last to enter the dirigible. Slowly, with her huge nose pointed skyward, she headed for the distant horizon.

Latinity is another thing we learned to shun. But it is not a very precisely bad thing, and hence not so funny. At least I can not go into hysterics when Dickens calls an ear an "auricular appendage," although some, I believe, have done so. Ring Lardner drops into this style somewhat surprisingly in his most humorous story, "The Facts."

> Bob's hirsute adornment having been disturbed by one of his spouse's digits during one of the orgies, he went upstairs ten minutes before dinner-time to effect repairs.

There is no sin of rhetoric more instinctively disliked than anticlimax, and there is none more naturally amusing, as you can see in this important truth from Robert Benchley:

> Readers of the humorous weeklies lolling about in their debilitating hot baths or toppling off luxurious club divans, have no idea of the sadness and heartaches which go into the fashioning of the

> little jokes which they thumb over so carelessly. It is not generally known, I believe, that one comic editor dies every eighteen minutes, or, at any rate, feels simply awful. . . .

Wallace Irwin in the guise of a Japanese schoolboy—and without too much concern about being either Japanese or schoolboy—put on a veritable riot of ingrammaticisms.

> Hon. Miss Maizie Jone, young lady of considerable antiquity & large average weight, promise pay me 10c hr. teach her bisickle ride. I teach her gently by up-hill; but by down-hill teaching become deliciously rapid because of nervousness enjoyed by hon. machinery. Japanese Boy is earnest to stop it & can not do until Baker Wagon ensue & leave Hon. Maizie broken among machinery. I am Hospital Corps for help; but Hon. Maizie become loudly thankless. Time there was ½ hr. & no pay.

That is enough, I hope, to indicate that if we were businesslike, we could go through a book on English composition, and show that every single thing condemned as "bad" by serious taste has been a source of pleasure in the comic writers. We could also go through a textbook in logic and show that a joke can be found—or if time presses, manufactured—to correspond to every fallacy, or rational unpleasantness, in Aristotle's list. Bugs Baer's Uncle John's argument that "you can always judge a man by what he eats and that therefore a country in which there is no free lunch is no longer a free country," will do as an example. All you have to do, if you want to invent a new kind of humor, is to find an old and firmly established way of being unpleasant which has not yet been exploited as a mode of play.

That is what Ogden Nash did. He took bad versification in all its cruder forms and made an elephantine frolic of it. Bad versification in its finer forms, the hyperdithyrambic meters and too elaborately pat rhymes, had long been made a source of laughter. Was it not in fact a little hard to keep from smiling at some of the long rhymes in Tom Hood's "Bridge of Sighs"? We were diabolically tempted, I remember, to say, "Handle with care," instead of, "Lift her with care." And in Poe's "Raven," we gave up the struggle.

> While I nodded, nearly napping, suddenly there came a tapping,
> As of someone gently rapping, rapping at my chamber door.

Those lines found their true place, I think, in the diary of the young woman psychoanalyzed by Dr. Jung. She was in love with an indifferent young officer on a boat, as I remember, and she just couldn't get that "contagious rhythm" out of her head.

When it comes to Poe's "Bells," the thing is so patently artificial as serious poetry that a question has arisen whether Poe himself was not fooling.

> Hear the sledges with the bells,
> Silver bells!
> What a world of merriment their melody foretells!
> How they tinkle, tinkle, tinkle,
> In the icy air of night!
> While the stars that oversprinkle
> All the heavens seem to twinkle
> With a crystalline delight,
> Keeping time, time, time,
> In a sort of Runic rhyme
> To the tintinnabulation that so musically wells
> From the bells, bells, bells, bells,
> Bells, bells, bells,
> From the jingling and the tinkling of the bells.

Taken seriously it is bad. But playfully it might be very good—almost as good as Eugene Field's merry verses about old Horace:

> It is very aggravating
> To hear the solemn prating
> Of the fossils who are stating
> That old Horace was a prude;
> When we know that with the ladies
> He was always raising Hades,
> And with many an escapade his
> Best productions are imbued.
>
> There's really not much harm in a
> Large number of his carmina,
> But these people find alarm in a
> Few records of his acts;
> So they'd squelch the muse caloric,
> And to students sophomoric
> They'd present as metaphoric
> What old Horace meant for facts. . . .

There is something very like comic juggling in such verses. They delight at once with playful singsong and with serious skill. Arthur Guiterman introduces a half-in-earnest sentiment into the mixture, and draws us back without losing the humor, toward Poe's "Raven" or "The Bridge of Sighs."

On order that must be obeyed
I sing of a dear little maid;
A mirthfully serious,
  Sober, delirious,
  Gently imperious
    Maid.

And first we'll consider her eyes
(Alike as to color and size);
  Her winkable, blinkable,
  Merrily twinkable,
  Simply unthinkable
    Eyes.

Then, having a moment to spare,
We turn our attention to hair;
  Her tendrilly-curlative,
  Tumbly-and-whirlative,
  Super-superlative
    Hair.

Forbear to dismiss with a shrug
Her nose, undeniably pug;—
  Her strictly permissible,
  Turn-up-like-thisable,
  Urgently kissable
    Pug.

Now, moving a point to the south,
We come to an Actual Mouth;
  A coral, pearliferous,
  Argumentiferous,
  Mainly melliferous
    Mouth.

Observe, underneath it, a chin,
Connoting the dimple within;
  A steady, reliable,
  Hardly defiable,
  True, undeniable
    Chin.

By all that is fair! it appears
We'd almost forgotten her ears!
Those never neglectable,
Tinted, delectable,
Highly respectable
Ears!

And last let us speak of herself,
That blithe little gipsy and elf,
Her quite unignorable,
Absence-deplorable,
Wholly adorable
Self.

Turning his back on all this humor of the "too utterly too too" in the matter of versification, a fault of excessive artifice when seriously presented, Ogden Nash adopted for his plaything the faults committed by a person who is not a poet and has no artifice at all. If you have ever tried to write rhymed verse, you will recognize in Nash's writing every naïve crime you were ever tempted to commit—artificial inversions, pretended rhymes, sentences wrenched and mutilated to bring the rhyme-word to the end of the line, words assaulted and battered into rhyming whether they wanted to or not, ideas and whole dissertations dragged in for the sake of a rhyme, the metrical beat delayed in order to get all the necessary words in, the metrical beat speeded up unconscionably because there were not enough words to put in. It is almost a mystic experience to find everything that as a poet you most despised, and that as a critic of poetry most set your teeth on edge, turned into rich delight by the simple process of going the limit with it in a playful mood.

I sit in an office at 244 Madison Avenue
And say to myself you have a responsible job, havenue?

What could be more simple? And what more delightful?

Look at the ancient Egyptians, they had thousands and thousands of years of prosperity and contentment, and they may have credited it all to Ra and Osiris and Isis.
But the real reason was that they just didn't get to hear about it and worry about it if somebody else was having a crisis.

Suppose for instance there was another European war tomorrow and we heard about it, we'd probably get into it without stopping to think should we?
But if we never heard about it until it was all over, we couldn't get into it very well, could we?
I'll certainly bet that if our ancestors had worried as much about other people's ancestors' troubles as we do about the troubles of people whose ancestors our ancestors didn't worry about the troubles of, they would never have had time to have any descendants, even Admiral Byrd or William Beebe.
And then where would we be?
So I think the best way to guarantee our own and our descendants' felicity
Is to abolish all means of communication, particularly those abetted by electricity.

I am tempted to say that no one who has not tried to write poetry can fully enjoy the works of Ogden Nash. To poets his humor is enriched by a rapturous feeling of *giving up the struggle,* which is not like anything elsewhere in the world. It is also, of course, enriched by values which have nothing to do with versification, for Ogden Nash is a fertile humorist and a thoughtful person. The new thing he has invented, however, the vehicle which carries all these values, is nothing but verse so awfully bad that you can not take it seriously.

In his first volume Mr. Nash acknowledged a debt to the "Sweet Singer of Michigan," Mrs. Julia Moore, whose verse was so bad that nobody except herself could take it seriously. She took it so seriously that a cult of mock-admiration arose, and she achieved a place of booby immortality in American literature. Stephen Leacock cites her verses as an example of what he calls the "supercomic." It is the thing usually described as "naïve humor," and he calls it supercomic because he thinks it must necessarily be funnier when a comic thing is naïve than when it is ingenious. He thinks this—at least so I judge—because he is trying his best to believe in a superiority theory of laughter. He could be dissuaded, I should think, by the simple device of asking him how much time he ever spent actually reading the works of the Sweet Singer of Michigan. He could surely be dissuaded by comparing a sample of her naïve verse with one from her ingenious disciple. Here, for instance, is something that Leacock quotes from the Sweet Singer about Lord Byron:

The character of Lord Byron
Was of a low degree,
Caused by his reckless conduct
And bad company.
He sprung from an ancient house
Noble but poor in deed.
His career on earth was marred
by his own misdeeds.

Here are a few lines from Ogden Nash on the same general topic:

In heaven and earth more than is dreamed of in our philosophy there are a great many things,
But I don't imagine that among them there is a wolf with purple and gold cohorts or purple and gold anythings.
No, no, Lord Byron, before I'll believe that this Assyrian was actually like a wolf I must have some kind of proof;
Did he run on all fours and did he have a hairy tail and a big red mouth and big white teeth and did he say Woof woof woof?
Frankly I think it very unlikely, and all you were entitled to say, at the very most,
Was that the Assyrian cohorts came down like a lot of Assyrian cohorts about to destroy the Hebrew host.
But that wasn't fancy enough for Lord Byron, oh dear me no, he had to invent a lot of figures of speech and then interpolate them.
With the result that whenever you mention Old Testament soldiers to people they say Oh yes, they're the ones that a lot of wolves dressed up in gold and purple ate them.

If humor did consist of, or depend upon, a feeling of superiority, it would be true that Mrs. Moore, to whose ingenuousness we are really superior, would have the advantage of Ogden Nash, whose ingenuity we should be proud to equal. The truth is that there is more humor in one couplet of Ogden Nash, like

Rumanians and Serbs
Get on my nerbs,

than in the whole life story and complete works of the Sweet Singer of Michigan.

Part Six

LAUGHING AT TOO-MUCH AND NOT-ENOUGH

CHAPTER I

Exaggeration

THERE IS ALWAYS something the matter with anything at which you laugh. And there are—need I argue?—innumerable ways in which something can be the matter with a thing. It can be dirty, dumb, daft, drunk, dilapidated, dark-faced, down-and-out—to mention a few familiar ones beginning with *d*. But after you have gone through the alphabet and listed all the adjectives which imply that something is the matter, and all the nouns they might apply to, you are not half through with the material of humor. For then you have to list all the ways in which a thing can be perfectly all right, except that there is too much or not enough of it. Ears, for instance, are perfectly all right, but a little too much of them is a great deal more than enough. Indeed, the merest hint of a slight excess equipment or carrying of spare parts in these regions will provoke a laugh.

> One day not long ago—says Frank Sullivan—I was in my study engaged upon some research when my seven-year-old niece, Ida, came romping in, seized a bottle of ink, and poured the contents over my head. The minx knows full well her old uncle hasn't the heart to scold her for interrupting him, and she takes advantage of it.
>
> "What is oo doin', nonkie?" she asked.
>
> I gave her a good kick in the shin.
>
> "Talk English, or get out of here," I ordered.
>
> "Well, hell's bells," she protested, rubbing the injured tibia, "all I wanted to know was what you were doing."
>
> "I am doing some research on inflation."
>
> "What's inflation?"
>
> "Don't you know?"
>
> "No. What is it?"

"Never mind. Do you know what fiat money is? Do you know at what figure France pegged the franc in 1927?"

"No."

"Do you know how to peg a franc?"

"Nope."

It was incredible. I was amazed. The world shaken by a tremendous economic upheaval, yet this girl, possible future mother of Presidents, knew nothing of inflation. I could scarcely believe my ears and told Ida so frankly.

"I can understand that," she said, gazing at the organs in question.

It is not so easy as that to make laughter out of eyes, because eyes as large as they come are not unpleasant. The nose is more of a quantitative problem, and the nose does rival the ears in the cordiality of its invitation to exaggerate. The first thing any clown or comedian thinks of in the dressing room is to put on some more nose. Nature, when she set out to make her comic masterpiece, W. C. Fields, gave him too much nose. And there is no mystery about this. The human nose is something of a protuberance, anyway. Other animals wear it more neatly sunk into the face. It takes only a little more of the human nose to be too much. And it is the *too* much—always and absolutely—not the *much,* that is funny.

Muchness, in fact—called *hyperbole* when it appears in serious literature—is one of the most affecting forms of speech. Understatement, or putting it mildly—called *miosis* by those who need another big word to remember—is still more forceful. It is only when putting it mildly is not quite putting it at all that this becomes funny. And it is only when exaggeration goes beyond some humanly reasonable bounds that it makes you want to laugh.

How beautiful are your steps in sandals
    O rapturous maiden!
The curves of your hips are like necklaces,
    the handicraft of an artist.
Your navel is a round bowl,
    in which liquor is never lacking.
Your belly is a heap of wheat,
    fenced in with hyacinths.
Your two breasts are like two fawns,
    twins of a gazelle.

Your neck is like a tower of ivory,
your head upon it is like Carmel.
Your eyes are pools in Heshbon,
at the gates of Bath-rabbim.
Your nose is like a peak of Lebanon,
overlooking Damascus.

That, you see, is beautiful and moving. And yet it would take only a mischievous grin, or the addition of a pair of ears in the same proportion, to turn the last line into comedy.

You're the top,
You're Mahatma Gandhi,
You're the top,
You're Napoleon brandy,
You're the purple light
Of a summer night
In Spain.
You're the National Gallery,
You're Garbo's salary,
You're cellophane.

That has the mischievous grin all the way through. At least I hope it has, for I never feel sure about these Broadway love-songs, whether they are meant to amuse the intelligent or express the serious raptures of boobs.

The contrast, at any rate, will make clear what is essential to a humorous exaggeration. There must be some thing or quality about which you are not deeply concerned, and a playful extension of it beyond what you can seriously accept. There is nothing inherently funny about crops growing and growing fast, but there is humor in this description of how they grew in the old days in the frontier country.

> Why, any one of them hot nights you could jist go into a little patch of fifty acres, clost to the house, an' hold your ear down, an' you could hear the young potatoes quarrelin', an' the old ones a grumblin' because they didn't lay along and stop crowdin'. Why, one day one of our squash vines chased a drove of hogs better'n half a mile, and they ran and squealed as if the old boy was after them. (Quoted by Constance Rourke in *American Humor.*)

Fred Allen was funny in the same way when he told of a scarecrow that "scared the crows so badly they brought back the corn they had stolen two years before."

Noel Coward's famous postcard from Paris with a picture of the Venus de Milo—"You see what will happen to you if you keep on biting your nails"—is of the same family.

Bob Lamont sent me this example of the current humor of the cattle country:

> A cowboy in a city restaurant ordered a steak well done, and when it came in he cut a slit in it, and turned to the waiter: "Do you call that well done? I've seen critters hurt worse than that get well."

That is a late echo of the wave of monumental "tall talk" which swept over this country from the West and Southwest in the eighteen-thirties and forties, and which gave rise in England to the opinion that the one thing American humorists know how to do is to exaggerate. I shall say something about that opinion in a little while. In fact, I shall say a chapterful. Here I merely want to point out that, however they may love to do it, Americans are not the masters of exaggeration. Exaggeration is a boisterous, Jove-like, lusty, life-embracing kind of playfulness. And Americans are far too busy being virtuous—at least in books—to master such an art.

Remember, for instance, the passage where Mark Twain spends the night hunting for a lost sock in a hotel room, and which concludes: "I glanced furtively at my pedometer, and found I had made 47 miles. But I did not care, for I had come out for a pedestrian tour anyway." That is a fair example of our exaggerative humor, and here is a piece of it:

> I started to get up, and knocked down an umbrella; it made a noise like a pistol shot when it struck that hard, slick, carpetless floor; I grated my teeth and held my breath—Harris did not stir. I set the umbrella slowly and carefully against the wall, but as soon as I took my hand away, its heel slipped from under it and down it came again with another bang. I shrunk together and listened a moment in silent fury—no harm done, everything quiet. With the most painstaking care and nicety I stood the umbrella up once more, took my hand away, and down it came again.
>
> I have been strictly reared, but if it had not been so dark and

> solemn and awful there in that lonely, vast room, I do believe I should have said something then which could not have been put in a Sunday-school book without injuring the sale of it.

There is certainly nothing lusty or boisterous in that last sentence. It is not a jovial exaggeration, but a facetious understatement. And it was not put there because it belonged there, but because Mark Twain, to say nothing of extending himself, dared not give us the faintest echo of what he actually said in that dark room. Around Elmira, where I grew up in his shadow, Mark Twain was as famous for his fertility and control of a stream of strong language in moments of crisis as he was for his books. He did come out of the Southwest, and bring with him the habit of overabundant characterization. But you will find no sample of it in his writings. He was, as Van Wyck Brooks says he was, clipped and afflicted with Puritanical gentility—not so much to the detriment of his serious work as of his abounding play. And that is true of all American boisterous humor, in so far, at least, as it got put between the covers of books. Rabelais, instead of trying to make those oaths funny by a kittenish allusion to a Sunday school, would have let you know how they resounded through the chamber, and out into the street, and rattled the battlements of the city, and how they rang the bells in the belfry, and shook the citizens out of their slumbers, and the priests out of conjunction with their flagons, and the lawyers out of the whores' beds. And then he would have started in letting you hear two or three of them, and then two or three more, and once he got started in that course he would not have stopped until he had exhausted a dictionary of malediction, and added two or three pages of unheard-of and up to that moment uninvented explosives. Nobody ever equaled Rabelais in the humor of exaggeration, and nobody with a leash on ever will.

From the unedifying spectacle of Mark Twain in full flight of exaggerative humor dropping to an insipid understatement for fear of introducing a little language into literature, it will do our ears good to turn back to a page from the master of exaggeration.

> At that time, which was the season of vintage, in the beginning of harvest, when the country shepherds were set to keep the vines, and hinder the starlings from eating up the grapes, as some cake-

> bakers of Lerné happened to pass along the broad highway, driving into the city ten or twelve horses loaded with cakes, the said shepherds courteously entreated them to give them some for their money, as the price then ruled in the market. For here it is to be remarked, that it is a celestial food to eat for breakfast, hot fresh cakes with grapes, especially the frail clusters, the great red grapes, the muscadine, the verjuice grape, and the laskard, for those that are costive in their belly; because it will make them gush out, and squirt the length of a hunter's staff, like the very tap of a barrel; and oftentimes, thinking to let a squib, they did all-to-besquatter and conskite themselves, whereupon they are commonly called the vintage thinkers. The bun-sellers or cake-makers were in nothing inclinable to their request; but (which was worse) did injure them most outrageously, calling them prattling gabblers, lickorous gluttons, freckled bittors, mangy rascals, shite-a-bed scoundrels, drunken roysters, sly knaves, drowsy loiterers, slapsauce fellows, slabber-degullion druggels, lubberly louts, cozening foxes, ruffian rogues, paltry customers, sycophant varlets, drawlatch hoydens, flouting milksops, jeering companions, staring clowns, forlorn snakes, ninny lobcocks, scurvy sneaksbies, fondling fops, base loons, saucy coxcombs, idle lusks, scoffing braggarts, noddy meacocks, blockish grutnols, doddipol-joltheads, jobbernol goosecaps, foolish loggerheads, flutch calf-lollies, grouthead gnat-snappers, lobdotterels, gaping changelings, codshead loobies, woodcock slangams, ninnie-hammer flycatchers, noddypeak simpletons, turdy-gut, shitten shepherds, and other suchlike defamatory epithets. . . .

I wish I could go on quoting this story, and tell you how those cake-bakers were driven off, and how they went back home and raised an army, the vanguard of which alone numbered "sixteen thousand and fourteen arquebusiers or firelocks, together with thirty thousand and eleven volunteer adventurers," and how they invaded the country of the shepherds, despoiling in particular the vineyards of an abbey where dwelt "a claustral monk, called Friar John of the funnels and gobbets," and what five solid pages of things happened to that army when this Friar John took after it with a stout cross made out of the stem of a sorb-apple tree. I would soon convince you that American tall stories are the short and simple annals of the poor compared to the adventures of the mind and imagination of Rabelais. But I must return to my subject, which is not American humor—I seem to remember—but the world-wide fact that too much even of a good thing, if taken playfully, is funny.

It remains to show that this kind of funniness, like all others, may or may not have a point. I suppose there was a point in the above exaggeration of a cake-bakers' fracas, if we were historical-minded enough to look it up. Probably Rabelais was taking a dig at some contemporary noble national crusade or conflict. And notwithstanding that the humor of his story has been enjoyed for four hundred years by men who knew nothing of his point, you would find that scholars still identify the humor with the point. The passage of time having separated them, leaving the humor in Rabelais' text and the point somewhere else in the library, we might, it would seem, make bold to infer that they are two things.

When these two things are flashed before us in one sentence, however, it is not so easy to perceive that they are two. Eugene Field's news note, for instance:

> Colonel G. K. Cooper went swimming in the hot water pool at Manitou last Sunday afternoon, and the place was used for a skating rink in the evening.

Or Stephen Leacock's opening of an essay on education:

> An education, when it is all written out on foolscap, covers nearly ten sheets.

Or Dorothy Parker's remark when told that Calvin Coolidge was dead:

> How can they tell?

Or Mark Twain's addendum when sending a greeting to ex-President Grant:

> He will remember me, because I was the person who did not ask him for an office.

Here exaggerative humor is hardly distinguishable from wit. And yet there is no tricking of the thought-process. There is no reason why these remarks are comic as well as caustic, except the reason that *too much* of anything, if plausibly brought in and playfully received, is comic.

CHAPTER II

Exaggeration as a Weapon: Caricature, Burlesque and Parody

THE EASIEST WAY to make things laughable is to exaggerate to the point of absurdity their salient traits. It requires no more ingenuity than is possessed by the multiplication table, and it does not matter whether the traits are good or bad. The laughing mirrors show how mathematical this kind of humor can be, and the mocking bird how unintentional.

For this reason parody, which may be described as the exaggerated imitation of a work or style of art, ought to be judged more severely than other comic forms. A mere plodding labor of self-mockery like Swinburne's parody of his own poems in *Nephelidia,* seems to me, but for the light on his character, quite a little less than worthless.

> From the depth of the dreamy decline of the dawn through a notable nimbus of nebulous moonshine,
> Pallid and pink as the palm of the flag-flower that flickers with fear of the flies as they float.
> Are they looks of our lovers that lustrously lean from a marvel of mystic miraculous moonshine,
> These that we feel in the blood of our blushes that thicken and threaten with throbs through the throat?
> Thicken and thrill as a theatre thronged at appeal of an actor's appalled agitation,
> Fainter with fear of the fires of the future than pale with the promise of pride in the past;
> Flushed with the famishing fullness of fever that reddens with radiance of rathe recreation,

> Gaunt as the ghastliest of glimpses that gleam through the gloom
> of the gloaming when ghosts go aghast? . . .

Compare with that the witty fancy in A. C. Hilton's parody of the same poet, his lines to "The Octopus":

> . . . O breast that 'twere rapture to writhe on!
> O arms 'twere delicious to feel
> Clinging close with the crush of the Python,
> When she maketh her murderous meal!
> In thy eightfold embraces enfolden,
> Let our empty existence escape;
> Give us death that is glorious and golden
> Crushed out of all shape!
>
> Ah, thy red lips, lascivious and luscious,
> With death in their amorous kiss!
> Cling round us, and clasp us, and crush us,
> With bitings of agonized bliss.
> We are sick with the poison of pleasure,
> Dispense us the potion of pain;
> Ope thy mouth to its uttermost measure
> And bite us again!

I do not mean to imply that a parodist to be good must be devastating. Many of them play with their subjects as lovingly as a cat with a catnip mouse. And the best of them are aware of this. Laughter and admiration, according to Arthur Symons, are the essential ingredients of parody, and Owen Seaman, a famous parodist, added "reverence" to the mixture. Carolyn Wells reminds us, more temperately, that the intent of the vast majority of parodies is "simply to amuse." These sayings of specialists are but the corroboration of our more general view of laughter.

What I would add to them is this: that since imitation is an easy and apelike trick and exaggeration a rather mechanical process, exaggerative imitation is within the scope of mediocre minds, and is more often a tedious perpetration than other forms of comic art. It is something that people who have no playful gift, but think they have, can learn to do. And it is something that people who have a gift can turn out in their indolent, if not inebriate, intervals. It is a parasite among the arts, and to justify itself must bear some blooms of independent truth or humor.

Independent humor is what raises Stephen Leacock's *Nonsense Novels* so high above the general run of parody. Within a scheme of subtle though extreme burlesque, his witty laughter flashes out in all directions, reckless of the scheme. It is good parody, but it is also a good show and you can enjoy it whether you ever heard of the originals or not. Here is a brief example:

GERTRUDE THE GOVERNESS: OR SIMPLE SEVENTEEN

It was a wild and stormy night on the West Coast of Scotland. This, however, is immaterial to the present story, as the scene is not laid in the West of Scotland. For the matter of that the weather was just as bad on the East Coast of Ireland.

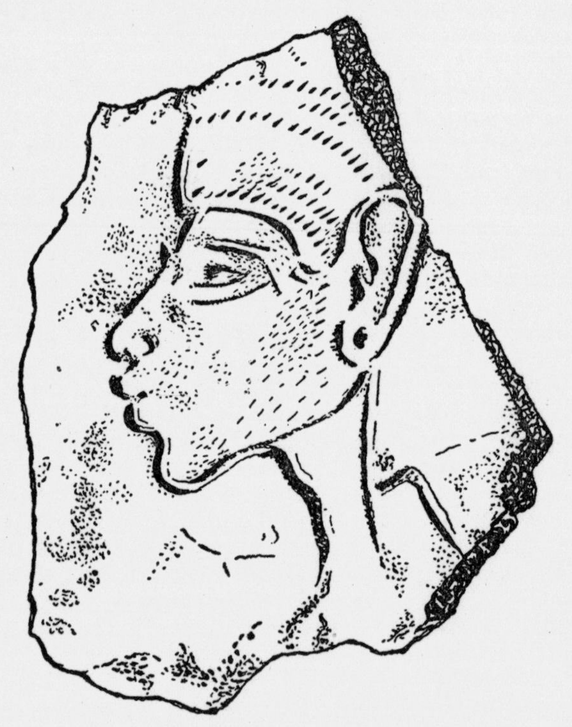

Akhenaton, a portrait in stone exaggerating the Pharaoh's weak points—the world's oldest caricature.

But the scene of this narrative is laid in the South of England and takes place in and around Knotacentinum Towers (pronounced as if written Nosham Taws), the seat of Lord Knotacent (pronounced as if written Nosh).

But it is not necessary to pronounce either of these names in reading them.

Nosham Taws was a typical English home. The main part of the house was an Elizabethan structure of warm red brick, while the elder portion, of which the Earl was inordinately proud, still showed the outlines of a Norman Keep, to which had been added a Lancastrian Jail and a Plantagenet Orphan Asylum. From the house in all directions stretched magnificent woodland and park with oaks and elms of immemorial antiquity, while nearer the house stood raspberry bushes and geranium plants which had been set out by the Crusaders. . . .

It was at this moment that a high dogcart, driven by a groom in the livery of Earl Nosh, might have been seen entering the avenue of Nosham Taws. Beside him sat a young girl, scarce more than a child, in fact not nearly so big as the groom.

The apple-pie hat which she wore, surmounted with black willow plumes, concealed from view a face so face-like in its appearance as to be positively facial.

It was—need we say it—Gertrude the Governess, who was this day to enter upon her duties at Nosham Taws.

At the same time that the dogcart entered the avenue at one end there might have been seen riding down it from the other a tall young man, whose long, aristocratic face proclaimed his birth and who was mounted upon a horse with a face even longer than his own.

And who is this tall young man who draws nearer to Gertrude with every revolution of the horse? Ah, who, indeed? Ah, who, who? I wonder if any of my readers could guess that this was none other than Lord Ronald.

The two were destined to meet. Nearer and nearer they came. And then still nearer. Then for one brief moment they met. As they passed Gertrude raised her head and directed towards the young nobleman two eyes so eye-like in their expression as to be absolutely circular, while Lord Ronald directed towards the occupant of the dogcart a gaze so gaze-like that nothing but a gazelle, or a gas-pipe could have emulated its intensity.

Was this the dawn of love? Wait and see. Do not spoil the story.

That gas-pipe represents the kind of thing that redeems parody, and carries it in the direction of what we call burlesque. Indeed I can see no particular reason for the word *burlesque* except to free us from

A STRIKE-BREAKING AGENCY

Rates

A tap on the nut.................... $10.00
A shot in the hoof.................... $15.00
Knockdown with a kick in the navel.... $7.30
A crowd clean-out, dead or alive....... $100.00

a set scheme of imitation, and remind us that exaggeration is and ought to be a boisterous and hilarious kind of play. It soon becomes sickly if meticulous.

The word *caricature* makes a more definite distinction than burlesque, not only because it applies especially to pictures, but because caricatures make fun of nature rather than other works of art. They are more creative than parody, as creative indeed as any strictly representative art can be. Nevertheless they are strictly representative, and their humor is fundamentally, even when elimination plays a vital part, exaggerative. It consists of "playing up" a trait to such an extreme that it becomes ludicrous. Of them too, therefore, I find myself inclined to demand a little more than mere playful mimicry, something besides likeness and overdrawing, some other humor, or some serious passion or opinion—better still, perhaps, some more exquisite discernment of character than I myself am capable of.

I can illustrate what I mean by "other humor," as well as by passion and opinion, with a rather crude drawing by Art Young—our undisputed leader in that social caricature which has gradually replaced the political caricature of the eighteenth and nineteenth centuries. Young's row of strike-breakers seems at first glance to represent exaggeration-as-a-weapon in an almost childish form. And yet there is a witty humor both in the names of these hired monsters, and in their portraits. They are not only overdrawn individuals, but grotesquely drawn types, ludicrous in their juxtaposition and contrast. They show that same leaning toward burlesque, toward free play and hilarity —if anything so filled with vicious meaning can be called hilarious— which makes Leacock's parodies rich.

The other way in which caricature rises above the art of the laughing mirrors is to make ludicrous some trait or aspect of a character that others would not see. It is here that David Low and Max Beerbohm excel, and excel so far that I can think of no American to place beside them—unless it should be Covarrubias or Peggy Bacon. Some of Peggy Bacon's caricatures in *Off with Their Heads!* are as subtle as they are funny, and she accompanies each, moreover, with a prose portrait quite as subtle as her drawing—quite as graphic too. Nothing else comparable to that slim volume exists in America. Al Frueh is ingenious to a degree, but he gets too far away from representative art to be either very incisive or very comic in his caricatures. They are touched with the non-humor of modernism. Covarrubias has a contagious hilarity, and perhaps better illustrates the fact that caricature is fundamentally an art of exaggeration. Boardman Robinson, whom I regard as the greatest draughtsman of our generation, is too much himself in his drawings to commit very often a perfect murder of anybody else.

To illustrate the varieties of crime open to the caricaturist, and how much at his mercy is the individual caricatured, I reproduce three caricatures of Sinclair Lewis. As he himself has a weapon of imitative mockery as keen as any one alive, there is a certain poetic justice in this. . . .

I shall say more of humor as a weapon, of its degrees and shades of sharpness, when discussing Satire in Part Seven. At present, under the pretext of field exploration in exaggerative humor, I am going to declare a recess, and ask the class to lay aside their textbooks and enjoy, or at least permit me to enjoy, a perfectly irrelevant and impertinent —not to say incompetent—excursion into American history.

Sinclair Lewis by Peggy Bacon

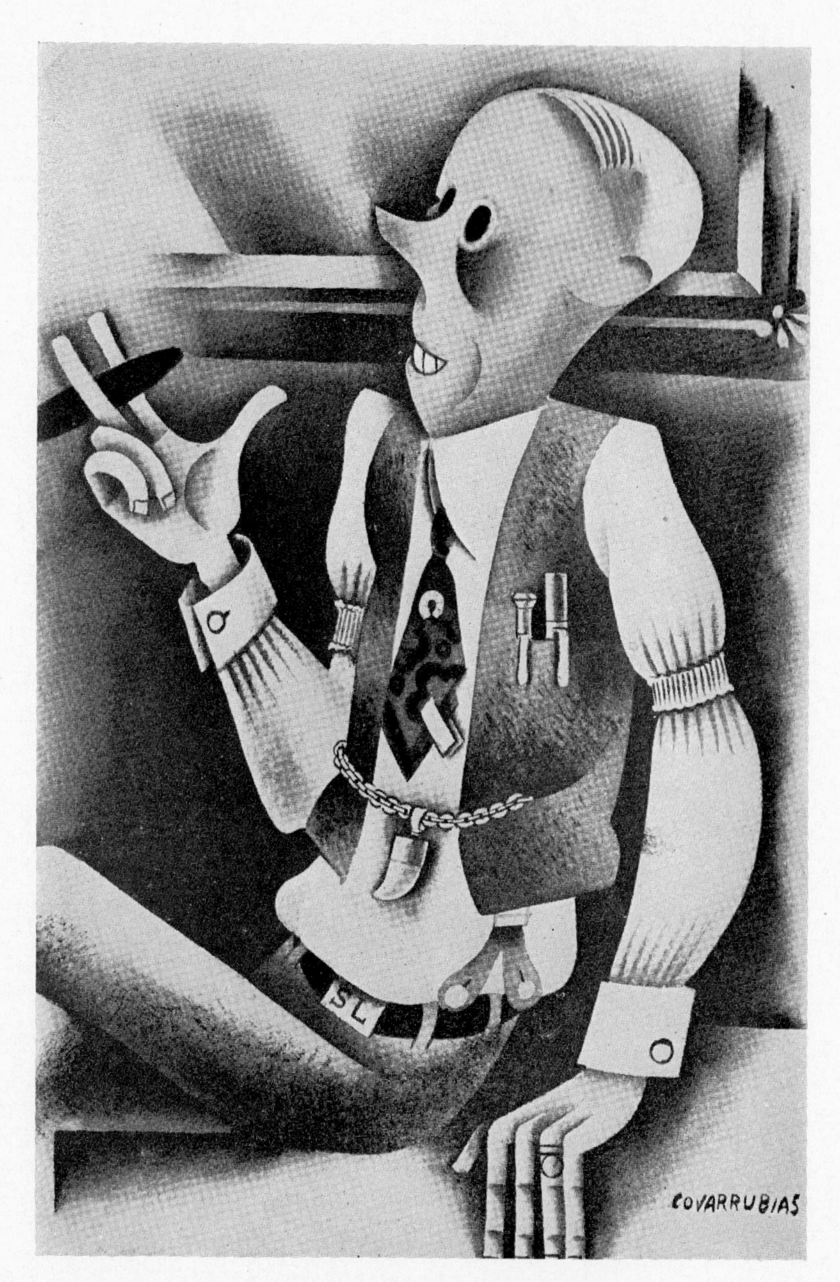

Sinclair Lewis by Covarrubias

Sinclair Lewis by Boardman Robinson

"Good heavens, Mother! Why make a mystery of things?"
(Illustrating page 262)

CHAPTER III

The American Blend of Humor— A Digression

ONCE I CALLED on a famous psychologist in Europe, and in the course of a not too psychological conversation received some advice.

"I want you to go home," he said, "and write a book on America, and I will tell you what to call it. *Misgeburt*—what is that word in English? No, not *monster*. *Miscarriage*—that's it. *The Miscarriage of American Culture*—that shall be the title of your next book, and you will tell the truth about the whole awful catastrophe."

We laughed, somewhat unsymmetrically, at this jest, and I asked:

"What makes you hate America so?"

"Hate it?" he said. "I don't hate America, I regret it. I regret that Columbus ever made the mistake of discovering it!"

It happens that I am as a patriot rather slow to boil. I think of myself instinctively as a citizen of the world and have the habit of discussing the defects and merits of my native land—except for its plumbing conveniences, about which I brook no two opinions—in a mood of cool appraisal. Therefore this violence of idea, in a great authority on the manner in which violent ideas are formed, stimulated rather than incensed me. America *has* failed to shine in most branches of human culture which transcend the mood of the matter-of-fact. We are a hard-surfaced folk, or have been. Our serious culture is like one of those modernist plays enacted on a bare stage with no backdrop and no scenery—and withal a sentimental play. We have used our brains well, but not our imaginations, not our emotional perceptions. We lack "depth"—whatever depth is—and we lack fineness.

I recognize all these facts and sense a validity in the viewpoint of the old-world critic. And yet as I left his study I settled back with a very comfortable feeling into being an American, and being a part of the process of creating an American culture. My feeling was not only comfortable, but also a little gleeful, a little on the laughing side. It was as though I had said to the old man: "It is just as well you don't understand our system—wait till the home stretch and we'll show you."

The basic thing historically is that America was born late, and spent her youth with grown-up brothers and sisters. She is precocious—or she is "old-wise," to translate a better German term. I mean in so far as she is wise at all, and not like all other countries full of dead men and clods. Our earliest heroes—Franklin, Jefferson, Washington, Tom Paine—were disbelievers in the legends in which all other early heroes lived and breathed. They were heroes of the matter-of-fact, and of will and resolution based upon a knowledge of it. A lot of religious and cultural top-hamper that came over with us on the ships, and then the long and pious effort of our second-rate geniuses to imitate it, have obscured this fact. Where other "national minds" were born in an atmosphere of imaginative belief, ours was born in an atmosphere of skeptical common sense. It was born with the industrial revolution and with modern science.

"Poets," said Benjamin Franklin, in a verse that was bad enough to make it plausible, "are the mere *waste paper* of mankind."

This does not mean that we are standing still at a goal. It means that we are moving in a different direction. We started in fact and are moving toward imagination; other cultures have moved the other way. I have no assurance where we shall come out. It may be impossible to work this process backward. But if it is not, then those other more imaginative cultures will fade out and die. For facts *are* facts, and once they are known you cannot with inward dignity deny them. I think and hope that American poets will find a way to unleash the imagination, and cultivate subtleties of feeling, without losing that inestimably precious sense of hard fact which is instinctive with us and not a thing that we have slowly had to learn. Nothing could be more interesting than to try to do this. No national mission, or adventure, could be more exciting.

That is why I felt comfortable in returning to my own nest of Americanness, after agreeing with so much that the great man in Europe said. Why I felt like laughing is not so easy to tell. It may be that I was retreating into the fastnesses of our own cultural territory. I was running up the flag on our sole impregnable fortress. For America *has* unleashed imagination and cultivated feelings in the one realm where, held down by that harsh sense of fact, she instinctively could—the realm of humor. "You may laugh at our crudity and make jokes about Columbus, but we could make a better joke and laugh with more imagination." That is perhaps what I was saying to the old man.*

It is no accident that Mark Twain and Abraham Lincoln—both men in whom humor took the place of ideological anchorings—became and have remained in the world's eyes the representative Americans. Their headstrong sensibleness, their steadfast confrontation of fact, and their adjustment through humorous emotion to the predicament in which facts steadfastly confronted place the wishful heart of man, is the keynote of our culture if we have one.

There was hardly a bolder and lonelier thing a man could do in Lincoln's place than crash through military discipline with acts of human mercy. There, if anywhere, he needed the support of angels or ideas. "Well, I don't believe shooting will do him any good," he would say to the indignant military. Or: "I put it to you to decide for yourself; if Almighty God gives a man a cowardly pair of legs, how can he help their running away with him?" And in this acceptance with a quizzical playful emotion of life's ultimate predicament, his mind would find rest, his will the requisite support. It is not a trivial or incidental thing to be as humorous as Lincoln was.

"I'm quite sure," said Mark Twain, "that . . . I have no race prejudices, and I think I have no color prejudices nor caste prejudices nor creed prejudices. Indeed, I know it. I can stand any society. All

* It is an opinion that I had already suggested in the chapter on "Poetic Humor" in my book, *The Sense of Humor* (1921).

that I care to know is that a man is a human being—that is enough for me; he can't be any worse."

In that, it seems to me, you have the whole temper and equilibrium of Mark Twain's mind, the ruthless vision—out of those hawk's eyes—and the laughter. You cannot separate the two as solemn critics do, and arrive at something called "Mark Twain's philosophy." Facts are awful, but you can be honest if you laugh—that was Mark Twain's "philosophy."

I am not saying that these attitudes are final, but just the opposite, that they are the starting point of a distinctively American culture, and that nothing is final. In order to see them so, however, it is necessary to disregard most of what has been done by the historians, for they call American culture everything that developed on this continent. I can find roots running back, but I think American culture as a distinct entity began not so very early in the nineteenth century. And it has its natural beginning, just as all national cultures have, in a mythology—a mythology which has been described, rather unfortunately, as the "tall talk" of the western frontier. If you want to see how much more it is than that, you should read a few pages of Lowell Thomas' sapless collection of *Tall Stories,* and compare them with a page of Constance Rourke's chapter on "The Gamecock of the Wilderness" in her book about *American Humor.* I spare you the sample from Lowell Thomas, but here is a page from Constance Rourke's rich book. She is describing the legends which grew up around the historic figure of Davy Crockett.

> The story of his life in one of the almanacs began by picturing his as a baby giant planted in a rock bed as soon as he was born and watered with wild buffalo's milk. Another declared that as a boy he tied together the tails of two buffaloes and carried home five tiger cubs in his cap. In another he wrung the tail off a comet, and announced that he could "travel so all lightnin' fast that I've been known to strike fire agin the wind." . . . On one of his adventures he was barred by an "Injun rock so 'tarnal high, so all flinty hard that it will turn off a common streak of lightnin' and make it point downward and look as flat as a cow's tail." Once he escaped up Niagara Falls on an alligator. "The alligator walked up the great hill of water as slick as a wild cat up a white oak."

In the end he became a demigod, and spoke in his own person:

> "One January morning it was so all screwen cold that the forest trees were stiff and they couldn't shake, and the very daybreak froze fast as it was trying to dawn. The tinder box in my cabin would no more ketch fire than a sunk raft at the bottom of the sea. Well, seein' daylight war so far behind time I thought creation war in a fair way for freezen fast: so, thinks I, I must strike a little fire from my fingers, light my pipe, an' travel out a few leagues, and see about it. Then I brought my knuckles together like two thunderclouds, but the sparks froze up afore I could begin to collect 'em, so out I walked, whistlin' 'Fire in the mountains!' as I went along in three double quick time. Well, arter I had walked about twenty miles up the Peak O'Day and Daybreak Hill I soon discovered what war the matter. The airth had actually friz fast on her axes, and couldn't turn round; the sun had got jammed between two cakes o' ice under the wheels, an' thar he had been shinin' an' workin' to get loose till he friz fast in his cold sweat. C-r-e-a-t-i-o-n! thought I, this ar the toughest sort of suspension, an' it mustn't be endured. Somethin' must be done, or human creation is done for. It war then so anteluvian an' premature cold that my upper and lower teeth an' tongue war all collapsed together as tight as a friz oyster; but I took a fresh twenty-pound bear off my back that I'd picked up on my road, and beat the animal agin the ice till the hot ile began to walk out on him at all sides. I then took an' held him over the airth's axes an' squeezed him till I'd thawed 'em loose, poured about a ton on't over the sun's face, give the airth's cog-wheel one kick backward till I got the sun loose—whistled 'Push along, keep movin'!' an' in about fifteen seconds the airth gave a grunt, an' began movin'. The sun walked up beautiful, salutin' me with sich a wind o' gratitude that it made me sneeze. I lit my pipe by the blaze o' his top-knot, shouldered my bear, an' walked home, introducin' people to the fresh daylight with a piece of sunrise in my pocket."

Is it any wonder that this childlike and savage imaginative explosion, crashing in on the refined habits of English literary humor of the genteel tradition, gave rise to the idea that exaggeration is the sole thing at which Americans laugh? Expressing, as Miss Rourke says, "an exhilarated and possessive consciousness of a new earth and even of the wide universe," these legendary heroes found no room to exist in British drawing rooms of the Victorian era. They were indeed too big for that. But among their own companions—and the companions of Davy Crockett are Theseus and Hercules, Thor and Baldur, Krishna and Balaram—these American heroes are not distinguished by size, but by humor. All mythical heroes have been exaggerations, but they have been serious ones. America came too late for that. Her demigods were born in laughter; they are consciously preposterous; they are cockalorum demigods. That is the natively American thing—not that her primitive humor is exaggerative, but that her primitive exaggerations were humorous.

I am not very strong on history—it is one of the things I have put off writing until I should have time to read up on it. But it seems to consist of riding some strong idea through a morass of facts that would bog you down and drown you if you were not mounted. And I should like to propose a brief history of American literature, of American imaginative culture, in which the idea would be that it is only about one hundred years of age, and did not arise as a gradual deposit of calcium in the backbone and vision in the eyes of nice white-handed New England teachers and preachers, mastering a graceful penmanship and learning to write almost as well as the English poets, but as a rough laughing growth springing up out of the struggles of the pioneers, and having its background in a humorous mythology, in legendary heroes taken as a joke. If imagination is what we failed of in our belated infancy, it is in this humorous mythology, rather than our sober poets, that we began vigorously to have it.

So far as concerns the origins of our literature, this idea that I am riding I find belongs to Constance Rourke.* But I should like to ride

* Though the American scene had been drawn, an American literature was hardly definable in 1834. Twittering poetasters and essayists, pretty story-tellers, and studious novelists were springing up by the dozen as if to refute the classic charge that the Americans were coarse. There was a great effervescence of what may be called the false-feminine; . . . English literature was accepted as the single great American heritage; and American literature was counted one of its provinces. . . .

Scant, fitful, sporadic as American literature has proved to be, it has had roots in common soil. Through the interweaving of the popular strain with that of a new expression on other levels a literature has been produced which, like other literatures, is related to an anterior popular lore that must for lack of a better word be called a folklore. No literal sequence followed from the comic mythologies, no simple, orderly completion. Extravagantly and willfully, as though it were possessed by the very essence of the comic spirit, American literature turned aside from these materials for the most part, and discovered it right on up to very recent times, and say that humor is not only the origin but the main achievement of our imaginative culture in so far as it has been distinctively American. It is in the humorists rather than the poets that imagination in its full vigor has flourished among us. That is what has made these humorists something of a sensation in the world. They did of course exaggerate. Imaginative humor runs out automatically into exaggeration. How could you play laughing havoc with the qualities of things, and not pile them up into quantities that also overwhelm the mind? The two things go together like size and shape—the inordinate quantity and the preposterous image. Ring Lardner said that "if the penalty for selling honest old beer to minors was a $100 fine why 2 to 14 years in a meat grinder would be mild for a guy that sells white pop on the theory that it is a drink." As a modification of the penal code that is indeed extreme, but it is also—is it not—fantastic? And the fantasy, not the extremeness, is what makes Ring Lardner's hand unmistakable in the writing of it.

> At high noon the wind was blowing a 2 inch gale backwards and neither scow would move, so the starter postponed it till along came a breath of fresh air, which was a ¼ to 2". Then away went the two sloops like a snail with paralysis.

> They were in Brock's inner office, the walls of which were adorned with autographed pictures of six or seven of the more celebrated musical comedy stars, and a too-perfect likeness of Brock's wife, whom he had evidently married in a dense fog.

> She smiled and Rita noticed her teeth for the first time. Most of the visible ones were of gold, and the work had evidently been done by a dentist for whom three members of a foursome were waiting.
>
> "Does she think," said Stu, "that just because she comes from the golden State she has to run around with a mouthful of nuggets?"

---

others of its own. The wealth of a native mythology was left behind, except as Melville used this, and a few other writers. Yet the Yankee, the backwoodsman in minstrelsy—though the influence there was less direct—the strollers of the theater and of the cults and revivals, the innumerable comic story-tellers and myth-makers, had made a groundwork for this literature.

(*American Humor,* pp. 160-62.)

That is the way Ring Lardner exaggerates. And here is Mark Twain:

> "Kings" and "kingdoms" were as thick in Britain as they had been in little Palestine in Joshua's time, when people had to sleep with their knees pulled up because they couldn't stretch out without a passport.
>
> I own millions and millions of feet of affluent silver leads in Nevada—in fact the entire undercrust of that country nearly, and if Congress would move that State off my property so that I could get at it, I would be wealthy yet.
>
> Twenty-four years ago, I was strangely handsome. . . . In San Francisco, in the rainy season I was often mistaken for fair weather.
>
> Pa's got a few buckshot in him, but he don't mind it 'cause he don't weigh much anyway.

You can find all the exaggerations you want in Baron Munchausen, but you cannot find a phrase to match those in any writer of English before Mark Twain. Even Lord Byron's wit was not lighted with these exploits of poetic humor. In Charles Dickens you could search all day for a phrase to print on the page with them. "Mark Twain can be quoted in single sentences," says Stephen Leacock, "Dickens mostly in pages." But all vigorously imaginative minds can be quoted in sentences—all of the tribe of Shakespeare. And American humorists, casual and unsustained as their flights are, belong to the tribe of Shakespeare. It is as though that revival of an Elizabethan gleam and range of vision which we call the romantic movement, and which occurred in poetry in England at the beginning of the nineteenth century, occurred a half century later in the United States and in humor instead of poetry.

More even than in individual writers this fact is evident in the humorous antics of our slang. To call a straw hat "the cow's breakfast," idle big talk "chin music" or "balloon juice" or "applesauce"; to describe a stupid man as "dead above the ears," a pretty girl as "an eyeful," a crazy man as "dippy in the dream box"; to say "climb on the bandwagon," "have the bulge on," "go chase yourself," "hit the hay," "park in his whiskers" (so far the ultimate exaggeration of a blow to the jaw), "a dewdrop" (understatement of the same), "caress the canvas," "bounce in with the bacon," "chew the rag," "dish the dirt," "wipe the earth with"—is to employ, with a humorous twist, the very language of Shakespeare. And the language of Shakespeare with a humorous twist is, in all essentials, the language of Rabelais. There is nothing else in the world, that I ever saw, so like a page of Rabelais as a page from a dictionary of American slang. A man who put that much imaginative vigor, and vigor of the tongue muscles, into serious speech would be one of the great poets of the world.*

Comic imagination, then, or what I prefer to call poetic humor, would stand not only at the beginning, but close to the center of my brief history of America's imaginative culture. Another feature of my history would be our humor troubadours. For America has not only a comic mythology; she has had her minstrelsy of laughter too, her jesting tramps or gleemen, who got about by making people smile instead of singing to them. Artemus Ward was the prince of this tribe, a traveling printer who could write "copy," and subsequently a platform entertainer. And he brought something from his eastern home that was not to be found at all in that loud humor of the pioneers. It was not exactly what we call a "dry New England wit," and I am not sure but he got it out of his own bosom rather than out of some

* American slang is not all, of course, comic, but very much of it is. And slang in general is so bathed in the mood of play that the uniquely imaginative character of our slang is a strong evidence, or an essential part, of what I am saying about our imaginative culture as a whole.

In his magnificent book about the *American Language,* H. L. Mencken quotes George Philip Krapp to the effect that "perhaps the most striking difference between British and American slang is that the former is more largely merely a matter of the use of queer-sounding words, like *bally* and *swank,* whereas American slang suggests vivid images and pictures." And Mencken illustrates this with the example of British and American college slang. "The vocabulary of Oxford and Cambridge seems inordinately obvious and banal to an American undergraduate. At Oxford it is made up in large part of a series of childish perversions of common and proper nouns, effected by adding *er* or inserting *gg.* Thus, breakfast becomes *brekker,* collection becomes *collecker,* the Queen Street Cinema becomes the *Queener,* St. John's becomes *Jaggers,* and the Prince of Wales becomes the *Pagger-Wagger.* The rest of the vocabulary is equally feeble. To match the magnificent American *lounge-lizard* the best the Oxonians can achieve is *a bit of a lad,* and in place of the multitudinous American synonyms for *girl* there are only *bint* and a few other such flabby inventions."

abstraction called New England. It was what underlies that dry wit in a laughter-loving rather than a caustic mind—a taste for pure absurdities. Artemus Ward liked to speak out before the public the kind of "foolishness" that is usually indulged at home. Phrases like "of the same similarness," or "Why is this thus? What is the cause of this thusness?" acquired a delicious drollness on his lips. He made people laugh by saying things that made absolutely no sense, or which there was absolutely no sense in saying.

> I was born in the state of Maine of parents.
>
> One of the peculiarities of my lecture is that it contains so many things that haven't anything to do with it.

He used to have with him, when lecturing on the Mormons, a panorama representing what he saw in Utah. In his picture the lion on Brigham Young's gate had a ridiculously elongated tail. He would point to it and say: "Yonder lion, you will observe, has a tail. It will be continued a few evenings longer." It appears that his British audience could hardly stay in their chairs when he pointed to one of the Nevada mountains and said in a modestly informing tone: "The highest part of that mountain is the top."

It is of course impossible to revive the alluring plausibility which his presence could impart to such a statement, how he could make the whole mortal being of a listener move with breathless playful expectation to this simple fall. We merely know that it was true. When it came to making humor humorous—and it very often does—Artemus Ward seems to have had no equal among men. No man on the platform was ever more successful or more loved.

I think the unique quality of his humor can be conveyed, after a fashion, by saying that his jokes were almost always blunt. If they had a point, he would slur it in the utterance so that you could hardly catch the gleam. And frequently they had no point. And frequently they would seem to lose their point, or forget all about it, and go wandering off in search of some ludicrous situation or image.

> "Does this railroad company allow passengers to give it advice, if they do so in a respectful manner?"

> The conductor replied in gruff tones that he guessed so.
> "Well, it occurred to me that it would be well to detach the cow-catcher from the front of the engine and hitch it to the rear of the train, for you see we are not liable to overtake a cow, but what's to prevent a cow from strolling into this car and biting a passenger?"

Artemus Ward was not perhaps more gifted than other American humorists, but his gift was more unusual. He was, like Poe among our poets, a prodigy. And like Poe he was so recognized in Europe as well as America. After his first London lecture in 1866, *Punch,* in an editorial ovation, advised "funny men on or off the stage, to hear Artemus Ward 'speak his piece' at the Egyptian Hall, and then, in so far as in them lies, to go and do likewise.

"To be sure Artemus Ward's delivery of fun is 'un-English.' But there are a good many things English one would like to see un-Englished. Gagging, gross, overdone low comedy is one of them. Snobbishness is another. The two go hand in hand. One of the best of many good points of Artemus Ward's piece is that it is quite free from all trace of either of these English institutions."

Those who think that British humor is a very subtle fluid whose quiet stream has been disturbed by the coarse, loud guffaws of the Americans, may learn something from these lines. The fact is that Artemus Ward so surprised London with the possibility of a gentle grace and mental quietness in platform humor that all English society was excited about it. Even the heavy-sitting queen was lifted by the general wave of enthusiasm.

"The most delightful fooling," she said, "that it has ever been our good fortune to hear. During his extraordinary prologue the audience fairly laughed till they could laugh no more, for the strange, quaint, quiet, gentlemanly humor of the lecturer was irresistible."

"Never was an American in London so beloved," said Moncure D. Conway, and Charles Reade nicknamed him "Artemus the delicious." "His jokes," said the London *Times,* "are of the true transatlantic type to which no nation beyond the limits of the States can offer any parallel."

It would be easy, with such a lead, to exaggerate Artemus Ward's Americanness. In his love for pure absurdity, he must take his place with Lewis Carroll as an event in world literature rather than an American event. Chesterton has said that the Victorians "discovered nonsense," and it is true that they were first in the pure love of it. But their nonsense derives some sense from the fact that it was designed for the entertainment of children. Their pointless jokes have always that point. That serious thought sustains many a true lady and gentleman in the considerable indignity of enjoying them. It gives moreover a flavor of condescension, almost a baby-talk flavor, to some of their finest foolishness. Artemus Ward's delicious absurdities were for grown-up minds. He loved nonsense with a manly and mature love.

Unfortunately for the world, he died in the midst of those lectures in London, when he had barely become conscious of his powers. No literary monument exists to perpetuate his rare spirit. Only in the memories of those who heard him, and in collected fragments—here too like the poetry of Edgar Allan Poe—is the original quality of his mind perceived. But almost as Poe stands at the source of a tendency toward "pure poetry," or poetry as an art and not a preachment, so Artemus Ward stands at the source of a tendency toward pure humor—toward the cultivation of absurdity so exquisite that it is treasured without condescension for its own sake.*

It is the blending of these two strains—the primitive vigor of imagination and the mature enjoyment of nonsense—that gives its distinct flavor to American humor. Both Mark Twain and Josh Billings were aware of this flavor, and tried to identify it by isolating the word "humor" for the purpose. Mark Twain said that the art of telling a "humorous," as opposed to a "comic," or a "witty" story, "was created in America and has remained at home." And Josh Billings apologized for the failings of this art by explaining that "Americans haven't had time yet to bile down their humor and git the wit out ov it."

Josh Billings was a crude character in comparison to Mark Twain—a "cracker-box philosopher," and on some subjects rather more of a cracker box than a philosopher. But he possessed these two gifts, the comic vision and the liberated taste for foolishness, in a degree that

* See note, page 353.

enabled him to create a new artistic form. He would appear in our brief and reckless history as the father of imagism. For he was the first man in English literature to set down on his page, quite like a French painter reared in the tradition of art for art's sake, a series of tiny, highly polished verbal pictures, and leave them there for what they might be worth.

> The crane is neither flesh, beast, nor fowl, but a sad mixtur ov all theze things.
> He mopes along the brinks of kreeks and wet places, looking for sumthing he haz lost.
> He haz a long bill, long wings, long legs, and iz long all over.
> When he flies thru the air, he iz az graceful az a windmill, broke loose from its fastenings.
>
> The gote iz a koarse wollen sheep.
> They have a good appetite, and a sanguine digestion.
> A maskuline gote will fite ennything, from an elephant down to his shadder on a ded wall.
> They strike from their but-end, insted ov the shoulder, and are az likely tew hit, az a hammer iz a nail hed.
> They kan klime ennything but a greast pole, and know the way up a rock, az natral az a wood-bine. . . .
>
> The Duk iz a kind ov short legged hen.
> They kan sale on the water as natral and eazy as a grease spot.
> Duks hav a broad bill which enables them tew eat their food without enny spoon.
> Thare aint any room on the outside of a Duk for enny more feathers.
> The duk don't kro like a rooster, but quaks like a duk.

There is little in New England poetry up to that date as graphic as some of this Poughkeepsie auctioneer's metaphors—nothing quite comparable to his statement that goats "know the way up a rock as natural as a woodbine," which is Homeric. Our history would make much of the originality of Josh Billings, and also of his crudity—for our whole history would be of something crude.

We should also devote a considerable and animated section to the great American art of laughing at oneself—that "humor of discomfiture written in the first person," which Leacock again says "absolutely distinguishes" Mark Twain from Dickens. It was not original with us, nor with anyone in history. But with us, I think, it first became a humorous convention. It first seemed the natural and appointed way to engage a reader in the joys of ridicule. One of the most interesting processes in cultural history, and most indisputable, has been the steady playing down of cruelty, and playing up of sympathy, in laughter. And this tendency of American humor stands at the height of that curious, and seemingly almost Christian, development. When you have taken upon your own person a defect or misfortune with

"Excellent—all but me!"

As Others See Us

(A celebrity-at-large and a self-caricature by Ralph Barton.)

which you propose to invite laughter, you are surely not inviting sneers. That is what Constance Rourke means, perhaps, by attributing to American humor as a whole a quality of "tenderness." A more complete and universal understanding of the mood of play would probably describe it better. We hold ourselves up to laughter because we believe in laughter. We understand it, and know how to distinguish it from snarling and showing of teeth. We believe in being humorous. We believe in it more with our souls than most civilized folk. And this, if my hypothesis about our general culture is correct, is because we have had the energy and the abounding spirits of a young nation, and yet our childhood fell in a day of skepticism instead of animal faith. We have made more of humor because deprived in infancy of serious childish fancies.

Such in outline would be my chapter on humor as the origin and almost the central stem of America's distinctly own imaginative culture. It would go on to tell, of course, how this native tree of laughter, rooted in a humorous mythology, grew to its height in Mark Twain and his contemporaries, and then about the time of his death suddenly burgeoned out all over the sky, and with a violent hilarity, and a certain thinning of the life sap, blossomed. We might call our chapter *The Root, Stem and Petals of American Humor.* It would not agree with the prevailing opinion that this recent phenomenon, this still continuing shower of arrantly hilarious laughter, known variously as the Newer Nonsense, the Larger Lunacy, the Higher Goofyism—or "Humor Gone Nuts," as Donald Ogden Stewart calls it—is an essentially new departure. It is the natural bloom of the tree. It was all foretold and predestined in the riotous mythology of the pioneers and in Artemus Ward's consecration of absurd nonsense—two things which might almost exonerate Columbus for his little mistake, a natural one after all when sailing west for India, in discovering America.

That would not be the whole of our history. It would say much of Edgar Allan Poe, stifled in this cold climate of fact because he lacked the gift of laughter. And it would say more of Walt Whitman, so like Mark Twain in his passion for democracy and fact, and yet unlike him as another world because instead of humor he relied on mystical belief. And with these strands to weave, it would say something about the future—about what might be done by a mind trained in fact and true to it, equipped as such a mind must be with humor, and yet not ill-at-ease in deeps of feeling and among fervent ventures of imagination, not ill-at-ease among revolutionary ideas, not condemned to make a final resting place of fact and laughter.

CHAPTER IV

Understatement

JUST AS WE CAN BE OVERWHELMED with too much of a thing, so we can be tantalized with too little. As we have seen, the overwhelming when performed in fun creates a jovial and boisterous laughter. The tantalizing gives a mischievous or droll effect. We call it understatement, but only because there is no word to describe a not-enoughness in more general terms. Statements are one kind of thing, but anything whatever that does not measure up to some accepted standard of size, degree, quantity or intensity, can be the cause of laughter. Charlie Chaplin's mustache may be described as an understatement in this sense, just as his shoes are an exaggeration. Gargantuans are an overstatement and Lilliputians an understatement of a man.

It is not funny to be little, however. The funny thing is to be *too* little. And a serious understatement stands in danger of becoming comic, just as a serious hyperbole did, only when it is extreme. In the fifth canto of Dante's *Inferno,* Francesca da Rimini describes in a very famous understatement the occasion of her sin. She and Paolo were reading the legend of Launcelot and Guinevere, and when they came to the passage where Guinevere's lips were kissed by her lover, Francesca says:

> "That day we did not read farther."

The words as they occur in the poem are moving in a high degree. And yet their understatement is so extreme that, like the exaggerations we quoted from the Bible, they would require little but a mischievous grin, or to be spoken by Mae West, in order to be comic.

> Then Abner Dean of Angel's raised a point of order, when
> A chunk of old red sandstone took him in the abdomen,
> And he smiled a kind of sickly smile, and curled up on the floor,
> And the subsequent proceedings interested him no more.

I hope the comparison is sufficiently blasphemous to drive home what has been said about the distinct existence of frivolity, or the play attitude—perhaps even to suggest the usefulness to education of some understanding in this direction. It will at least show that the sole thing laughter requires of an understatement is that it should be so far under as to be, for the real business of saying the thing, no good.

Here is Mark Twain writing to the New York Society of California Pioneers in 1869. He is in humorous mood, and the mood is conveyed three times by the mere inadequate expression of something whose extent is obvious.

> Elmira, October 11, 1869.
>
> If I were to tell some of my experience, you would recognize California blood in me; I fancy the old, old story would sound familiar, no doubt. I have the usual stock of reminiscences. For instance: I went to Esmeralda early. I purchased largely in the "Wide West," "Winnemucca," and other fine claims, and was very wealthy. I fared sumptuously on bread when flour was $200 a barrel and had beans for dinner every Sunday, when none but bloated aristocrats could afford such grandeur. But I finished by feeding batteries in a quartz mill at $15 a week, and wishing I was a battery myself and had somebody to feed me. My claims in Esmeralda are there yet. I suppose I could be persuaded to sell.
>
> I went to Humboldt District when it was new; I became largely interested in the "Alba Nueve" and other claims with gorgeous names, and was rich again—in prospect. I owned a vast mining property there. I would not have sold out for less than $400,000 at that time. But I will now. Finally I walked home—200 miles—partly for exercise, and partly because stage fare was expensive. Next I entered upon an affluent career in Virginia City, and by a judicious investment of labor and the capital of friends, became the owner of about all the worthless wild cat mines there were in that part of the country. Assessments did the business for me there.

> There were a hundred and seventeen assessments to one dividend, and the proportion of income to outlay *was* a little against me. . . .

That is the conversational rough ore of funny understatement. The following from the "Danbury News Man" is a little more subtle:

> A traveler would have missed the noon train yesterday, had he not stepped on a peach pit at the head of the depot stairs.

Lincoln's well-loved story about the dog who swallowed a bomb with the fuse attached and was scattered all over the landscape, deserves recording here. "Rover was a good dog," his master said, "but as a dog I am afraid his days of usefulness are over."

> There was a bear,
> And there was a boy named Benjie;
> The bear was bulgey,
> And the bulge was Benjie.

That brief elegy too, aside from a pun on the two meanings of the verb *is,* derives its humor from a quantitative defect. Neither in eloquence nor in elaboration is it quite equal to the occasion it describes.

Of course the "quantities" we treat of here are not usually of the kind contemplated by science. They are "intensive" rather than "extensive" quantities. When Mark Twain speaks of "a misunderstanding conducted with crowbars," you can not put that word *misunderstanding* on the scales and determine just how much less it weighs than it ought to. You do, however, instantly perceive it not as an inappropriate, but as an inadequate word. It belongs to a series—misunderstanding, dispute, altercation, quarrel, row, set-to, scrap, fight, battle—whose scope of meaning, or whose "psychic weight," varies on a scale. The series as a whole is appropriate, but this member stands low—it stands too low—in the scale.

The trapeze joke reproduced on p. 182, and regarded by *The New Yorker* staff as one of their three best, is another example of the comically inadequate. Here again the words belong to a series. The series may be described as apologetic, and apologies are certainly in order. But this particular member does not measure up in degree of

compunction to the size of the crisis. You can not say that the exclamation is irrelevant; it does not break in upon the situation, or explode it with a rank ineptitude. It travels along in the right direction, seemly and correct, and yet not quite far enough. The result is almost a demure, a self-containing, kind of humor.

That is why it is dear to the heart of the New Yorkers, who are so given over to the ideal of "playing down" jokes—a decadent ideal, although productive of the best caption writing yet achieved—that they would almost feel pained if they saw somebody laugh out loud while reading their magazine. They go in for the reserved smile, and for what Dave Freedman calls the "tittamatitta," a laugh localized mainly above the Adam's apple and in the $5.50 audiences. The "yokchadebokcha," or belly laugh, to be heard in the galleries and dangerous to the pants buttons, Freedman thinks has all but died out of American literary humor since about 1910.

"The élite nowadays," he says, "think it is vulgar to laugh loud. I think it is vulgar to be élite."

People who take jokes seriously—and that, I sometimes believe, is the majority of grown-up people—would probably think it fantastic to describe that trapeze joke as "played down," or "demure," or in any other way except as cruel or sadistic. They will think the same thing about this from Ring Lardner's description of the "Halloween pranks that were a feature of hospital life" at the "Polyandry Hospital."

"Oop—sorry."

> The patient in Room 18 had been almost fatally burned in an apartment house fire. A crowd of twenty other patients and nurses gathered outside his door and yelled "Fire!" till he jumped out the window. As Room 18 was on the fifth floor, you can imagine his surprise.

I pause to explain, therefore, that I am not discussing the cruelty of these jokes, which may or may not be enjoyed by those who laugh, but their humor. And their humor derives from the fact that the phrases "Oop—sorry" and "You can imagine his surprise," although having plausibility and arising naturally, are keyed too low. They are keyed totally and absolutely too low. In order that this should happen, it was necessary that the situation be keyed high. That is the part played by "cruelty" in making these jokes humorous. And it makes them humorous for people who are not sadistic, as well as for people who are.

What really is to be learned from such jokes is the magic power possessed by a playful understatement. We all know it is not funny for a patient to jump out of a hospital window, much less for a flying trapeze artist to plunge to earth in a circus. Such things are too wrenchingly terrible to be comic. But this little trick of the not-enough can make us laugh no less.

What understatement more often does, and exaggeration too, is to enable us to "see the humor" of a situation that is in itself laughable.

> Waiting to be whipped—says Josh Billings—iz the most uninteresting period of boyhood life.

Well, waiting to be whipped is funny, if you do not happen to be too closely involved in it. But it is the playful exaggeration contained in the word *period,* and the mischievous inadequacy of the word *uninteresting,* which makes you smile—if you will be so kind—at this remark of Josh Billings.

Mark Twain provoked a like smile in the passage we quoted on page 22 about his boyhood terror. I climbed in the window, he said, "because I had a delicacy about going home and getting thrashed." Indeed understatement was the sole technique employed by Mark Twain in that passage in order to turn his terror into fun. He suddenly began to understate what he had been so abundantly stating before.

> I went away from there. I do not say that I went away in any sort of a hurry, but I simply went—that is sufficient. I went out at the window, and I carried the sash along with me. I did not need the sash, but it was handier to take it than it was to leave it, and so I took it.

It is our hard, rapid, unliterary way of slapping it down, rather than our leaning toward exaggeration, that makes American humor seem a little crude. Understatement has been one of our chosen tricks from the beginning. Manipulated without Mark Twain's naturalness, it has been, in fact, something of a bad habit. The manner in which Bill Nye describes his trip to the barn in advance of his dog, Kosciusko, might seem crude to some critics, but, if anything can be exact in this liquid region we are staking out, it is the exact opposite of exaggeration.

> The second year that little Kosciusko was with us, I shaved off a full beard one day while downtown, put on a clean collar and otherwise disguised myself, intending to surprise my wife.
>
> Kosciusko sat on the front porch when I returned. He looked at me as a cashier of a bank does when a newspaper man goes in to get a suspiciously large check cashed. He did not know me. I said, "Kosciusko, have you forgotten your master's voice?"
>
> He smiled sarcastically, showing his glorious wealth of mouth, but still sat there as though he had stuck his tail into the door-steps and couldn't get it out.
>
> So I waived the formality of going in at the front door, and went around to the portcullis, on the off side of the house, but Kosciusko was there when I arrived. The cook, seeing a stranger lurking around the manor house, encouraged Kosciusko to come and gorge himself with a part of my leg, which he did. Acting on this hint I went to the barn.
>
> I do not know why I went to the barn, but somehow there was nothing in the house that I wanted. When a man wants to be by himself there is no place like a good quiet barn for thought. So I went to the barn, about three feet prior to Kosciusko.
>
> Noticing the stairway, I ascended it in an aimless kind of way, about four steps at a time. What happened when we got in the haymow I do not now recall, only that Kosciusko and I frolicked around there in the hay for some time. Occasionally I would be on

> top; and then he would have all the delegates, until finally I got hold of the pitchfork, and freedom shrieked as Kosciusko fell.

It had been my intention to illustrate this book exclusively with American humor, letting even Charles Dickens in only for the purpose of comparison, but when it comes to humorous understatement, it would be a pose not to pay my loyal and most treasonable respects to P. G. Wodehouse. If anybody has achieved a crystal-clear and cool perfection in the art of comic narrative he has; and understatement is the very life and fiber of his style. Wodehouse can make anything in the world laughable by merely withholding the precisely necessary amount of warm language. And when a thing is laughable, his instinct to enhance the laugh by pinning some meticulously inadequate expression on it, is unfaltering.

> To find oneself locked out of a country house at half-past two in the morning in a pair of lemon-colored pyjamas can never be an unmixedly agreeable experience.
>
> Few things so speedily modify an uncle's love as a nephew's air-gun bullet in the fleshy part of the leg.
>
> Except for that slight bias toward dishonesty which led her to steal everything she could lay her hands on which was not nailed down, Aileen Peavey's was an admirable character.
>
> The fascination of shooting as a sport depends almost wholly on whether you are at the right or the wrong end of the gun.
>
> Naturally, when baronets are threatening to pour vitriol down her neck, a refined and sensitive young girl cannot pick her words. This sort of thing must of necessity interfere with the selection of the *mot juste.*

These sentences will recall the Wodehouse style to those who know its cadences. Aside from his own style, however, Wodehouse fills his books with characters whose every utterance falls short in warmth or comprehensiveness of what the situation asks. He finds these characters in force among the British squirarchy, whose inane pursuits he loves to ridicule. The Honorable Bertie Wooster, whose glib and easy-sliding brain contrasts so sharply with that of his keen servant, Jeeves, is a perpetual wellspring of this kind of humor. Even when stiffly standing on his rights, as in the interview with Sir Roderick Glossop about the banjolele, Bertie is laughable not only because of the triviality of the issue, but because he is really not up to a scene of indignation. He lacks weight even for the description of it.

Well, if that was the attitude he was proposing to adopt, well, I mean to say. My geniality waned. I drew myself up coldly, at the same time raising a stiff eyebrow. And I was just about to work off the old To-what-am-I-indebted-for-this-visit gag, when he chipped in ahead of me.

"You ought to be certified!"

"I beg your pardon?"

"You're a public menace. For weeks, it appears, you have been making life a hell for all your neighbours with some hideous musical instrument. I see you have it with you now. How dare you play that thing in a respectable block of flats? Infernal din!"

I remained cool and dignified.

"Did you say 'infernal din'?"

"I did."

"Oh? Well, let me tell you that the man who has not music in his soul . . ." I stepped to the door. "Jeeves," I called down the passage, "what was it Shakespeare said the man who hadn't music in his soul was fit for?"

"Treasons, stratagems, and spoils, sir."

"Thank you, Jeeves. Is fit for treasons, stratagems, and spoils," I said, returning.

He danced a step or two.

"Are you aware that the occupant of the flat below, Mrs. Tinkler-Moulke, is one of my patients, a woman in a highly nervous condition? I have had to give her a sedative."

I raised a hand.

"Spare me the gossip from the loony-bin," I said distantly. "Might I enquire, on my side, if you are aware that Mrs. Tinkler-Moulke owns a Pomeranian?"

"Don't drivel."

I am not drivelling. This animal yaps all day and not infrequently far into the night. So Mrs. Tinkler-Moulke has had the nerve to complain of my banjolele, has she? Ha! Let her first pluck out the Pom which is in her own eye," I said, becoming a bit Scriptural.

He chafed visibly.

"I am not here to talk about dogs. I wish your assurance that you will immediately cease annoying this unfortunate woman."

I shook the head.

"I am sorry she is a cold audience, but my Art must come first."

> "That is your final word, is it?"
> "It is."
> "Very good. You will hear more of this."
> "And Mrs. Tinkler-Moulke will hear more of this," I replied, brandishing the banjolele.
> I touched the buzzer.
> "Jeeves," I said, "show Sir R. Glossop out!"
> I confess that I was well pleased with the manner in which I had comported myself during this clash of wills.

Is it not a kind of emotional understatement to speak of one's own most centrally located segments as one would of the poker or the dinner bell? "I shook the head," "I wiped the brow," "I put the foot down"—a brilliant invention of Mr. Wodehouse. And Bertie has a similar trick of introducing abbreviations into his narrative just when the subject matter calls for warmth.

> I don't know how long it was that I stood there rooted to the s. It may have been quite a stretch. Despair was gripping me. . . .

Bertie's underweighted despair was caused by the fact that, in endeavoring to escape from Mr. J. Washburn Stoker's yacht in the middle of the night, he had blacked himself up like one of the orchestra, and was now unable to find his valet or get into the house where he belonged.

> What with platoons of scullery maids having hysterics every time I went near the back door, it seemed impossible to connect with Jeeves tonight. It was just as impossible to go the rounds of the neighbourhood, calling on perfect strangers and asking for butter. I mean, you know yourself how you feel when a fellow you've never met drops in at your house with his face all black and tries to touch you for a bit of butter. You just aren't in sympathy.

For Americans there is a particular pleasure in these too extreme, and therefore funny, understatements. They are the extreme of something in the British cultivated classes which repels us—their habit of pretending not to have the feelings that a simple human being has. It seems to us as if with them the juvenile ideal of "being a sport" had obliterated the mature and more important thought of being real. I remember in *Journey's End* when the young soldier is dying in the dugout, he looks up and asks: "What's that rumbling noise?" His friend answers with an inflection that can be conveyed only by the word *trippingly:* "The guns are making a bit of a row." In the awfulness of the moment, under the approaching shade of death, that carefully bred trick of vapidity, that gentlemanly inability to state adequately any fact fraught with emotion—to say simply, "Those are the guns"—had for me the taste of a perversion. The Germans are sentimental; the French are hard and intellectual; the cultured British are Germans pretending to be French; and that pretense is distasteful to the Americans, who carry the idea of being downright to the point of being crude. For that reason when it is stressed enough to become funny, we read into the fun a serious satisfaction. We taste the style of Wodehouse as a satire on this cultural habit which we do not like.

I do not know to what extent Wodehouse would go with us there. A born humorist will make fun of almost anything if the fun is good. At any rate, it is not only the saps he ridicules who are so fertile of inadequate remarks. His very heroes and heroines are so molded as to generate the same humor. Jeeves himself is so perfect a servant as to be almost divine in his superiority to this world's alarms. No conceivable situation resulting from the escapades of his light-headed master will provoke in him what might be described biologically as an "adequate response." In still another way the incomparable Psmith—"the *p* is silent as in *pshrimp*"—keeps us laughing by an inexhaustible underproduction of emotive language in time of trouble. He has not the Olympian erudition of the inimitable Jeeves, but as an all-round efficiency expert, a man who can do anything—and will, for a price—he is endowed with an equally supernatural incapacity for getting het up.

> "Well, look here . . . look here . . . Well, look here," said Freddie, "will you steal my aunt's diamond necklace?"
> Psmith placed his monocle in his eye and bent gravely toward his companion.
> "Steal your aunt's necklace?" he said indulgently.
> "Yes."

> "You do not think she might consider it a liberty from one to whom she has never been introduced?"

A very different character is Miss Pauline Stoker, beautiful and headstrong daughter of an American millionaire. And yet she too is possessed of such coolness in calamity that it seems impossible to shake an exclamation out of her mouth.

> I stooped to pick up the candle, and the next moment I had uttered a startled cry.
> "Don't make so much noise!"
> "But there's a corpse on the floor."
> "There isn't. I should have noticed it."

That is Pauline. Or rather that is the kind of humor for which Pauline exists.

I hope I am not conveying the impression that Wodehouse is monotonous in his adherence to the inadequate expression. On the contrary, one of his most delightful arts is that of dropping a red hot and unregenerately American slang phrase right into the middle of his most British paragraph.

> William Mulliner had never tasted alcohol in his life. He had promised his late mother that he would not do so until he was either twenty-one or forty-one—he could never remember which. He was at present twenty-nine; but wishing to be on the safe side in case he had got his figures wrong, he had remained a teetotaller. But now, as he walked listlessly along the street towards the corner, it seemed to him that his mother in the special circumstances could not reasonably object if he took a slight snort. He raised his eyes to heaven, as though to ask her if a couple of quick ones might not be permitted; and he fancied that a faint, far-off voice whispered, "Go to it!"

Wodehouse has all the arts of humor, but he never gives way long to the mood of abundant characterization. He is always aloof; he is always withholding the word. He is at the opposite extreme from Rabelais. Even when exaggerating, he does it in the manner of one making a precise and upon the whole too careful estimate. He understates his very exaggerations, so that even here the flavor of something playfully not quite delivered is kept up.

> With a soft sigh such as might have proceeded from some loving father on the steppes of Russia when compelled, in order to ensure his own safety, to throw his children out of the back of the sleigh to the pursuing wolf pack, he took the pipe from his mouth, collected his other pipes, his tobacco and his cigars, wrapped them in a neat parcel and, summoning the charwoman who cleaned his studio, gave her the consignment to take home to her husband. . . .
>
> I turned to Aunt Agatha, whose demeanor was now rather like that of one who, picking daisies on the railway, has just caught the down express in the small of the back.
>
> He started to get pink in the ears, and then in the nose, and then in the cheeks, till in about a quarter of a minute he looked pretty much like an explosion in a tomato cannery on a sunset evening.
>
> So there was nothing of the lion leaping from its den about the way I now left the bedroom, but rather a bit more than a suggestion of a fairly diffident snail poking its head out of its shell during a thunderstorm.

Those phrases "a soft sigh," "rather like," "pretty much like," "rather a bit more than a suggestion of a *fairly* diffident"—so alien to the manner of American exaggerative metaphor—are wholly characteristic of Wodehouse. He is the sly and mischievous, as opposed to the boisterous, joker. He is the man who holds out something and seems to give it, and yet also to some extent withholds it, or refuses to give it, or give himself with it.

It is an art closely akin to what is called by comedians the "dead pan" delivery. Indeed I think the whole discussion about "how to tell a story," whether to add to its contagion with your own laughter, or add to its comicality with a grave expression, draws some illumination from this contrast between the jovially too much and the mischievously too little. Artemus Ward was seen to laugh uproariously when composing his lectures, but in delivery—to quote Charles Reade —"the refined, delicate, intellectual countenance, the sweet, grave mouth, from which one might have expected philosophic lectures, retained their seriousness while listeners were convulsed." Josh Billings advised comic lecturers, "when they lay a warm joke, not to act as a hen doth when she has uttered an egg, but look sorry and let someone else do the cackling." Stephen Leacock is equally impressive on the other side. "I always try to appear as happy as possible while I am lecturing. I take this to be part of the trade of anybody labeled a humorist and paid as such. I have no sympathy whatever with the idea that a humorist ought to be a lugubrious person with a face stamped with melancholy. This is a cheap and elementary effect belonging to the level of a circus clown. The image of 'laughter shaking both his sides' is a truer picture of comedy. Therefore, I say, I always try to appear cheerful at my lectures and even to laugh at my own jokes."

There is of course no chosen way to tell a story; it is a matter of wielding your special self with skill. But I think it is quite obvious that the boisterous Falstaffian style, in which one adds a full measure of laughter to one's jokes, accords better with the humor of the overmuch. It belongs to the same kind with it. The dead pan delivery is itself almost a kind of understatement.

CHAPTER V

Understatement as a Weapon: Irony

THE WORD IRONY has been a sort of peg in the hall closet of literature. It has had anything and everything hung on it at one time or another. I have on my desk a book called *Irony, An Historical Introduction,* in which I have counted twenty-six different meanings attributed to this long-suffering term.* The author confesses that he has "used the word *irony* in a different meaning with every writer" he has discussed, and avows that this is "a difficulty which appears to be inherent in the subject." To the literary mind in search of ideational pasturage, this is of course no difficulty at all, but a bonanza. But coming to it from the direction of the psychological laboratory, or at least a reading of the reports of laboratories—for that is as far as our own scientificness goes—it is impossible not to wish a little system might be introduced here and this word relieved of a part of its burden.

It was originally, in the old Greek, a colloquial and somewhat slangy term for a foxy way of talking. The *eiron* was the soft-spoken, poker-faced boy, canny and restrained, who always had something more in mind than he was telling you. On the comic stage he was set off against another character called *alazon,* a loud-mouthed, blustering, swanking, cock-and-bull-story-telling lad like Davy Crockett or his biographers. It is characteristic of the Greek view of life that the triumph of the *eiron* over the *alazon* became almost a settled convention of their comic theater. And it was through that comic theater,

* It is by J. A. K. Thomson of Cambridge University, and has been, notwithstanding its elusiveness, of great value to me.

more resembling a highly imaginative Fourteenth Street burlesque show than anything on Broadway, that this slang term *eiron* got lifted into literature. It came in hand in hand with the word *alazon,* and its meaning was largely determined by this companionship. My Greek dictionary defines *eiron* as "a dissembler, one who says less than he thinks," and *alazon* in its adjective form as "swaggering, boastful, braggart," and as a noun, "false pretender, impostor, quack."

So you see the Greeks were keenly sensitive to these two qualities of humor we have been discussing, the humor of big talk and of understatement. Comedy, you might say, was born into the world as a playing off of the one against the other. And the word *irony* arose out of this crude clash. It described the "taking down" of the big talker by the man who says less than he means.

American humor also arose in history with this contrast plainly to be seen. The New England Yankee with his "dry" humor—we call it dry as we do a dry wine, I judge, because its geniality is not sweetened by smiling—is the American *eiron.* And the loud-mouthed backwoodsman, "gamecock of the wilderness," with his tall tales and preposterous asseverations of prowess, is the *alazon.*

> Do you know, sir, that Daniel Boone was so tall and had such strength in his arms that he could toss a kicking buffalo over his shoulder?
>
> Paul Bunyan, my friend, stood fourteen feet high in his bare feet, and carried a rifle the size of a pine sapling.
>
> I honor him the more, sir, for what he did, learning that he was a small man.

That is *alazoneia,* the insolence of the unmitigated liar carried to the absolute, and not to be accommodated by mortal nerves except with laughter. Of American *eironeia,* the remark of Calvin Coolidge to a secret service man who accompanied him on hunting expeditions is a fair example. After every shot fired by the President, this man would hand him a fresh-loaded rifle and somewhat self-importantly break the old one and peer down the barrel. The President deflated him finally by saying, in his small squeaking voice:

"Find a hole there, Colonel?"

Coolidge was in character as the mouthpiece of this New England humor, for he was himself as a president of the United States something of an understatement. In many minds, I suspect, a feeling for this harmony of speech and person underlay the warm affection in which he was held. He was popular as a character in the national comedy.

Unfortunately our national comedy, which ought to have brought into conflict these two characters, the laconic Yankee and the loud-blowing western pioneer, never got written. Here as elsewhere American literature is unachieved. The rough ore exists, but no poet powerful to refine it—no audience to demand that it be refined. These things will come when we get tired of chopping and building and scooping in money. We started our civilization at the wrong end. We are traveling not only toward imagination, but toward a primitive simplicity. You see it in architecture. You begin to see it in the movies. You will see a great poetic comedy on these shores before they sink. It will differ from the Greek comedy in its better sense of the intrinsic humor of the *alazon*—its better sense, too, of his serious merit when excess of talk is backed up with adequacy of character. There is a narrow monotony in the Greek conception of comedy as a perpetual showing up of the overbold. The contribution of our pioneer spirit would be an occasional healthy pleasure in seeing the *eiron* get a "sock on the jaw."

I do not mean, of course, that the contrary rule was absolute even in Athens, or that the Greeks could not appreciate the fun in absolute swagger. Aesop has a fable which might well be entitled "Mrs. Braggart Sees It Through," although like a true Greek he draws the opposite moral. Some foxes gathered by the river to drink—a river which enters the sea at Miletus. Owing to the rush and roar of the waters they dared not go in. But one of them, jeering at the cowardice of the others, and avowing herself a nobler breed of animal, sprang gallantly into the flood. As she was swept out from the bank and downstream, the canny foxes shouted:

"Don't go away and leave us all alone! Come back and show us the way in!"

"Sorry!" she answered. "I have business in Miletus—I'll show you later!"

Aesop's moral reads: "Applies to those who bring danger to themselves by their *alazoneia.*" But we, if we paused to draw the moral at all, should say, "It's a great life if you don't weaken," or words to that effect. We give our hearts to the reckless fox. We could never have conquered a continent if we had not.

But to return to the history of the word *irony*—and the subject, if I remember, of our book—the next step upward was its employment to describe the unique mental attitude of the philosopher, Socrates, as he appears in the dialogues of Plato. Plato's dialogues were a kind of drama, a drama in which ideas rather than men were in conflict. And the plot of these dramas obeys upon the whole the convention of the Athenian comedy. Socrates is the *eiron,* and he is continually "taking down" the pretenses of the various schools of contemporary thought as represented by the other characters. He does this in the main by professing to be a very ignorant person asking questions. He seems to be almost a beggar of information. And of course he is. But that is not all he is. He is also the most brilliant thinker in the world, and his questions are exquisitely designed to expose the ignorance and inconsistency of these learned authorities with whom he talks.

Protagoras makes a long disquisition on the question whether virtue can be taught or not, and after quoting it, Socrates, who is here reporting the conversation, proceeds:

> At length, when I saw that he had really finished, I gradually recovered consciousness, and looking at Hippocrates, I said to him: O Son of Apollodorus, how deeply grateful I am to you for having brought me hither; I would not have missed the speech of Protagoras for a great deal. For I used to imagine that no human care could make men good; but I know better now. Yet I have still one very small difficulty which I am sure that Protagoras will easily explain, as he has already explained so much. For if a man were to go and consult Pericles or any of our great speakers about these matters, he might perhaps hear as fine a discourse; but then if any one has a question to ask of any of them, like books, they can neither answer nor ask; and if anyone challenges the least particular of their speech, they go ringing on in a long harangue, like brazen pots, which when they are struck continue to sound unless someone puts his hand upon them; whereas our friend Protagoras can not only make a good speech, as he has already shown, but when he is asked a question he can answer briefly; and when he

> asks he will wait and hear the answer; and this is a very rare gift. Now, I, Protagoras, have a little question that I want to ask of you, and if you will only answer me that, I shall be quite satisfied. . . .

This "little question," of course, leads Protagoras into a considerable morass, and in his flounderings the "little questions" still pursue him.

> I thought that Protagoras was getting ruffled and excited; he seemed to be setting himself in an attitude of war. Seeing this, I minded my business and gently said:
>
> When you say, Protagoras, that things inexpedient are good, do you mean inexpedient for man only, or inexpedient altogether? and do you call the latter good?
>
> Certainly not the last, he replied; for I know of many things, meats, drinks, medicines, and ten thousand other things, which are partly expedient for man, and partly inexpedient; and some which are expedient for horses, and not for men; and some for oxen only, and some for dogs; and some for no animals, but only for trees; and some for the roots of trees and not for their branches, as for example, manure, which is a good thing when laid about the roots, but utterly destructive if thrown upon the shoots and young branches; or I may instance olive oil, which is mischievous to all plants, and generally most injurious to the hair of every animal with the exception of man, but beneficial to human hair and to the human body generally; and even in this application (so various and changeable is the nature of the benefit) that which is the greatest good to the outward parts of a man, is a very great evil to his inward parts; and for this reason physicians always forbid their patients the use of oil in their food, except in very small quantities, just sufficient to take away the disagreeable sensation of smell in meats and sauces.
>
> When he had given this answer, the company cheered him. And I said: Protagoras, I have a wretched memory, and when anyone makes a long speech to me I never remember what he is talking about. As then, if I had been deaf, and you were going to converse with me, you would have had to raise your voice; so now, having such a bad memory, I will ask you to cut your answers shorter, if you would take me with you. . . .

That is the flavor of the Socratic irony as overtly jocular as you will find it. In general the dramatic elements are played down to such a degree that a thoughtless reader might hardly see the smile that underlies them. Nothing farther from the fantastical and obscene slapstick of the comic theaters could be imagined. But nevertheless Plato's dialogues are conceived in a spirit of comedy. To a person with intellectual interests they are often delicately humorous. The hero himself, when put on trial for corrupting the youth, is made to explain his popularity by saying that people "like to hear the cross-questioning of the pretenders to wisdom—for it is amusing." That was Plato's opinion. It was very likely also a statement made at his trial by the real Socrates. And it is so true—this drama of the seemingly humble and ignorant questioner puncturing the pretenses of the authorities has so deeply and peculiarly amused mankind ever since—that the word *irony* in all European dictionaries is defined, offhand, by an allusion to Plato's Socrates. Our own *Century Dictionary* says:

> "Simulated ignorance in discussion: a method of exposing an antagonist's ignorance by pretending to desire information or instruction . . . characteristic of Socrates, with reference to whom the term was first used."

The term *eiron* was not first used of Socrates, as we have seen. Nor was it first used with special reference to knowledge and ignorance. It was first used to describe any comic character who makes you laugh by *understating himself*, and makes you laugh in particular at the man who overstates himself. And it is to this earlier use of the term that I think we ought to go back for a definition.

I assembled so many quotations from Wodehouse in the previous chapter because I wanted to establish the flavor of comic understatement as a thing that exists and can be identified. It can be identified as the humor of the not-enough in general, before ever it appears in the form of understatement. And it can be identified in playful understatements before these are employed as weapons against an adversary.

Let us remember again that children are laughing at all kinds of ineptitude long before any preoccupation with the status of a self could come to be. They are laughing as Artemus Ward's friends used to laugh when they dropped around to his room on Sunday morning, and were entertained with such impromptu "sermons" as this, delivered with the utmost gravity:

> A bean pole, legitimately used, is an instrument of good, yet if it be sharpened at one end and run through a man it will cause the most intense pain and perhaps produce contortions. The wick of an unlighted candle may safely be manipulated, but if you light that wick and thrust your hand into the blaze and keep it there half an hour a sensation of excessive and disagreeable warmth will be experienced. . . . On the same principle we can easily hold in our arms an infant, and experience delight in doing so; but it would be very difficult for us to perform a similar experiment with a corpulent old gentleman who is in a state of unconscious inebriety, while the delight afforded by the performance in this instance would hardly be worth mentioning. All these things seem wonderful at first blush, but science makes them as clear as clear can be.

When you have sufficiently unlimbered your infantilism and sloughed off your accretions of sound judgment as to know, or remember, that such exploits in understatement for understatement's sake can be droll in a peculiar way, then you will see why the same thing when employed as a weapon has a way of wounding that is quite its own. You will see too that the victim, the person who is "made a fool of" by an irony, may be a very shadowy and unimportant creature. He may play the role rather of a pretext for the humor of understatement, than an adversary to be brought down by it. Take, for example, this suave and orotund pronouncement with which Wodehouse begins a chapter of his masterpiece, *Leave It To Psmith.*

> In any community in which a sensational crime has recently been committed, the feelings of the individuals who go to make up that community must of necessity vary somewhat sharply according to the degree in which the personal fortunes of each are affected by the outrage. Vivid in their own way as may be the emotions of one who sees a fellow citizen sandbagged in a quiet street, they differ in kind from those experienced by the victim himself.

Here all will agree, I think, that the humor lies essentially between Wodehouse and his readers. A victim is there, but he is not what we are smiling at. He is not at least its focal point. The center of levity—to put it still more technically—falls outside the victim.

In the following irony the victim moves in considerably closer to the center:

> Several of his [Lordship's] best friends were residing in those palatial establishments set in pleasant parks and surrounded by high walls with broken bottles on them, to which the wealthy and aristocratic are wont to retire when the strain of modern life becomes too great. And one of his uncles by marriage, who believed that he was a loaf of bread, had made his first public statement on the matter in the smoking room of this very castle.

There you have the same suave and orotund, and yet totally inadequate, description of a catastrophe. You have the playful humor of understatement. But this humor is now subtly and yet definitely enjoyed "at the expense of" a certain person, or a certain caste of persons. The very fact that their serious predicament has been understated to the point of absurdity makes us see their woes as laughable, not tragic. The understatement, being funny itself, "makes fun" of them. It makes them the butt of an oblique and delicate and velvet ridicule.

> Mr. Coe—says Artemus Ward—unintentionally dislocated his neck a few years since by falling from a scaffold in Illinois, a rope being twined about his neck at the time. There was a large crowd present, including the sheriff of the county.

A glimpse of the atom of irony may be seen in our familiar trick of deflating a violent denunciation by saying: "I judge you don't like him," or words to that effect.

> "Blast him!" muttered Mr. McTodd with indescribable virulence.
>
> Psmith eyed him inquiringly.
>
> "Correct me if I am wrong," he said, "but I seem to detect in your manner a certain half-veiled annoyance. . . ."

There the center of levity falls, I should say, close to the midriff of the victim.

This question of the center of levity is so important in the estimation of ironies—and of all hostile jokes—that I want to illustrate it once more. I will take an example of a purely playful understatement from *Life on the Mississippi.* After describing with humor his first lesson in piloting at the hands of Mr. Bixby, Mark Twain proceeds:

The watch was ended at last, and we took supper and went to bed. At midnight the glare of a lantern shone in my eyes, and the night watchman said:

"Come, turn out!"

And then he left. I could not understand this extraordinary procedure; so I presently gave up trying to, and dozed off to sleep. Pretty soon the watchman was back again, and this time he was gruff. I was annoyed. I said:

"What do you want to come bothering around here in the middle of the night for? Now, as like as not, I'll not get to sleep again tonight."

The watchman said:

"Well, if this ain't good, I'm blessed."

The "off-watch" was just turning in, and I heard some brutal laughter from them, and such remarks as, "Hello, watchman! ain't the new cub turned out yet? He's delicate likely. Give him some sugar in a rag, and send for the chambermaid to sing, 'Rock-a-bye Baby!' to him."

About this time Mr. Bixby appeared on the scene. Something like a minute later I was climbing the pilot-house steps with some of my clothes on and the rest in my arms. Mr. Bixby was close behind, commenting. . . .

To a humorless person I suppose there would be nothing in that passage but history. The concluding words are, after all, an accurate, if slightly succinct, account of the actual order of events. And yet they are sly and delightful to our sense of humor for the mere quantity of what they do not say. They are sly and delightful, but not strongly ironical. The victim being, in the first place, the author himself, a boy whom we already love, and his sin of not wanting to get up being one with which we have sympathized since birth—where in fact it originated—we do not laugh so much at his expense as with his help. We enjoy *with him* the comedy of understatement.

Compare with that the following comment by Ring Lardner on the calling of a baseball game in the World Series:

No doubt my readers has been tipped off by this time that the 2d game of the big serious was called on acct. of darkness but a great many of them may not know that the umpires and club owners was called a lot of different names which I will not repeat here but suffice it to say that none of them was honey, dearie and etc.

The boys that had paid $5.50 and up to see a ball game did not

> seem to think it was dark enough for the umps to step in and stop it. Personly I will not express no opinion as some of my best friends is umpires, but will merely state that I started out of the press box the instant it was over and by the aid of a powerful candle which I generally always carry to world serious games when Shawkey and Barnes is scheduled to pitch, why I was able to find my way down to the field where I run plum into A. D. Lasker who had forgot to light his headlights. Will further state that nobody who I passed on the way out to 8th Avenue had yet put on their pajamas or made any other preparations that would indicate the fall of night and even when I got down to park's row, pretty near a hr. after the game's untimely end, I was still able to grope my way to the office by feeling along the sides of buildings and was seated right here at my typewriter writing this article before the hoot owls and nightingales begun to emit their nocturnal sqawk.
>
> However, one of our fellow passengers on the bus downtown was Billy Evans, an umpire himself, and while he admitted that he had not saw none of the outfielders signaling to each other with flares, still and all he says the polo grounds is a terrible hard place for the athletes, and a specially the batters, to see a ball when they's the slightest twinge of darkness. As far as that is concerned there is 2 or 3 of the boys on each of the contending clubs that dont seem able to see the ball any too good even at high noon.

Taken at its face value, that too is little but a playful understatement of the fact that it was broad daylight when the game was called. It is humorous, and it would be humorous if purely playful—if, this fact being known, the humorist were, like Artemus Ward above, merely failing in diverting ways to state it. But besides being humorous, it is hostile. These reiterated and more and more extreme failures to state that it was broad daylight, these increasingly intense mock arguments to prove that it was at any rate not quite pitch dark, pile up into an irresistible assertion that it was not even verging toward twilight, and constitute a series of crescendo thrusts at those who called the game upon the pretense that it was. I said that Wodehouse understates his exaggeration; Lardner here exaggerates his understatements. He gives us irony in its raw and bitter form. And yet he is still within the definition we have proposed—still wielding, in fact, the essential art of Socrates. He is making fun of "the authorities" by understating his own position to the point of absurdity.

CHAPTER VI

Sarcasm and the Irony of Fate

HAVING GOT RING LARDNER and Mark Twain into the same pen with Socrates, we would seem to have finished our task of defining irony. We were telling the history of the word, however, and that history has been significant since Socrates. It has followed two roads, a low road and a high road. The low road has brought it out in the vicinity of the word *sarcasm,* with which its relations are badly in need of adjustment. The high, or high-brow, road has led it up into the heaven of pure intellectuality, where it can not be defined, and can "mean a different thing with every writer," and will therefore stand in no danger of attaching itself to any real fact and hindering the proliferation of ideas in the literary mind.

Let us take the high road first. It began in the discovery that there was something akin to ironic humor in the attitude of Greek audiences toward their tragedies. The subject of Greek tragedy, by and large, is the destruction of the overambitious man through jealousy of the gods. It taught much the same moral as their comedy, the moral of moderation or restraint. And *hubris,* the word they employed to denote an ambition swollen to the point of impious insolence, might be described as the serious counterpart of *alazoneia,* the mood deflated by the *eiron* in their comedies. Moreover the audience who watched this insolent man swaggering to his doom, were fully aware what was coming to him. There was no "mystery story" here. The plots were all well known to everybody; they were known like Jack and Jill. Therefore the audience looked upon this tragic hero's projects and proud talk with a certain detachment. Between audience and author there existed an understanding that was like a serious joke at his expense. They both knew how far the truth fell short of what he was saying. The gods, the fates, the course of things, *the facts he did not know,* were present to them all the time, unobtrusive, inexpressive, neither frowning nor smiling—"dead pan" in short—but like the *eiron* meaning more the less they said, and in the end triumphant.

We, with our excited exclamation, "Don't tell me how it comes out, I'm going to see it!" can hardly imagine the mood of the spectators of a Greek drama. That drama had grown up out of a religious rite performed by the whole community in a sacred precinct which had been of old their threshing floor. And this sacred precinct, this place-of-public-worship-turned-into-a-theater, was still opened only on the Lord's Day. It was opened by the priests of Dionysus and Apollo. The performance as a whole was ritual rather more than drama. It is no mitigation of the passion in a ritual to know how it is coming out. But when the ritual takes the form of a dramatic presentation of some historic person's life, a peculiar situation arises in the minds of those who watch it. They participate in the passions and propulsions of the hero, but without sharing the hazard. They participate somewhat as one does in the drama of a bullfight, having the knowledge of a superior being that the chief protagonist is doomed to die. And this peculiar emotional situation was of course exploited by the poetic ingenuity of the playwrights. They would even at times exchange with the audience a gruesome wink at the expense of their doomed hero. Œdipus has unknowingly slain his own father in order to become the husband of his mother, and when an arriving messenger asks for him, the chorus replies:

> "He is within, but here is his wife . . . and mother . . . of his children."

You might almost describe these typical Greek tragedies, if you did not care much about incest nor feel disturbed when people chop up their close friends and relatives, as practical jokes played by the author and enjoyed by the audience upon some haughty character who needs "taking down." The author and the audience are "wise" to the situation—they are "on"—and the hero is not. From this fact, and because of its similarity to the tricks played by the *eiron* upon the *alazon,* there arose among those who read the plays in after years the phrase "tragic irony."

For us the phrase may serve merely as another evidence that the comical and painful are not objectively distinct. Every kind of humor can be matched by a kind of pain. Everything that is tragic may be comic if you contrive to take it playfully. Hemingway has shown it to be true of bullfights. And now we see it of the tragedies of Sophocles and Euripides. The example above was "ironic" because the chorus said less than they meant. But when King Œdipus is led on by the gods to the point of issuing a decree of banishment against the murderer of his father, not knowing he is banishing himself from his own kingdom, that is not irony, but—if you persist in the analogy with the comic—a crude practical joke. We have nothing to learn, then, from the phrase "tragic irony," but just what Socrates insisted on at the Symposium, that "the genius of comedy and tragedy is the same" —which is a way of saying that our theory of humor is the right one.

For those, however, who devised this phrase, it seemed to give irony a wholly unique place among aesthetic qualities. And they began to describe irony in ways that had nothing whatever to do with humorous understatement, and little to do with humor, and toward the end, indeed, little to do with anything at all that is real. We need not follow this high road in all its windings. Suffice it to say that as a result of the peculiar set of facts we have described, and I think adequately explained, irony came to be identified with such widely differing things as philosophy, liberty, self-mastery, self-escape, divine elevation, logical beauty, intellectual transcendence, the contrast between what is and what ought to be, the "paradox of the great and good," the "smile of the sphinx," the "severing of the infinite from the finite world," and so on up to the peak of the stratosphere. The peak was reached, and the German flag planted there, by Friedrich Schlegel, who believed with his master, Fichte, that "the Ego," having created this world of mere empty appearance—*whose* Ego has never been determined—could sit aloof and smile at it in a humorless way, and indeed is doing so all the time in every work of art. Art itself, in that remarkably egotistical picture of being invented by the German romantic philosophers, becomes irony.

While these confused agglutinations of soul-vapor were gathering round the word on the heights, the humble good sense of mankind was arriving, as you know, at the perception that irony is close kin to sarcasm. It was also convincing itself that there is such a thing as an "irony of fate." Those are the two clear conclusions arrived at on the low-brow road. And if our definitions, besides bringing Mark Twain and Ring Lardner and Socrates all under its wing together, can make room in there for "fate" also, or the course-of-things, and then explain the exact relation of the whole family to sarcasm, I think it will have done its work. It will be as well established as anything can be in this fluid region where words are of necessity often loosely used.

Most people today, if you ask them what irony is, will say a mild, or veiled, or not passionate sarcasm. "Covert sarcasm" is what the *Century Dictionary* says after finishing with the Socratic meaning. And sarcasm, or attacking a person by praising him in a false tone, is familiar to us all. "You're a fine friend, you are! You're loyal and true!" This is one of our most ancient forms of Christian communion, so ancient that those words "yoú are" with the peculiar accent may almost be described as a negative adverb. There is nothing of pleasantry in this manner of greeting a fellow mortal, nothing that belongs to our subject. It has, on the contrary, a particularly searing, or "flesh-tearing" quality, because it not merely denies him the virtue in question, but clothes him in it—showing him, so to speak, in the guise of a proper man—in the very act of stripping it off.

In order to become humorous, a sarcasm like everything else in the world has to develop a defect which can be taken playfully. The words have to be so false, foolish, illogical, inappropriate, inadequate, or extravagant in their eulogistic meaning that they obviously can not be taken seriously. Their failure to mean what they say thus becomes a joke, and their meaning-the-opposite is the point of the joke.

> Are you lost daddy I arsked tenderly.
> Shut up he explained.

That is an atom of humorous sarcasm. You have only to imagine a humorless person reading it—"Why! but he *didn't* explain! Saying shut up is *just the opposite* of explaining!"—in order to see that this is true.

"When it comes to sarcasaming," said Mark Twain's Connecticut Yankee, "I guess I can keep my end up." And he proved it by describing to King Arthur's subjects how justly the taxes were distributed in the country he came from.

> If you take a nation of 60,000,000 where average wages are $2 per day, three days' wages taken from each individual will provide $360,000,000 and pay the government's expenses. In my day, in my own country, this money was collected from imports, and the citizen imagined that the foreign importer paid it, and it made him comfortable to think so; whereas, in fact, it was paid by the American people, and was so equally and exactly distributed among them that the annual cost to the 100-millionaire and the annual cost to the sucking child of the day laborer was precisely the same—each paid $6. Nothing could be equaler than that I reckon.

There again you have only to say it in all seriousness, in order to see what, in all playfulness, makes it funny.

> The affair between Margot Asquith and Margot Asquith—says Dorothy Parker—will live as one of the prettiest love stories in literature.
>
> If definitions of happiness can keep Professor Phelps on his toes that is little short of dandy . . .

These bits from her book criticisms in *The New Yorker* of ten years ago will show that when it comes to sarcasaming, Dorothy Parker too can keep her end up. They will show what a wholesome caustic this harsh art can be. And they will show what its essential mode of operation as a weapon is—to say something that collapses automatically when taken at its face value, leaving, so to speak, the value of the other end just where the face had been.

"The more it
Snows-tiddely-pom,
The more it
Goes-tiddely-pom

> The more it
> Goes-tiddely-pom
> On
> Snowing.
>
> "And nobody
> Knows-tiddely-pom,
> How cold my
> Toes-tiddely-pom
> How cold my
> Toes-tiddely-pom
> Are
> Growing."

The above lyric is culled from the fifth page of Mr. A. A. Milne's new book, *The House at Pooh Corner,* for, although the work is in prose, there are frequent droppings into more cadenced whimsy. This one is designated as a "Hum," that pops into the head of Winnie-the-Pooh as he is standing outside Piglet's house in the snow, jumping up and down to keep warm. It "seemed to him a Good Hum, such as is Hummed Hopefully to Others." In fact, so Good a Hum did it seem that he and Piglet started right out through the snow to Hum It Hopefully to Eeyore. Oh, darn—there I've gone and given away the plot. Oh, I could bite my tongue out.

Why does this crudest kind of hostile wit seem so much like irony, which is the most subtle? To answer this question let us compare the above abrupt and total annihilations with the more indirect and almost tenderly administered poison in the following. It is about the arrival in New York of the "Grand Duchess Cyril of Russia."

> When the good ship of Paris reached New York the duchess disembarked by way of the steerage gangplank and most folks said how clever she was to outwit the newspaper boys and etc., but some of the deeper thinkers suspects that the reason she disembarked by way of the steerage gangplank was, well, on account of it being right there. (Lardner.)

Does not that answer the dictionary's description of a slightly veiled, or coolly toned, or "covert" sarcasm? Would you not, from the mere feeling of it as you read, describe it as a pointedly ironical, rather than a sarcastic, remark?

It differs from the remarks quoted from Dorothy Parker in just this, that instead of meaning the opposite of what it says, it means more than what it says. The gangplank was there—that is quite true—but that is not *enough* to make sense. And so you add, smilingly, a little more. And instead of the harsh jolt of jumping to the opposite, you experience the sly and gradual humor of apprehending the understated.

It remains only to show that "fate," or the course-of-things, has a habit of making fun of man in this same delicate way. And that is not difficult. Things play, of course, all kinds of jokes on man, and they are all in common parlance called the irony of fate. But fate is especially given to this trick of leading him along by understating her intentions. And man, if you will consider his character and costumes, seems to have been brought on the stage for the express purpose of adding humor to the joke.

That man is an *alazon,* that he swaggers about this planet with his head swathed in a cloud of honorific emotions and self-elevating intellectual constructions, pouring out a flood of grandiose language on every subject under the sun, must be apparent to anyone who has read history. A good ninety per cent of our human brain-work is expended in building balloon cushions between ourselves and the hard facts. Yet the facts rarely stand up in a shouting mood and contradict us. They lie low; they say little; their humility is remarkable. They will agree in a measure to any "construction" we want to put upon them. They often seem, indeed, to be nodding their heads in approval when we are stalking and swaggering our worst, dressed all up, and making weighty gestures and orations, passing laws, and inventing religions and systems of universal philosophy. They agree, they go along with us, raising a minor question now and then, significant if we were "on," but never obstreperous in their objection. All the while they know very well that we are top-heavy, and are riding for a fall.

It is only necessary thus to think of fate—of the facts and forces, I mean, that determine events—as a person, in order to see that toward mankind he is an ironical person. He consents to our waging a universal war for democracy and world peace—he permits us to put that "construction" upon him—knowing very well that we are promoting militarism to the point of dictatorship and doing our best to abolish democracy from the earth.

That is, perhaps, a sarcasm, rather than an irony of fate. A better example of fate's irony is the story of Napoleon Bonaparte. It is the best possible example, because Napoleon made a conscious effort to outwit this Socratic jester by himself taking the standpoint of the hard facts. He tried not to be an *alazon.* He invented the word *ideology* to describe all those cloudy intellectual constructions by which other great men had been intrigued to their doom. He succeeded too, by comparison with the revolutionary idealists whom he superseded, in being very matter-of-fact—so much so that he seemed for a time to be the very expression of the developing facts, the child, as they said, of destiny. But he was not matter-of-fact enough. He carried a plenty of ideological mist, although of another kind, in his own head. And so fate made a fool of him, much as Socrates did of Protagoras, assenting to his grandiose propositions with remarkable humility, humoring him, going along with him—asking him at times, it even seemed, for information as to the proper course for history to take—only to show him up as a self-deceived, inflated toy in the long run.

That is the irony of fate—or as we now say more wisely, of the facts that are beyond our control. They say little but mean much.

Napoleon's word *ideology* was taken over by Karl Marx, who made another and far more stupendous effort to base himself upon the hard facts, to find out "the forces that control history," to associate his purposes with fate. Never was a man more determined not to be fooled by grandiose ideas, not to be "utopian," not to be an *alazon,* than Karl Marx. And fate has humored him—even more remarkably than she did Napoleon. Her ironic smile is still visible only to an attentive eye. That to Marx's followers the word *ideology,* a term of violent abuse to him, has become a good word, and they describe his own philosophy—alas, too well—as "the ideology of the proletariat," will indicate the scope and nature of the jest.

That, however, is another book. Here it must suffice to say that only science can outwit the irony of fate. Science is nothing, indeed, but an attempt to outwit this jester—to base man's emotional ambitions, no matter how "insolent," how "swaggering," upon an unemotional and undeluded grasp and definition of the relevant facts. Where this is possible, and to the extent that it is possible, the *alazon* may triumph, the joke may be turned against fate. And yet the facts, even when known and molded to our desires, continue to say so much less and mean so much more than we do when we talk about them, that I am afraid their irony will never die. They say, indeed, nothing at all. And that, if you can make it mean a great deal, is the supreme irony.

Part Seven

THE PREVAILING TOPICS OF LAUGHTER

CHAPTER I

Playthings of the Moment

THE READER, if he is still there, has now considered all the general forms of adult play. Our science, in this formal sense, is finished. But there are certain materials, or themes, which predominate significantly in laughter. Grown-up people have their playthings just as children do. They have their playthings of the moment, their "topics of comedy," about which everybody for a time is brimful and bursting with laughter, and all a jest need do is open the tap and let them laugh. And they have certain perennial natural subject matters of hilarity, like insults and sexual allusions, which prevail so universally that any one of them may seem, on a quick view, to be almost a definition of the comic.

As to the playthings of the moment, it is beyond our science to explain what brings them into favor and retires them. The causes are as various as the results. It is more necessary for the humorist than for anybody else to be up-to-date—that is all that can be said. The fashions in humor have complete command of our taste exactly because they have no deep roots. They can not be influenced by considerations, because entertaining considerations is work. Humor is play, and it has to happen at the first glance or never happen at all. That is why "antique funnyings in print bring on a pleasant melancholy," as Booth Tarkington so deftly says.

To me Mark Twain's "Jumping Frog of Calaveras County"—until he translated it back from French into English—was a rather mediocre piece of journalism, and I note he thought so too. And yet because of some momentary predisposed hilarity toward "western" jokes, this "squib," this "villainous sketch," as he described it, leapt across the world and made him famous, almost, overnight.

Another historic piece of American humor, Artemus Ward's "The High Handed Outrage at Utica," which Lincoln read to his cabinet with such gusto just before reading them the Emancipation Proclamation, hardly provokes a smile today. We sit like the impregnable Stanton, or Salmon P. Chase, wondering what the President could see to laugh at.

> 1 day as I was givin a descripshun of my Beests and Snaiks in my usual flowry stile what was my skorn & disgust to see a big burly feller walk up to the cage containin my wax figgers of the Lord's Last Supper, and cease Judas Iscarrot by the feet and drag him out on the ground. He then commenced fur to pound him as hard as he cood.
>
> "What under the son are you abowt?" cried I.
>
> Sez he, "What did you bring this pussylanermus cuss here fur?" & hit the wax figger another tremendjis blow on the hed.
>
> Sez I, "You egrejus ass, that air's a wax figger—a representashun of the false 'Postle."
>
> Sez he, "That's all very well fur you to say; but I tell you, old man, that Judas Iscarrot can't show hisself in Utiky with impunerty by a darn site!" with which observashun he kaved in Judassis hed.

Our totally changed attitude toward the characters of the Bible is what has drained the color out of this, as out of much poetic humor of the period. We can not experience the clash of emotional atmospheres involved in applying the name "Judas Iscariot" to a palpable object seized by the feet and dragged about right here in Utica, New York. Calling Judas a "pussylanermus cuss" would have been ludicrous to any live mind then. It would moreover have derived a meaning-value from the very fact that this change of attitude was in the wind. The jest tuned in, so to speak, on a live issue, and the issue is now dead.

A still more famous American joke was Artemus Ward's answer when Maguire of the San Francisco Opera House telegraphed: "What will you take for forty nights on the Pacific Coast?" He answered, collect: "Brandy and water."

There is more than one reason why that joke has lost its savor. Telegraphing, in the first place, was a more momentous and expensive thing then than it is now. The Pacific Coast was noted for its drinking bouts. The typical choice of the hard drinker was brandy and water. (You have to change that to "whisky and soda" to get so much as a smile out of a contemporary audience.) Brandy and water was, moreover, the accepted symbol for what they called a "spree"—also an outworn entity. The duration of a "spree," instead of being a stale question that somebody's maiden aunt might excite herself about, was the living topic of sophisticated comedy. Those world-famous sprees of gold-encumbered miners coming down the mountains to the Pacific Coast were, in fact, the very symbols of all reckless and abandoned fun. When Artemus Ward, in collapsing a lecture agent's "What will you take?" with no answer at all, replied to a bartender's "What will you take?" with an answer that proposed to extend one of those celebrations for forty days and nights—the same period that Christ starved in the desert—he touched the very mainspring of the nation's laughter. He tapped a vein, indeed, that ran right back into that humorous tall talk, that cockalorum mythology, in which the nation's own authentic comedy began. With the change in all these attitudes and circumstances, the living spirit has departed from his words, but the form is still there, the skeleton, of a royal joke. *In pace requiescat.*

If a truly witty and rich jest can so fade with changing circumstances, what is to be expected of those droll remarks that prosper merely because they touch a topic about which everybody feels like laughing? The topic of educated women, of mules, of Mormons, of church sociables, of "swear words," of "mentioning in polite society" certain more or less obvious attributes of nature, were at various times a magic key to laughter in the topmost circles of our sophistication. Josh Billings gives us the surprising information that he has "seen people that would rather die and be buried than say bull," but "they wouldn't hesitate to say *male cow.*" "Old maids" were fountains of hilarity in those days. We do not believe in them any longer, either. Our joke is on the person who does—the preacher who got up in his pulpit one Sunday morning and said: "To refute certain slanders that have been going around this community I am going to ask every woman in this congregation who is a virgin to stand up." A deathlike silence ensued. "Have no fears," he said. "In the eyes of the Lord, and for the good name of our parish, I call upon you to testify." Nobody moved. The parson's eyes traveled anxiously over his congregation. He swallowed hard. Finally a young woman with a baby in her arms rose hesitantly in a rear pew.

"But my good woman," he said, "do you understand my meaning? You have a child in your arms."

"Well, you wouldn't expect this little baby to stand up all by herself, would you?" she said.

People for whom the chastity joke has reached that stage of fermentation are not going to laugh heartily at the fun Josh Billings had in remarking: "There are many singular beings in this world, but I fancy the singularest are the spinsters." It is a poor joke, but if we still had a vivid play-interest as well as a sturdy belief in the singularity of spinsters, we should be satisfied with the mere fact that it *is* a joke, and is *about* something we want to laugh at. It is a far better joke than Groucho Marx's recent one about the Dionne quintuplets:

> "Don't you know what duplicates are?"
> "Sure. It's five kids up in Canada."

And yet that pitiable joke, merely because it reminded us of our present playthings, was greeted with a roar of laughter.

An elderly friend of mine, a spinster of seventy-odd, went to a party where everybody dressed to represent a famous book. She wore a simple black gown with a placard across her abdomen reading: THE DIONNE QUINTUPLETS.

Guess the title of the book. . . .

It Can't Happen Here!

So much the better, you see, if you can touch *two* lively topics of the day—and a topic of eternity besides.

After eluding-prohibition had taken the place of having-a-spree as a laugh topic, Will Rogers one day proposed a nation-wide subscription for a "consolation cup" to be presented to Sir Thomas Lipton, the perennial loser of the international yacht race. Ring Lardner answered:

> Bill Rogers' scheme won't satisfy the old man or me either. Bill suggested that everybody chip in $1.00 apiece and send it to Mayor Walker, whose duty it would be to use the proceeds in the purchase of a consolation cup for Sir Thomas. In the first place, Mr. Lipton lives in a country where you don't have to pour your consolation into a cup even in the main dining room. In the second place, suppose everyone but Bill Rogers did send a $1.00 to Mayor Walker; that would only make something like $120,000,000 and the Mayor would face the alternative of being called a cheap skater or paying for the saucer out of his own pocket. In the third place, I understand that Bill is already sorry he conceived the idea; its publication brought him back into the limelight and tore away the blanket of obscurity he has been trying to hide behind for the past fourteen years.

That still has a flavor for us, but what will be left of it eighty years hence? A footnote will explain the "reference" about a cup in the main dining room, and the solemn footnote will be funny, but never again the cup. A second footnote will explain the point of the concluding sarcasm, and perhaps settle the question whether Will Rogers got his idea from the Lipton Tea Company and whether he got anything else with it. And that will not be funny, but still, I hope, of serious concern to critics.

A woman in Washington during Roosevelt's inauguration asked a policeman for a comfort station. "Madam," he replied with a polite gesture, "there's one just around the corner." "Here, don't give me any of that old Hoover stuff!" she said, "I'm in a hurry!"

Imagine a learned commentator in a foreign language two thousand years hence getting out his spectacles and encyclopedias, delving in the "original sources," and trying to bring that joke to life by finding out *about* it. As well try to strike fire by explaining the principles of combustion. Laughs won't live on the knowledge *about* a thing; they live in the perception *of* it. You can learn to love—at least they say so —but you laugh at first sight or not at all.

Stephen Leacock should remember this when making his probably true, but certainly extreme remarks about the primitiveness of Aristophanes' wit, and the vast improvement that historic times have seen in humor. We can not, even with the laugh-killing help of the commentators, find out what the fine edge of a half of Aristophanes' jokes was, to say nothing of tasting their live flavor.

I myself have presided over the decline and almost death of Leacock's own early masterpiece, the story called *My Financial Career.* It must have been first published in the nineties, for I can remember my mother, who was a humorous and heretical minister, causing her congregation to writhe, shout and wriggle in their pews more like Holy Rollers than respectable Congregationalists, reading this story to them after prayers. It was from her I learned its fatal power. And I will now confess that for seventeen years I have made a large part of my living, to say nothing of my success in life, by reading this piece to the public. It is a piece about a man who goes into a bank with fifty-six dollars to open an account, but is so shy and so stricken dumb by the grandeur of the institution, that he comes out after a series of excruciating experiences, with his money still, or again, in his hands. I always preceded it with a quotation from Bergson's book on laughter, and pretended that I was reading it in order to convince the audience by their own feelings that his derision theory is false. I have convinced them, too, for they always loved the man who went into the bank. But that was not why I read it. I read it because it was the one thing in this world that I could count on as Elijah counted on the Lord. It stood there in the middle of my lecture like the shelter of a great rock in a barren land. They could despise me, if they wanted to, and glare me down, and get ready to give me the stratosphere or drive me off the platform with bricks. But they could not hold in when I read them that story, and they could not recover their animosity after I got through reading it. Leacock stood between me and death by refrigeration more times than I can possibly thank him for—until 1930.

In 1930 I began to notice a slight cooling of the welcome to his story. The trouble seemed to center around the word *rattled* in the very first sentence: "When I go into a bank I get rattled." "That is old-fashioned slang," I said to myself, and I wondered if it would be a sacrilege to bring that up to date. But that old-fashioned slang began to cast its killing shadow farther and farther forward into the story.

A chill seemed to be running through the whole piece. By 1931 even his question to the manager, "Can I see you—alone?" no longer drew a yell. And "I don't know why I said 'alone,' but without it the thing seemed self-evident," provoked only a titter. By December of that year, they wouldn't stand up and shout at "Good morning, I said, and stepped into the safe." And after Roosevelt's inauguration—in the spring, namely, of 1932—even "What! are you drawing it all out again?" was received as a mild and tolerable pleasantry. I won't say that the story is dead even now. I insist upon believing it immortal. But from being my prop and refuge, my shelter in the arms of eternal humor, and my principal source of income, for nigh twenty years, it has become a thoughtful memory of how funny it was to be shy in the presence of a bank before the banks themselves turned purple-red and hid their heads in shame.

Besides these alterations in the terms of laughter which we can explain, there are many which we can not. The grown-up child's attachments shift capriciously from one plaything to another as the infant's do. In a preface to *Of Thee I Sing,* George Jean Nathan speaks of "facetious allusions to Congress" as an outmoded type of humor superseded by this piece—a crack, I suppose, at Will Rogers. But facetious allusions to the vice president are old enough, as old, at least, as Mark Twain's return in 1900 from his sojourn abroad (see his speech to the Lotus Club), and a large section of *Of Thee I Sing* is devoted to carrying that time-honored joke to its limit in a spirit of raw and Rabelaisian slapstick. That is highly commendable, and suggests that America may not always be an ambitious novice in the art of exaggeration, but it is not a new play topic.

Will Rogers, although he stuck to the "rustic" attitude, and spoke with a mild flash of scorn about the "little New York boys" and their up-to-dateness, had actually a keener sense of the kinship between humor and the present moment than any other humorist I know. He was the only person I ever spoke to, besides Joe Cook, who felt, as I do, that there is something almost a little alien to the perfect spirit of humor—to his own humor, at any rate—in the mere act of "telling a story."

"A very funny thing," he said to me, "but I can't tell a story. I never told a story in my life. My humor always pertains to now."

He illustrated the nowness of his humor with a local variant of the vice-president joke, which is worth adding to our memories of him. He had recently, when I lunched with him, been up in the north of California to speak at a Democratic rally. It was during an illness of the governor, and the lieutenant governor preceded Rogers on the platform. In a rather clumsy effort to poke fun, the speaker said that he would not try to make any jokes since the biggest joke in California was scheduled to follow him. "Like all conceited actors," he added, "I see he is whispering to his companion now, instead of listening to me and trying to learn something."

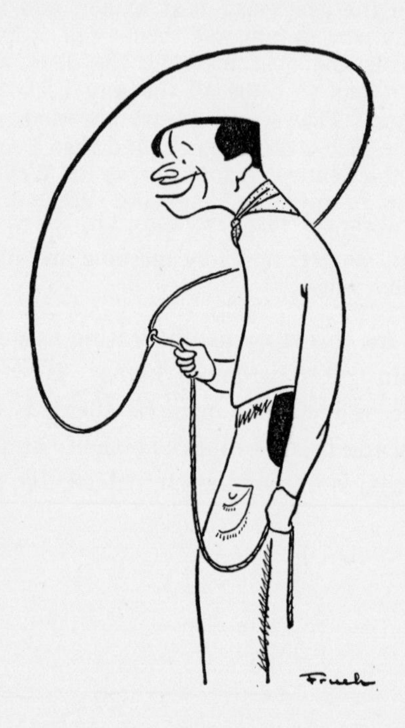

When he sat down the chairman said: "I won't waste any time introducing Will Rogers for I know you are only waiting for his comeback."

The come-back sounded like this:

> "First of all, ladies and gentlemen, I want to apologize. It is quite true that I was whispering to the lady next to me, and I feel very bad about it. I am sorry. The reason it made such a disturbance was that I asked her a question. I asked her, I said: 'Who is that man talking?' And she said, 'I don't know.' And then she turned and asked the gentleman next to her, and then he turned and asked the lady next to him, and then—well, it had to go all the way down the aisle and over there by the door, and then when they found out, it had to come all the way back: 'Why, it's the lieutenant governor!' That sounds pretty big when you say it, and that's why it made such a disturbance. And then I says to the lady, I says: 'Oh, it's the lieutenant governor, is it? Well, what does *he* do?' 'Oh he don't *do* anything,' she said. 'What do you mean,' I said, 'don't do anything? Don't he even get up in the morning?' 'Oh yes,' she said, 'he gets up every morning and inquires whether the governor's any worse.' "

Although he told me this story as illustrating how his jokes "pertain to now," it also illustrates perennial humor. It would have tickled Aristophanes' public as it did his own. Its theme is personal prestige. Its point is "getting the better" of an opponent. And that, as we shall see in a few moments, is one of the eternal jocular preoccupations of the race.

CHAPTER II

Matrimony and Other Painful Pleasures

BEFORE DISCUSSING the perennially prevailing topics of laughter, I have to explain what I mean by the topic of a pointed joke. Some jokes have two topics and some only one. Some, I mean, start off talking about one thing, and fool you by ending up in another. Others talk about the same thing all the way through, but fool you as to what they are going to say about it. I call them two-track and one-track jokes.

President Lincoln, with a "meaning no offense, gentlemen," told some ministers who came to see him a story about a Negro boy who was making "mud pies" with his toe.

"What are you making?" an onlooker asked him.

"A church," he said. "Can't you see the pews and the pulpit?"

"Why don't you make the minister?" the onlooker asked.

"Ain't got enough mud!" the boy said.

You might classify that joke under "mud pies," or "Negro architecture," but you would more likely classify it under "ministers"—especially when the ministers were right there to get the point. It is a two-track joke. And generally speaking the "topic" of a two-track joke is the topic upon which it comes to rest—if I may so describe the atmospheric conditions prevailing after Lincoln got through telling that story.

A man and a girl were out automobile riding together, and something happened to the machinery. They both got out and crawled under the car to fix it. After a while a cop tapped them on the shoulders and said: "I beg your pardon, did you know that your car had been stolen?"

That again is a two-track joke, and its topic is not automobile accidents, but sex and concentration. And so, in general, when I speak of the "topic" of a joke, I refer to the meaning or emotional satisfaction which gives it point, and this may or may not have anything to do with the theme on which it starts off.

In jokes which have only one topic, it is apt to be a topic about which we have two conflicting attitudes of feeling. One-track jokes have often, therefore, an intimate warmth and excitement about them. They seem to run deeper than two-track jokes. Thurber and White are distillers of poetic humor rather than concocters of jokes, but they play one very neat trick on the topic of matrimony which I want to quote as an example of this.

> The impracticability of two people living apart—they argue—becomes apparent in the matter of the old 1916 Cadillac touring car which they own. On separating, the husband will generously give the car to his wife to use, but that doesn't alter the fact that he, and he alone, knows what you have to do when the car "does that funny thing." Thus, the husband is apt any time during the day to pick up the phone and hear his wife's voice:
>
> "Dear, I'm on the Merrick Road between Bellport and Patchogue, and the car is doing that funny thing again." This means dropping whatever work he is doing, taking a cab to the Penn station and a Long Island train to the scene of the breakdown. This also shows up in his work. It never could happen if husband and wife were living together, because in that case they would never be on cordial enough terms for him to let her use the car.

There is only one subject of discussion here, and there is, moreover, no logical trick or inconsistency in what is said about it. In so far as it appeals to "the intellect pure and simple," the argument is unimpeachable and is no joke. But it happens that when a man is arguing in a sociological tone of voice about the advantages of living together, our matrimonial emotions inevitably start sliding toward the *yes* end. By the time we reach the words, "It could never happen if husband and wife were living together," we are practically in tears of tender consent. Those tears are dried with a suddenness that would crack the skin if we had not in us also a confirmed wish to break out of the house and set bombs under this whole business of institutionalized felicity.

> A very nervous young man came in with a girl to get a marriage license, and the clerk, taking down the data, murmured: "Parents' consent?"
>
> "Parents' consent!" he said. "Who the hell do you think that is in the door with a shotgun, Daniel Boone?"

A two-track joke which relies for its point on the same rebellious emotion, will seem, other things being equal, a little less delicately droll. For instance, a man was describing a terrible catastrophe that occurred in his house, a gas heater having exploded and blown everything into the street, and to convey an idea of the devastating force of the explosion, he said: "It was the first time I've seen father and mother go out of that door together in twenty years!" Perhaps the humor lies here more in the image than the trick—the swift and perfect reconciliation!—but the trick consists of arousing an interest in a thing remote from matrimony, the size of an explosion, and satisfying a reverse-interest in matrimony in the act of disappointing that.

I suspect that this difference between one-track and two-track jokes might play a considerable role if a thorough-going science of humor ever came to be written, men having found out what actually takes place in the brain and body when they think and feel.

Our present business with it—aside from making clear what we mean by the topic of a joke—is to remark that any subject matter upon which we have two contrasted or conflicting attitudes of feeling, becomes by that very fact a natural material for one-track jokes, and therefore a prevailing topic of laughter. Matrimony, sin, virtue, doctors, religion, priests, policemen, swear words—it is a long and changing list, and we may as well let "marred life" stand for the whole tribe.

> Marred life is a job just the same as like a telegraph operator or a embalmer and every employ is entitled to 2 wks. vacation per annum and if the husband takes a 2 wks. vacation trip every sum-

mer and vice versa, why they will get so as they won't miss their regular jobs ½ as much as if they was on it all the wile. For inst. I knew a couple where the husband use to go South for a mo. every Winter and one time she didn't know he was still missing till one night in August when a bat got in the house and she screamed and nobody told her to shut up . . .

They's no fun playing tennis unless the guy on the other side of the net has got a racket and the same goes for a connubial quarl and my advice is for the husband to call up home just before he leaves the office and ask the spouse if she is feeling brutal this evening and if she ain't she better be, because by the time he gets the right number they won't be nobody half to wait till dog days to see him froth at the mouth . . .

Finely, try and forget once in a wile that you are marred and go out somewheres together for a good time. Don't go to a dance or a card party or a good show or the opera, but pick out something that the both of you can enjoy, like for inst. a 3 cushion billiard match or a cock fight or to watch the high school football five practice. Remember always that you swore at each other at the altar that each was taking the other from bad to worse and may the best man win. (Lardner.)

CHAPTER III

Satire and Sympathetic Humor

Once you understand that humor has its roots in play, it is no surprise to learn that jokes whose point lies in the downing or "degradation" of a rival, or potential rival, are the commonest of all jokes. The question who gets the better of whom is at issue in the majority of games and recreations, from the frolics of a litter of kittens to the bridge parties of a twitter of Colonial Dames. This is not due to the nature of play, but to the nature of the playing beast. It is life itself, the character of those species which have succeeded in keeping it going, that is predominantly rivalrous. Life is full of egoism and hostility; life is avid of sudden glory and superiority. We do not say on that account that life consists of these things, and we have no better cause to say that humor does. It is natural and quite inevitable that a creature whose principal serious occupation is getting ahead against rivals should, when he pauses to "make fun," most often and most successfully make fun *of* somebody. Jibes are not the essence or the origin of laughter; they are merely the easiest kind of joke to crack.

Irvin S. Cobb told me that the "biggest laugh" he ever got out of an audience was got with a jibe at Will Rogers, and Will Rogers confirmed this by saying it was the biggest laugh he ever heard laughed. They had both been invited to a dinner in New York, and each was to be introduced by an appropriate celebrity. Will Hays, the virtue specialist of the movies, introduced Will Rogers, and he did so with oil and flowers. His peroration ran somewhat as follows: "And I want to say to you, ladies and gentlemen, that when this Oklahoma cowboy first strolled in here from the open spaces, it did not take New York long to discover, and rejoice in the discovery, ladies and gentlemen, that Will Rogers had something under the old ten-gallon hat besides hair!"

Cobb jumped to his feet without an introduction. "Ladies and gentlemen," he said, "I am moved. I am touched. I want to endorse from a full heart these glowing words that have been spoken, and I want to add that I think it was high time somebody in this broad land of ours said a good word for dandruff!"

It is a rough jest, but nobody with experience in extracting laughter from after-dinner audiences will doubt that it had the effect reported. The moment it is understood that play is in order—and could it be better understood than with these two famous jokers present?—it is understood that "taking a crack" at somebody is in order. It is in order to see which of two people is going to "get the better" of the other. And that is not because humorous feeling is a feeling of superiority, but because a contest is the liveliest kind of fun.

It is not a joke to assert, no matter how convincingly, that a man has no brains, although if he can not answer, it is enjoying superiority over him. It is a joke to endorse a flowery tribute of praise, to set all minds moving in the direction of an encomium, and then with an unexpected trick of mind and tongue *present them* with the assertion that he has no brains. The humor lies in the trick, not the assertion.

Repartee is a manly sport conducted with this kind of wit. It is word play taking the place of sword play. It is a duel fought with the points of jokes.

> Go 'way, I can't talk to an idiot!
> Come here, I can! (Cantor.)

> The Tankard of Ale pointed the stem of his pipe accusingly at his adversary. One could see that he was deeply stirred.
> "He's talking rot about smoking."
> "I am talking sense."
> "I didn't hear any."
> "I said that smoking was dangerous to the health. And it is."
> "It isn't."
> "It is. I can prove it from my own personal experience. I was once," said the Lemon Squash, "a smoker myself, and the vile habit

reduced me to a physical wreck. My cheeks sagged, my eyes became bleary, my whole face gaunt, yellow and hideously lined. It was giving up smoking that brought about the change."

"What change?" asked the Tankard. (Wodehouse.)

Then they came over and hunted me up and I will confess I wouldn't of known him. Him and I is the same age to the month, but he seems to show it more, some way. He is balder for one thing. And his beard is all white, where mine has still got a streak of brown in it. The very first thing I said to him, I said:

"Well, Frank, that beard of yours makes me feel like I was back north. It looks like a regular blizzard."

"Well," he said, "I guess yourn would be just as white if you had it dry cleaned." (Lardner.)

Jack Goodman and Albert Rice have recently published a little book on repartee called *I Wish I'd Said That,* a book which ought to live forever for the slogan at its masthead: "It has been our unwavering policy to waste no time in thinking." That having been a matter of policy, and not an oversight as is so often true of essays on the comic, the genial authors will not mind my remarking that they neglected to notice exactly what they were talking about. They represent as an example of improved technique in repartee what is a most precise example of the difference between repartee and serious retort.

Many too many people—they say—have answered the line "I have nothing to say!" with the obvious retort: "You never have!" The betterism technic should be tried on this sort of remark. Why not answer, for instance, "I know, but just how are you phrasing it this time?"

The second answer is repartee because it plays a trick on the opponent's mind, seeming to acquiesce in his superior pose, and yet evolving out of that very act the thought which floors him. The art of hostile repartee might be defined as follows: One person makes a statement honorific to himself and/or degrading to his opponent; his opponent so manipulates the words, or logic, or emotional tenor, of the statement as to collapse that pattern, and substitute one which distributes the honors in a reverse sense.

A highly placed member of the Convention during the French Revolution attempted to wither an opponent of lower origin by asking:

"Is it true, as I have been told, that the member from X——
is a veterinary?"
The member from X—— replied:
"Yes, Monsieur. Are you ill?"

Put yourself in the place of the first speaker and try to think of a reply, and you will see what a hazardous and thrilling sport this is. And if you want to see how different it is from merely jabbing a person who is not armed and in the game, compare that retort with the reply of Dr. Johnson—or was it Dean Swift?—to the woman who said, "You know I never can keep my nails clean in London": "Perhaps, madam, you scratch yourself."

Or compare it with John Randolph's answer to the man who remarked, on being introduced to him, "I had the honor of passing your house this morning": "Thank you."

Those were pretty raw insults, but still they were not fired point-blank. They trick the mind that hears them, and contain a trace, no matter how remote, of roguishness. They are not only mean, that is, but mischievous. That is how they differ from saying, "Madam, your body is dirty," or "I hope you will never enter my house." And no matter how savage a satire may become, this difference remains, and can be felt by all those not too seriously hurt to feel it.

It is essential, if understanding is to lend anything to the enjoyment of satire, that this fact be understood. Satire is a name we give to any form of jocularity that finds its point in worsting an opponent. It is humor as a weapon. It is not contrasted against caricature or irony, but comprises them. It comprises every kind, except perhaps the crudest ridicule and mockery, of "making fun of." I shall devote a special chapter to this important phase of manufacture. But in order to approach it with the proper equilibrium, I must first discuss that kind of wit which does not make fun *of*, but merely makes fun, and also that whose point, or final resting place, is admiration or a sympathetic feeling.

As there are many who still contest the existence of such wit, I will point out not only that there is such wit, but that there is a manly sport of fencing with it. There is a game of repartee in which the aim is to get the *worse* of an opponent, or to so manipulate the tenor of a statement as to hand the honors to the other. I call it a manly sport because it is played not only by all sorts of people affectionately disposed to each other, but continually by witty men in their association with women. An example may be found in Ring Lardner's account of how he revolutionized the ticket-selling industry.

> A beautiful widow with two children asked for tickets to Peekskill.
>
> "Madam," I said, "Peekskill has many attractions, but I think you would find Ardsley just as nice, and it's nearer and cheaper."
>
> "All right make it Ardsley," said she, "and how about my kiddies? Are they half fare?"
>
> "Not half as fair as their mummy," said I.

Everybody must have played, in season and according to his abilities, this game of complimentary repartee. It differs from derogatory repartee in no respect whatever, except that instead of dealing a mischievous blow it pays a mischievous tribute.

> "Do you believe in love at first sight?"
>
> "No. Do you?"
>
> "No. That is just why I want to see you again." *

The practical joke is there, the trick played on the mind, but the point arrived at is a tribute, not a degradation.

Suppose a comedian goes to the telephone, calls a number, and says: "Hello, please connect me with the brewery," and then after a moment's pause takes a tumbler and draws a glass of beer out of the instrument. That is a pun, you might say, on the word *connect,* and its point, or serious value, if it has one, lies in that glass of beer. The comedian has it, and the audience hasn't. Where is the degradation? Where is the downing of a rival? The jest is not in any sense, or from any point of view, satirical. And it is typical of a million jests to be seen in the moving pictures every day. More than half the serious pleasure which backs up the comic shocks in both *Popeye the Sailor* and *Mickey Mouse* is a pleasure in the ease with which *they* get satisfactions that we should like to have. We are laughing at their comi-

* Line spoken by Roland Young in *Ruggles of Red Gap.*

Art Young

Having Their Fling.

(The cartoon on the World War for which Art Young was arrested and tried twice in the United States Courts.)

cality, and yet we can not have those satisfactions except through sympathy.

There is one excuse and one only for the opinion that laughter as such is hard and hostile. That is the fact that laughter is not serious. Compassionate humor must not be too compassionate, or it will run out into pathos. But the same thing is true at the other end of the spectrum. Satire, if it is too bitter, runs out into hot scorn. There is a certain range of feelings which can be enjoyed playfully, just as certain wave-lengths can be perceived as light, and if you pass beyond this laugh spectrum at either end the humor disappears. Once that fact is understood, the last pretext for identifying comic laughter as such with satire is removed. And it has to be removed, as I shall show in the next chapter, before you can properly appreciate satire itself—the variety of its tones, its unique sharpness as a weapon, or its steady pressure in enforcing cultural standards.

To my mind the overstressing of ridicule in laughter belongs to a juvenile stage of development. It belongs to the period, both in the individual and the race, when prestige and self-glorification are of disproportionate concern. Dr. Kimmins reports, on the basis of a statistical study that "the misfortunes of others as a cause of laughter" rise to a high proportion at the age of seven and after that gradually decline.* It is well known that derisive humor also plays a stupendous role in primitive society, and that this role has diminished with the development of mind and culture.

The "fear and horror of ridicule"—says Paul Radin in his *Primi-*

* "With children of 7 years of age," Kimmins says, "about twenty-five per cent of the boys' stories, and sixteen per cent of the girls' are of this nature. At 8 years of age there is a decrease to about eighteen and ten per cent respectively. At 9 and 10 years there is further very considerable reduction, and beyond the age of 10 the proportion is negligible."

Clara O. Wilson, of the University of Nebraska, confirmed this finding from the other side. She found that "laughter accompanying recognition of one's own predicament tends to increase until the child is about seven, then decreases." (*A Study of Laughter Situations among Young Children.*)

Seven years is also the age most often mentioned by Jean Piaget in discus[illegible] the child's development from "egocentric thinking" to an adult self-and-[illegible] consciousness. (*The Child's Conception of the World,* 1929.)

Thomas Nast

"Let Us Prey."

A PUN THAT WAS TOO SERIOUS TO BE FUNNY.
(*Nast's life was threatened, and he was offered $50,000 to desist from these pictorial attacks on the Tweed ring.*)

tive Man As Philosopher—"is . . . more potent and tyrannous than the most restrictive and coercive of positive injunctions could be." And he explains this not on the ground that comic laughter as such is derisive—that question he leaves expressly to the psychologists—but on the ground that primitive society is "permeated with a thirst for prestige and naive self-glorification."

"It is ridicule and not indignation and horror that assails a man who attempts to change a detail in a ceremony, to tell a story in some new and original manner, or who acts counter to some definitely accepted belief and custom, and it is the same fundamentally ill-natured laughter that greets him when he becomes unwittingly the victim of some untoward accident. To avoid it a man will go to any length. He may even commit suicide in consequence of it. . . ."

Mankind has traveled a long way from there to the delicate self-ridicule of Bob Benchley, or the state of affairs described by Robert J. Burdette in his defiant limerick:

> There was a young man from Cohoes
> Wore tar on the end of his nose,
> When asked why he done it,
> He said for the fun it
> Afforded the men of Cohoes.

Dwight Morrow, they say, once got on a suburban train and could not find his ticket. The young conductor recognized him and said:

"It's all right, Mr. Morrow, you can give us the ticket some other time."

"It may be all right for you, young man," he said, "but how am I to know where I'm going?"

Like seven-year-old children, the human race as a whole has had to grow up to that larger range of humorous enjoyments which was its animal birthright. It has had to overcome a temporary and juvenile preoccupation with self-and-other feelings, and recover its own infant gift of pure playful mirth. The people who have most fully recovered this are, naturally, those exceptionally endowed with humor. And accordingly we find among professional humorists and comedians an extremely small number who have any tolerance at all for the derision theory. I have listed as many of their opinions as I could conveniently find or collect on pages 329-43, and they constitute, I think, a strong corroboration of the view we have arrived at by setting out from the laughter of babies. The most mature and the most immature would, in their vast majority, agree with Jimmy Cagney who exclaimed, when I asked him if he thought there was hostility or a feeling of superiority in all laughter:

"Christ no! If anything can hand me a laugh I love it!"

CHAPTER IV

Degrees of Biting

THE BEST WAY TO APPROACH SATIRE, if you want to enjoy it, is to take a firm grasp of that phrase "make fun of." No satirist is so bitter that he is not making fun. And the person, thing or institution of which he is making fun may occupy a whole range of positions from that of mere pretext for a laugh to that of mortal enemy to be slain with ridicule if possible—and if not, then cleave him with a heavier weapon.

Approaching satire in this way, you have open to your understanding the range of enjoyment that is open to your feelings. There is no mitigation of the joy of buffeting other people, and biting, and mangling, and chewing them up into a fine pulp. There is also no distortion of those hilarities to which the conception of some other person, or some person-in-abstract, is necessary, but in which a wish to condemn or cast a shadow on him is as far away as the moon.

Of these latter William L. Alden's treatise on "The Smith Rolling and Crushing Machine," provides, I should think, a convincing example.

> The patent office—it begins—contains numerous models of machines framed with the utmost skill, but intended for purposes for which no man will ever desire to employ them, or which are hostile to the best interests of the community . . .
>
> It is to this latter class of inventions that the recently patented "Smith Rolling and Crushing Machine" undoubtedly belongs—unless, indeed, the nature and object of the invention have been grossly misrepresented. As its name implies, it is obviously intended for diminishing the number of Smiths. It is understood that it con-

sists of a series of heavy rollers resembling those by which iron plates are rolled, and also a pair of gigantic grindstones of novel pattern and enormous power, the whole being set in motion by a 12-horse-power engine. Its method of operation is at once simple and effective. The operator takes a Smith of any size, and, adjusting the gear of the rollers to the exact width to which it is desired to roll the Smith, gently inserts his head between the rollers. The machine is then set in motion, and in the brief space of fifty-eight seconds the Smith is rolled to any desirable degree of thinness. If a Smith is to be crushed, he is placed in a hopper communicating with the grindstones, and after a rapid trituration, varying from two minutes to five minutes, according to the size and toughness of the Smith, he is reduced to a fine and evenly ground powder, in which such foreign substances as buttons or shirt-studs can be detected only by the most delicate chemical tests. . . .

I suppose that sadistic people, if not named Smith, and masochistic people if so named, will have their quaff of pleasure in vividly imagining the operation of this machine. But it would be fantastic to describe the humor on that account as a satire directed against people named Smith. It is the humor of a sustained mock-solemn claim to sense in a state of continual collapse into ludicrous nonsense. If people named Smith took offense at it, we should tell them that they had no sense of humor. Or we should ask them: Can't you take a joke? And if you can't, would you mind withdrawing while we have some fun?

A step from this play-humor at the violet end of the satire spectrum will bring us to the art that we call "kidding." And we have invented this term, suggestive of purely frivolous capers—*caper* itself being the Latin word for *goat*—because we need to specify that although in form satirical, it is in feeling friendly. The victim is there; he is a little more substantially our target than the Smiths were above. But still we are not really firing at him, we are entertaining him. Let us hear a little of this genial kidding from Mark Twain's earliest and not most subtle toast, "To Woman."

Human intellect cannot estimate what we owe to woman, sir. She sews on our buttons; she mends our clothes; she ropes us in at the church fairs; she confides in us; she tells us whatever she can find out about the little private affairs of the neighbors; she gives us good advice, and plenty of it; she soothes our aching brows; she bears our children—ours as a general thing. . . .

> I repeat, sir, that in whatever position you place a woman she is an ornament to society and a treasure to the world. As a sweetheart, she has few equals and no superiors; as a cousin, she is convenient; as a wealthy grandmother with an incurable distemper, she is precious; as a wet nurse, she has no equal among men. What, sir, would the people of the earth be without woman? They would be scarce, sir, almighty scarce.

That is "making fun" with the accent on the fun. And lest this be misunderstood, Mark Twain concludes it with a "jesting aside"—an amateurish phrase, but one that brings its meed of evidence to our hypothesis of the play attitude—and with a fulsome tribute to that mother of all sentimentalism, the idea of the mother.

Let us move a jog toward the hot end of the spectrum now, and hear Mark Twain make fun of the "New England Society of Philadelphia," make fun of ancestor worship and the whole reverential rigmarole that goes with it. And let us hear him at good length, for here we touch a thing that he has elsewhere lashed with whips of earnest scorn. He is still sunny and genial. He is still "kidding," to employ our strictly technical term, but there is, as William Dean Howells said of *The Prince and the Pauper*, "a bottom of fury to his fun."

> I rise to protest. I have kept still for years, but really I think there is no sufficient justification for this sort of thing. What do you want to celebrate those people for?—those ancestors of yours of 1620—the Mayflower tribe, I mean. What do you want to celebrate *them* for? Your pardon: the gentleman at my left assures me that you are not celebrating the Pilgrims themselves, but the landing of the Pilgrims at Plymouth Rock on the 22nd of December. So you are celebrating their landing. Why, the other pretext was thin enough, but this is thinner than ever; the other was tissue, tinfoil, fish bladder, but this is gold leaf. Celebrating their landing! What was there remarkable about it, I would like to know? What can you be thinking of? Why, those Pilgrims had been at sea three or four months. It was the very middle of winter: it was as cold as death off Cape Cod there. Why shouldn't they come ashore? If they *hadn't* landed there would be some reason for celebrating the fact. It would have been a case of monumental leatherheadedness which the world would not willingly let die. If it had been you, gentlemen, you probably wouldn't have landed, but you have no shadow of right to be celebrating, in your ancestors, gifts which they did not exercise, but only transmitted. . . .

They were a mighty hard lot—you know it. I grant you, without the slightest unwillingness, that they were a deal more gentle and merciful and just than were the people of Europe of that day; I grant you that they are better than their predecessors. But what of that?—that is nothing. People always progress. You are better than your fathers and grandfathers were (this is the first time I have ever aimed a measureless slander at the departed, for I consider such things improper). Yes, those among you who have not been in the penitentiary, if such there be, are better than your fathers and grandfathers were; but is that any sufficient reason for getting up annual dinners and celebrating you? No, by no means—by no means. Well, I repeat, those Pilgrims were a hard lot. They took good care of themselves, but they abolished everybody else's ancestors. . . . Yes, they were a hard lot; but, nevertheless, they gave us religious liberty to worship as they required us to worship, and political liberty to vote as the church required. . . .

O my friends, hear me and reform! I seek your good, not mine. You have heard the speeches. Disband these New England societies —nurseries of a system of steadily augmenting laudation and hosannaing, which, if persisted in uncurbed, may some day in the remote future beguile you into prevaricating and bragging. Oh, stop, stop, while you are still temperate in your appreciation of your ancestors! Hear me, I beseech you; get up an auction and sell Plymouth Rock! The Pilgrims were a simple and ignorant race. They never had seen any good rocks before, or at least any that were not watched, and so they were excusable for hopping ashore in frantic delight and clapping an iron fence around this one. But you, gentlemen, are educated; you are enlightened; you know that in the rich land of your nativity, opulent New England, overflowing with rocks, this one isn't worth, at the outside, more than thirty-five cents . . .

Yes, hear your true friend—your only true friend—list to his voice. Disband these societies, hotbeds of vice, of moral decay—perpetuators of ancestral superstition. Here on this board I see water, I see milk, I see the wild and deadly lemonade. These are but steps upon the downward path. Next we shall see tea, then chocolate, then coffee—hotel coffee. A few more years—all too few, I fear—mark my words, we shall have cider! Gentlemen, pause ere it be too late. You are on the broad road which leads to dissipation, physical ruin, moral decay, gory crime, and the gallows! I beseech you, I implore you, in the name of your anxious friends, in the name of your impending widows and orphans, stop ere it be too late. Disband these New England societies, renounce these soul-blistering saturnalias, cease from varnishing the rusty reputations of your long-vanished ancestors—the super-high-moral old ironclads of Cape Cod, the pious buccaneers of Plymouth Rock—go home, and try to learn to behave!

That Mark Twain could wield the colors at the hot end of the spectrum is well known. His "Unspoken War Prayer" will illustrate how far satire can remove itself from "kidding":

> Oh, Lord our Father, our young patriots, idols of our hearts, go forth to battle. Be Thou near them! With them—in spirit—we also go from the sweet peace of our beloved firesides to smite the foe.
>
> Oh, Lord, our God, help us to tear their soldiers to bloody shreds with our shells; help us to cover their smiling fields with the pale forms of their patriot dead; help us to drown the thunder of the guns with the wounded, writhing in pain; help us to lay waste their humble homes with the hurricane of fire; help us to wring the hearts of their unoffending widows with unavailing grief; help us to turn them out roofless with their little children to wander unfriended over wastes of their desolated land in rags and hunger and thirst, sport of the sun-flames of summer and the icy winds of winter, broken in spirit, worn with travail, imploring Thee for the refuge of the grave and denied it—for our sakes, who adore Thee, Lord, blast their hopes, blight their lives, protract their bitter pilgrimage, make heavy their steps, water their way with their tears, stain the white snow with the blood of their wounded feet! We ask of One who is the spirit of Love and Who is the ever-faithful refuge and friend of all that are sore beset, and seek His aid with humble and contrite hearts. Grant our prayer, oh Lord, and Thine shall be the praise and honor and glory, now and ever. Amen.

What I am trying to show is, that if you imagine all laughter to be hostile, you not only deny the varieties of humorous experience in general, but you fail to understand the range of feelings open to the satirist himself. You ignore the degrees of biting. Mark Twain's jests about women were too laughing to be called hostile; his thrusts at the war-makers are too hostile for laughter.

A worse thing you do, however, if you identify laughter itself with biting, is to falsify the color of satire even when it is most merciless. If comic laughter as such is but a veiled hostile attack, then a slashing satire is a more direct unleashing of this attack. It approximates the tense behavior of the snarling animal. The essential feeling-quality of

Cornelia Barns

"Poppa, do they allow boids to build nests in trees?"

satire, however, to those who love it knowingly, lies in the fact that it is not tense or snarling. It is not a direct attack. It is not an *attack* at all. It denies the victim that honor. It denies him that extraordinary compliment. It destroys him without attack, without tense behavior. It destroys him without taking him seriously. It destroys him as a plaything, a toy, a thing but for the pure fun of destruction hardly worth destroying. That is why it is so devastating. That is why it is so much more devastating, when successful, than any snarling onslaught could be.

To realize this, let us hear Dorothy Parker destroy Margot Asquith, a thing worth going back some years to hear.

> That gifted entertainer, the Countess of Oxford and Asquith, author of "The Autobiography of Margot Asquith" (four volumes, neatly boxed, suitable for throwing purposes) reverts to tripe in a new book deftly entitled "Lay Sermons". . . .

Is a further word necessary? And could you accomplish so swift and perfect a destruction by going after a countess with snarls, or with any remote evolutionary descendant of snarls, such as hammer and tongs? Could you accomplish it by seriously declaring, and much less concentrating your forces to prove, that her volume is tripe? Does not the absoluteness of the zero to which Mrs. Asquith is here reduced rest essentially in the fact that she has not received the tribute of such an attack—that, on the contrary, a little frivolous amusement has been indulged in by two people profoundly undisturbed about her, and yet Mrs. Asquith is no more?

"You thought I was going to say *type,* didn't you? Well, *presto chango,* and the more fool you, I said *tripe,* and still it makes sense!"

That is the little jest that has been enjoyed between the author and her readers—that is elemental humor—and yet somehow combined with, or growing out of that, almost as though by accident and to the surprise of all, the Countess of Oxford and Asquith has disappeared. She has sunk without a trace. Without disturbing the waters she is gone.

Either I am abnormal and a departure from the human race, or that is what happens in satirical humor. That is how it differs from serious polemic. That is both its strength and its weakness. And if this be true, what could more completely falsify it than to insist that elemental humor *is,* when understood, a serious attack?

I do not mean to exaggerate the harm that can be done by a false theory. It can not change the nature of our feelings. What it does is to illumine them with a colored spotlight that destroys their finest tints.

There is one more count against this derision theory before I have done. It not only blurs the varieties of satire, and dulls us to its sharpest edge. It also underestimates its practical value—the very value upon which the derision theorist insists. There is no doubt that hostile humor, all the way from savage ridicule to subtle irony, does play a vital role in social evolution. We "laugh down" what is rigid and inflexible, as Bergson says. We laugh down also what is too limp or flexible, as he quite fails to say. We do this more effectively and on a grander scale than would be true if comic laughter did consist of hostile criticism. The pervasive and persisting force of ridicule derives from the fact that, while involving hostile criticism and appealing to that interest, it appeals to a more sustained and universal interest, the interest in having playful fun. Two people who are "having fun" at the expense of a third are extremely unconcerned to count the expense. They are far less quick to tire or stray off, or desist at the bidding of sympathy, than they would be if they were seriously scolding him. Scolding people is, in fact, for most of us, a bore. But having fun at their expense is having fun. Here again the play-interest stands in the center of the problem. It is the fact that comic laughter as such is not corrective work but aimless play that makes laughter which is corrective such a tireless weapon and a cleansing broom.

Dorothy Parker by Peggy Bacon

CHAPTER V

Slapstick and Aggressive Humor

ONE OF THE MINOR REASONS why humor theories have gone wrong, is that they have failed to distinguish between getting the better of a person in a contest and hitting him over the head with an ax or a thrashing machine. There is of course a similarity here, and it is not always easy to distinguish the two kinds of delight. But there is also a vital difference. Ascendancy is not the same thing as bodily aggression. A feeling of superiority, or of pride in the fact that somebody else is a damned fool—the only pride most of us have access to—is not the same thing as joy in other people's pain. Both these gratifications enter frequently into the composition of a joke, and by bunching them together and calling the whole thing "superiority" or "sudden glory," the idea that some such generalized ego-emotion *is* humor has been given more plausibility than would naturally fall to so narrowing an idea.

There is always in the antics of circus clowns a high proportion of swattings and kickings and shootings and bumpings and fallings from trapezes, chariots, and galloping jackasses. There is a strong appeal to the repressed sadisms of the audience, their desire to see somebody, as they so delicately put it, "get it in the neck." Burlesque shows and popular comedies the world over are full of these play-cruelties, and there are innumerable "funny stories" which rely for their point on the same pleasure.

"My wooden leg pained me terribly last night."
"How's that?"
"A friend hit me over the head with it."

"Why did you hit your husband with a chair?"
"I couldn't lift the table."

Officer: "Did you know you missed that old man by an inch?"
Driver: "That's all right, I'll get him going back."

That these jokes in which humor tastes of cruel glee belong in a different class from those in which it tastes of triumph, or the degradation of a rival, was demonstrated by Richard N. Sears in the Harvard psychological laboratory. He put a series of jokes before various groups of students, and asked them to estimate these jokes on a scale according to their comic merit. I think one of his principal results was to demonstrate that students inducted into a laboratory for experimentation are in no state of mind for mirthful laughter. They seem rarely to have estimated a joke on the ground of its jocular merit, but always on the ground of their serious attitude toward the subject matter. We shall have to have a playatory, I am afraid, before we shall ever get down experimentally to the very nub of this question. And before we can do that, we shall have to find out what a playatory is.

However, this very fact makes more convincing Mr. Sears' demonstration that the people who give a high rating to jokes containing an "act of aggression," form a different group from those who especially enjoy jokes like the following, which end in the "ascendancy" of one person over another.

Grace: "I didn't accept Bob the first time he proposed."
Mabel: "No, dearie, you weren't there."

Lady (to street-car conductor): "At which end shall I get off?"
Conductor: "Either end, Madam—both ends stop."

The latter joke I get from Carolyn Wells, who presents it in the preface to her *Outline of Humor* as a "mild example" of the state of mind exemplified in the man who, telling the story of a burning house, said: "I saw a fellow up on the roof and I called to him, 'Jump and I'll catch you in a blanket!' Well, I had to laugh—he jumped and I didn't have no blanket!" Which shows how badly the discrimination established here by Mr. Sears was needed. Only the blind force of a traditional notion could make a person as sensitive as Miss Wells confuse the two ways of taking pleasure exemplified in the outcomes of these two stories.

According to my view it is quite natural that people addicted to aggression jokes should not be the same ones who adore jokes ending in ascendancy. For although both these pleasures occur frequently in combination with the comic feeling, they occur frequently for contrary reasons. Ascendancy jokes are the most frequent of all for the reason given in the last chapter—that rivalry is the commonest form of play. It is "more fun" than other diversions, and it is more fun, not because it is different from serious life, but because it is the same thing cast loose from cares and consequences. Aggression jokes derive their peculiar delightfulness from the fact that we have cruel impulses which we can *not* unleash in serious life, cultural standards being here at variance with our instincts, and they sneak forth and take a furtive drink of satisfaction when we play. Aggressive jokes, that is to say, belong with risqué and ribald jokes rather than with satire. They release organic drives that have been repressed, and are full of spring, and go off with a particular bang, and fill the mind with a rank and noisy kind of glee. Slapstick belongs with obscenity; and from Aristophanes to Minsky that is where you will find it at its best.

CHAPTER VI

Risqué and Ribald Jokes: Freud's Theory

IT IS HARDLY NECESSARY TO REMARK that "sex" in a broad sense is one of the interests most often drawn upon to give point to a joke. It fulfills this function well, not because it has any special innate connection with laughter, but because it is a vigorous and unflagging interest, and yet one which we hold down. It can be relied on to intrude into our minds upon the slightest pretext when other meaning-patterns come to grief. And its intrusion, although superficially distressing if taken seriously, is also seriously desired. The very force which suppresses it contains the wish to bring it forth—an inner situation much like that depicted in the story of the couple under the bushes and the park policeman.

> Policeman: "What are you doing in there?"
> The Citizen: "Nothing."
> Policeman: "Come out here and hold this flashlight!"

The whole life and nature of man in civilized communities is a veritable set-up for sex jokes. They are easy to make, and no special theory is needed to explain them. What they need most, in fact, is to be rescued from a theory that puts them in a false light. As this theory has behind it the prestige of Sigmund Freud, who has made the greatest contributions to self-knowledge made in modern times, and as it is widely regarded as the last word on witty jokes, I am going to criticize it at some length. This will be a slight departure from the program of our textbook. I can not guarantee it will not tempt the impetuous reader into a few moments of hard work. I beg him, at least, not to be misled by the title of this chapter into thinking we are going on a binge.

Freud's idea of the unconscious action of repressed impulses explains so many peculiar things that one naturally gets to assuming, especially if one has been reared in the Godlike bad habits of German philosophy, that it explains everything. For instance, Freud discovered that primitive myths are prone to occupy themselves with incest. The King's son is forever getting stowed away as a baby in some cold cranny, being pulled out by a passing shepherd, reared to young manhood in a hut, and then coming back to town and one day while strolling around the family mansion just by pure accident killing his father and marrying his mother. This sort of thing happens in myths too often to be a coincidence. And when you realize that our violent resistance to the idea of incest is not instinctive—it is not a part of our animal inheritance, but of our acquired trick of being human—you can readily believe that interests of this kind, repressed in infancy but unconsciously effective, have played their part in molding these myths. But this is far from saying, as Freudians are prone to, that these repressed interests "explain" all myths and the very existence of mythology.

The same thing may be said of those slips and errors of everyday life about which Freud has written such a sly book. Every once in a while you meet somebody coming out of the subway, or dashing for a train, and you both start to pass each other on the same side. Then you both, being of equal intelligence, shift simultaneously to the other side. Then you shift back again, also simultaneously. Then one of you decides to shift quicker than he did before, and so does the other. And then you, being the more collected of the two, decide to stand stock-still until the other goes around, but he also, being more collected than you, decides to do the same thing. Then you both smile and remove your hats and say, "Beg pardon!" And then you start again. But each of you during that exchange of courtesies has been thinking, "Now, next time I'm going to make my getaway on the *wrong* side, and I'm going to make it quick before he has time to move!" So you both bolt for the wrong side and collide once more, and back off in surprise like a couple of slightly bellicose roosters. Then you give up intelligence as a bad job and fall back on custom, both moving forward, this time on the right side, and very slowly, with the dignity and cautious equilibrium with which a cat goes into battle.

Now it is a mere matter of mathematics that this sort of thing will happen every once in a while, no matter what the repressed fantasies, fixations, complexes, infantile predispositions or polymorphous perversions of the libidos of the two cats or roosters may be. It is mathematics that the two, if their judgment, reaction time, cerebrospinal connections and nerve and muscular co-ordinations and life history are sufficiently similar, will never get by each other, and never have—that they are still there dodging back and forth and pausing at intervals to raise their hats and say, "Beg pardon!"

Freudians are prone to ignore the simple geometry and arithmetic of these coincidences and imagine that they always are caused by unconscious impulses of sex or aggression. It would be truer to say that, for the very reason that they are normal and inevitable, such incidents are sometimes manufactured or exaggerated by hysterics with high pressure fantasies in "the unconscious," in order to let off surreptitiously a little steam.

All this sounds obvious enough, but it is an obvious sound much needing to be made where psychoanalysts are gathered together and going good. And Freud's attempt to explain witty pleasure as due to a release from inhibitions—complicated though it is by the notion of an "economy of psychic expenditure," which he got by way of Lipps from Herbert Spencer—is an example of the same error. It is not too much to say that if Freud had been of French or Anglo-Saxon culture, he would never have imagined that his doctrine of repressed impulses *explains* witty jokes. He would have been content to point out that witty jokes, like myths and dreams and daydreams, slips and errors, art and poetry, are frequently employed as vehicles of expression by repressed impulses. He would have added that jokes which do release such impulses evoke "big laughs" and fill the laughers with a rank and racy kind of glee. That would have been a valid contribution to our science.

I was once lecturing in support of the Soviets in Garden City, Long Island, which is a conservative and somewhat Episcopalian suburb of New York. After my lecture, an elderly gentleman in evening clothes rose from his seat, and in a voice trembling with indignation and outraged virtue, said that he wanted to ask me just one question about Soviet Russia:

"Is it true that in that barbarous country a man can go into some kind of an institution which they call a marriage bureau, and get divorced from his lawfully wedded wife by the simple device of paying down ten or fifteen cents?"

Prompted by some demon that I wish would stand by me oftener, I replied:

"No, it isn't quite so cheap as that, but don't give up hope, it will only cost you half a dollar."

To the audience that was, I suppose, a superiority jest; its point was that I got the better of the indignant gentleman. But what made me recall it here was its success with the gentleman himself. Its effect upon him was miraculous. He sank back in a state of joyous collapse, and sat there beaming on me all the rest of the evening. A safe majority, I suppose, of those who violently oppose divorce, in their inmost being violently want one.

That is the kind of thing Freud's doctrine of unconscious motivation makes so clear. Jests often liberate the surging wishes prisoned in us. They remove our lid of culture, and let us be, in fun at least and for a second, animals.

Even this much of Freud's theory can not stand, however, unless we loosen and enlarge his view of the nature of these animals. Freud thinks that all, or practically all, the tendencies released by wit from "the unconscious," can be described as sexual or aggressive, and that these two, indeed, "can be united under one viewpoint." Perhaps the simplest way to advance a broader view would be to remind him that aggression itself—and sex also—besides being animal instincts, are ideal standards against which some people are in suppressed revolt. Motives of flight are as proper to the human animal as motives of attack. They are as rigidly censored by our culture, and often in as dire a thirst of expression. Whatever else we got out of the World War we got the proof of that. And just as "shell shock" is a distinct variety of hysteria, so a distinct kind of humor is that which releases us from the necessity of pretending to be aggressive. Mark Twain was forever making jokes whose point was a frank confession of cowardice. He made them in *Life on the Mississippi,* in recounting his own abortive participation in the Civil War, in his stories about boys. He made them in describing in *The Innocents Abroad* his trip down into the Jordan valley.

> It was such a dreary, repulsive, horrible solitude! It was the "wilderness" where John preached, with camel's hair about his loins—raiment enough—but he never could have got his locusts and wild honey here. We were moping along down through this dreadful place, every man in the rear. Our guards—two gorgeous young Arab sheiks, with cargoes of swords, guns, pistols and daggers on board—were loafing ahead!
>
> "Bedouins!"
>
> Every man shrunk up and disappeared in his clothes like a mud turtle. My first impulse was to dash forward and destroy the Bedouins. My second was to dash to the rear to see if there were any coming in that direction. I acted on the latter impulse. So did all the others. If any Bedouins had approached us, then, from that point of compass, they would have paid dearly for their rashness. We all remarked that, afterwards. There would have been scenes of riot and bloodshed there that no pen could describe.

I suppose there are many stern souls of heroes—I wish I knew how many—who will feel contempt mingle with their amusement here. There are many more who will pretend to feel it, for even in a joke they dare not be caught in the company of fear. But there are plenty too, like me, who will find in this joke a frank release from the demands of aggression as a cultural ideal.

Soldiers especially will be found in this indulgent class, not because they are less aggressive than others, but because they are more nagged by the ideal. They have a famous tenderness for sayings that relieve them of the pretense of heroism. "Keep your mouth shut and your bowels open and never volunteer," has been a motto of the bravest. "Never bone when you can bugle," the slogan attributed to General

Hugh Johnson when at West Point, has been quoted to the general's discredit, but I think it would make most soldiers like him better.

Not only aggression, but sexuality also, is a cultural ideal. Its demands are rigorous and many people find it hard to meet them. I suspect that a release from these imperious demands was provided to a considerable body of the population by Theodore Dreiser's famous joke on the forces of law and order in Kentucky. He went down there, you remember, to investigate a rebellion of the miners of Harlan County, and was arrested, other pretexts lacking, on a charge of illegal cohabitation. His answer, published widely in the press, was that he was not only not guilty, but not physiologically able to be. A heroic joke, in my opinion, and conspicuously colored with the gleeful feeling of release.

What Freud's theory first needs is to be cured of the German habit of explaining the entire universe every time you explain a fact. The effort of any animal to be human is bound to be a strenuous one, and to involve patching, and padding, and sewing up, and binding-around, and holding in by main force, on all sides. The momentary vacation afforded by a joke is, therefore, as various as it is valuable.

CHAPTER VII

About Nonsense and about Children: Freud's Theory Some More

FREUD'S GREAT SIN AGAINST HUMOR, and against the art of enjoying it, is that he makes it all furtive. He thinks, as we have seen, that there is no humor in the playful nonsense of children, and that humor arises only when grown-up people elude their ideals of rationality and other inhibitions, and escape back into that non-humorous childish fun. "Wit, comic and humor," he says, "are all striving to bring back a pleasure that has been lost." He does not explain why this nonsense which is not comic to a child, should be comic when it is furtively returned to by an adult. He merely explains why there is more pleasure in it—namely, because the psychic energy with which we were holding ourselves from it is released. This pleasure of release when it arrives in consciousness just seems to wear a sheepish expression. . . . I can think of no other way to describe the total adventitiousness of comic feeling in Freud's picture of a joke. He never mentions it, so far as I recall, but once, and that is when he says: "The child lacks all feeling for the comic."

Now I think Freud was brought to this rather fantastic opinion about children, not by observation, but by the fact that he can not himself see that pure nonsense is ever comic. And that, as I have explained, is because he does not take a sufficiently discriminating look at nonsense. He does not distinguish leading a mind on and landing it nowhere, which is a funny trick, from talking gibberish, which is a bore. The nearest thing to gibberish enjoyed among adults is what our comedians call "double talk." It consists of coming in and starting some earnest and rather excited speech, and then having it gradually lose its outlines, and while still sounding *like* earnest speech, turn into an unintelligible jumble of syllables. I have never heard him, but I have been authoritatively told that Sid Gary's double talk is "two hundred times funnier than Jimmy Durante." At any rate it is funny. And so is Beatrice Lillie's unsuccessful attempt in *At Home Abroad* to order "two dozen double-damask dinner napkins" from a department store clerk. It is by far the funniest thing in the show, and it differs from gibberish only in its plausibility, its perfectly sincere, engaging and magnetic *proposal* to make sense.

I think that if Freud would bear this difference in mind, and also hear a good comedian do an act of this type, he might be led into a friendlier attitude toward nonsense. And once arriving there, he would not make the mistake of denying that such well-known children, for instance, as Lewis Carroll and Carolyn Wells and Donald Ogden Stewart and Walt Disney, lack all feeling for the comic. At any rate, it is this erroneous opinion about children—and about nonsense—that underlies his whole unnatural and unwholesome view of wit and laughter. He has denied that our baby—or Miss Washburn's, or whosever baby it was—finds it funny to be tossed out toward its mother's arms and suddenly yanked back. And having done that, he has—naturally enough and quite inevitably—denied the funny feeling to the human race. He has said, in effect: You think jokes are funny, but they are not, they are merely furtively enjoyed.

Only the other day I was talking to the mother of a child of four. We were standing in her front yard, and the child was running about dragging a broken rake or tailless mop, or some long-handled shaky instrument. We heard him chuckling and laughing to himself several times, and his mother finally asked him what he was laughing at. "It makes such a funny noise," he said, "kolunkit, kolunkit, kolunkit!" He was quite right; it was making a funny noise. We were only too dull or practical or preoccupied to notice it.

Professor Seward in his *Paradox of the Ludicrous* described two or three of the jokes enjoyed by his infant daughter, Helen. When but a month or more over two years of age, she suddenly decided not to call a well-known visitor by her real name. "'Who is this, Helen? Miss . . .' would be the encouraging suggestion; and the reply shot back was 'Bug.' . . . If mother began, 'This little pig went to . . .' 'Bug' would come the answer. 'And this little pig stayed . . .' 'Bug' with a twinkle of gleeful mischief."

To my mind this gag is quite as good as many of those put on the stage by the Marx Brothers, and even those printed in books by some of our most successful humorists. Let us read a bit of Joe Cook's *Why I Will Not Imitate Four Hawaiians,* that book which he talked off impromptu, in the presence of a stenographer, much, I imagine, as a child talks nonsense to himself but aided by the presence of his elders.

THE STORY OF MY LIFE—SO HELP ME

> First of all, I am worth millions of dollars. The fact that I was born in a private family proves that my parents must have been well-to-do. My tender age, at the time of birth, created quite a bit of favorable comment. I was the only child in kindergarten that chewed tobacco. The parents of all the other little boys and girls begged me to teach their children this delightful habit. Gertrude Ederle was the first woman to swim the English Channel.
>
> At the age of eighteen, my father asked me if I would mind going to work. He kept on asking me this favor for five consecutive years, but I had a mind of my own.
>
> Finally, my mother said, "Well, father, if the boy won't go to work, why don't *you* go out and look for a job?"
>
> Father effected a compromise by agreeing to hunt up something as soon as we had used up the money from the accident insurance company, for grandma's falling off the roof. Father really pushed her off but he was only fooling.

Does the statement, "Gertrude Ederle was the first woman to swim the English Channel," contribute anything of more relevance to Joe Cook's *Life—So Help Me* than "Bug!" does to "This little pig went to market"? Is it not the same rudimentary kind of gag?

I asked the author why he put that phrase in, and he said: "It just came into my head and I saw that it was funny—I don't know why."

I can not say I find either of these irrelevancies very funny—Helen Seward's or Joe Cook's—but I did find a similar thing funny when reading, as a sidelight on this chapter, Thurber and White's *Is Sex*

Necessary? To make its quality apparent I shall have to quote this passage also at some length.

> And now we come to Sex.* Woman, observing that her mate went out of his way to make himself entertaining, rightly surmised that sex had something to do with it. From that she logically concluded that sex was recreational rather than procreational. (The small, hardy band of girls who failed to get this point were responsible for the popularity of women's field hockey in this country, 1911–1921.) As though in a vision, the "right to be sexual" came to women. They fell to with a will. For thousands of years they had been content merely to be amiable, and now they were going to be sexual. The transition from amiability to sexuality was revolutionary.** It presented a terrific problem to Woman, because in acquiring and assuming the habits that tended to give her an equality with Man, she discovered that she necessarily became a good deal *like* Man. The more she got like him, the less he saw in her. (Or so he liked to think, anyway.) Just as soon as she began to put her own sex on an even basis, she found that he lost interest. Her essential Narcissism (pleasure of looking in a mirror) was met by his Begonia-ism (concept of the potted plant). Things got so that Woman spent *all* her time admiring herself in mirrors, and Man, discouraged, devoted himself quietly to raising begonias, which are fairly easy to raise. Sex atrophied.
>
> But, as I say, sex was in the transition stage. Woman soon began to outgrow her Narcissism and was satisfied to snatch quick glances of herself in makeshift mirrors, such as the backs of watches, the shiny fenders of automobiles, plate-glass windows, subway weighing machines, and such. Convinced that sex was not sin, she set out joyously to study it. How hard she studied has recently been apparent, even to persons who read only a few books a year.
>
> New York became the capital of the sexual revolution. It was conveniently located, had a magnificent harbor,*** a high mortality rate, and some of the queerest-shaped apartments to be found anywhere. There are apartments in New York in which one must step across an open bathtub in going from the kitchen to the bedroom; any unusual layout like that arouses sexual desire and brings people pouring into New York from other cities. New York became the Mecca for young ladies from the South and from the Middle West whose minds were not quite made up about sexual freedom, but who thought that if they could once get to New York and into an irregular apartment, the answer might come to them.
>
> Their mothers were against it.

* Are you glad?

** Zaner claims it was also amusing.

*** New York has one of the finest harbors in the world.

> "Now what can you get in New York that you can't get right here at home?" their mothers said.
>
> "Concerts, new plays, and the opera," the daughters invariably replied. There has never, to my knowledge, been a case of a young lady telling her mother that she wanted to go to New York because she was seeking an outlet for her erotic eagerness. It was always concerts that she wanted. Often it turned out to be concerts that she got.

The irrelevancy that I found especially funny there, and so funny that I laughed aloud, was the footnote about New York's harbor. And to the best of my introspective judgment, I found it funny because it had so blankly and absolutely nothing to do with the argument. It differs from Joe Cook's irrelevancies, and Helen Seward's, only in wearing a more plausible aspect. It sounds altogether *like* a relevant and important footnote, and that fact certainly entered into my perception of its humor.

I once enjoyed a half hour's conversation with Freud, and the sharpest image I retain is of him leaning his head way back with his funny bent nose pointed toward the ceiling and "laughing like a child." That is not only my most vivid memory, but those are, by an odd chance, the words I wrote down in a notebook to describe it. Freud, although a trifle crisp and crotchety, I imagine, when opposed, is a jolly laugher when he feels good, and he ought to know better than to turn this whole science upside down so that the subject-matter drops out of it by saying that children never find things funny. They find them funny more often, and they laugh comically upon a less exquisite provocation, than we do. That is exactly what makes it plausible to say they "have no feeling for the comic." They do not require that comic things should mask a serious thought, or tap a deeper reservoir of feeling, in order to give sanction to a good loud laugh.

This is THE MUSE OF NONSENSE:
  See!
 Preposterously Strained is She;
 Her Figures have nor Rule nor Joint
 And so it's Hard to See the Point!

Gelett Burgess

CHAPTER VIII

That Comicality Is Not Release: Freud's Theory Still

THERE ARE OTHER WAYS, besides establishing the facts about nonsense and about children, to prove that Freud is wrong in identifying comic pleasure with release from adult inhibitions. This pleasure, according to him, is due to a liberation of the psychic energy that had been employed in keeping up these inhibitions. It will be more intense, therefore, the stronger the impulses that were inhibited. And jokes which release one of the two major impulses, the sexual and the aggressive, enabling it to "elude the censor," will of course be funniest of all. And they will be funny only because of that "censor," and of the fact that he has been eluded.

A simple way to prove that this whole picture is fanciful would be to remark that obscene jokes flourished to their highest, and were enjoyed with the most abounding laughter, in the ages when there was no censor working actively against them—that is, in practically all ages preceding the nineteenth century. "The notion of obscenity," says Professor Sumner in his *Folkways*, "is very modern." And Mark Twain's Connecticut Yankee made the same observation when he woke up in Arthur's court. "Many of the terms used in the most matter-of-fact way by this great assemblage of the first ladies and gentlemen in the land would have made a Comanche blush. Indelicacy is too mild a term to convey the idea. However I knew that the highest and first ladies and gentlemen in England had remained little or no cleaner in their talk . . . clear up to a hundred years ago; in fact clear into our own nineteenth century—in which century, broadly speaking, the earliest samples of the real lady and real gentleman discoverable in English history—or in European history, for that matter—may be said to have made their appearance." The reason for this sudden and late appearance of delicacy and of "real" ladies and gentlemen, according to Professor Sumner, is the "mode of life under steam and machinery . . . houses larger, plumbing cheaper . . ."

There may be some extremeness in this assertion. The tendency to concealment gratified by larger houses and cheaper plumbing must have been there always. But to whatever extent it is true that "the notion of obscenity is very modern," it is certainly not true that obscene jokes depend for any essential value upon their being obscene—upon their accomplishing the feat, that is, of eluding a censor. The comicality is there all the time, whether the censor is or not.

We need not rely, however, upon that historic argument. Let us take a joke which is "indelicate" today, because it suggests to our minds, and even makes an approach to mentioning, a locale in the body that we think proper to keep mum about. And let us see if we can not demonstrate with our feelings that this adroit suggestion is not what makes it funny.

The question is asked: What is the difference between a fly and a bee? And the answer: You can't button a bee.

Formally considered, that is a pun upon the equivocal word *fly*. And so far as the verbal trick goes, the location of the article of apparel designated by that name is irrelevant. If it happened that we called the lapel of an overcoat, or the loose end of a cloth belt, a "fly," the joke would be there just the same, although without "suggestiveness." And would it not be, while less sly and waggish, rather more droll? The conundrum form is always bad, but the idea of "buttoning a bee," if maneuvered into our apprehension with the charm and plausibility with which Lewis Carroll could have done it, would, I think, consort with the best in *Alice in Wonderland*. It belongs in *Alice in Wonderland*. To my mind, at least, its droll humor is rather smeared over and lost in the serious excitement of releasing some rays from a repressed "tendency."

I think I can best prove my point against Freud by thus making it felt, and so I will quote another piece of whimsical humor—one that shows in a quite different way the irrelevance of a released tendency to comicality. This is from E. B. White, himself posing as a kind of Dr. Freud:

> So many children have come to me and said, "What shall I tell my parents about sex?" My answer is always the same: "Tell them the truth. If the subject is approached in a tactful way, it should be no more embarrassing to teach a parent about sex than to teach him about personal pronouns. And it should be less discouraging."

There again you have a piece of nonsense, plausible nonsense, and it derives some rays of a pleasing color from the repressed topic of sex. But its whole jocular operation is irrelevant to that fact. As a joke, what it does is to exaggerate to the point of absurdity two thoughts quite unrepressed, namely, that children are getting terribly sophisticated and that parents are pretty stupid.

A still more convincing way to prove that what makes a sexual joke comic is the playful trick and not the release from inhibitions, is to show that it is just as funny when you are led to expect a sexual thought and *fail to get it,* as when the trick works the other way.

> A man who stuttered badly came to the Briarcliff Golf Club one day and told the secretary that he loved golf, but was shy about his stuttering and found it lonesome to be on the links without a companion. The secretary said, "I know just the solution—there is a lady plays here frequently who stutters too, and I am sure you would get along fine together." A match was arranged and they met on the green and prepared to play. The man said that he would like to introduce himself first. "My n-n-n-name is P-p-p-pe-pe-peter" he said smilingly, "but I am not a s-s-s-s-sssaint!" She smiled in response. "M-m-m-my n-n-n-na-na-name is M-m-m-m-ary," she said, "but I am not a v-v-v-v-v-v-v-v-v-v-v-v-v . . . v-v-v-very good player."

You will find that joke, in the hands of a good story teller, as sure fire as any in the whole arsenal of impropriety. And yet what does it do exactly? It makes you think you are going to get a release of "sex" from inhibitions, and then fools you. Of course the story as a whole is a release, provided you are really squeamish on the subject of virgins. The story is colorful because of our interest in what it pretends to be going to say, not because of what it says. But the color is all there before the joke is. The story is funny because it disappoints that very interest, and leaves it unappeased. If the comic pleasure depended upon a release of such interests from "the unconscious," you could hardly be comic by offering to release one and then slamming the door in its face.

The same thing is proven for "aggressive" humor by one of the best gags in Charlie Chaplin's film *The Immigrant*. While the ship steams into port he hangs over the rail retching and squirming in what seems a very death agony of nausea—hangs so far over, and stays so long, that only those really addicted to the sufferings of others can keep on laughing at this old gag, and then suddenly comes up in triumph with a fishline and a big live fish. That fish, and that instantaneous and total change of roles between the actor and the audience, are greeted with a roar of laughter. And yet the joke is wholly on the audience. They thought they were indulging a tendency to enjoy the sufferings of others, but found instead that the actor was playing a trick upon that very tendency.

I wish the defenders of the derision theory, as well as the Freudians, would go to see this picture, and hear an entire theaterful of people enjoy the sudden frustration of their sadistic impulse with more gusto and a louder laugh than they accorded to its satisfaction.

Charlie Chaplin himself rejects the idea that "there is hostility in all laughter." "Of course they are often sympathetic with me while they laugh!" he exclaims. And I think that exclamation worth more than quite a long volume of professorial apologies for laughter.

But to return to Freud: there is, if you can bear to see me murder two more jokes, a still better way to prove that his theory is wrong. I think I can prove not only that eluding the censor has nothing to do with the comicality of wit, but that all those peculiar devices for making "sense in nonsense," which Freud considers the indispensable "technique of wit" and upon which his theory rests, are quite unnecessary to it.

My first joke is one that seems made for Freud's theory:

> An unhappy man was advised by a friend to take a wife, and his reply was: "Whose?"

From our viewpoint that was a quick practical joke played on the friend—and on everybody else who hears it—a meaning-tendency being set up in their minds and deftly brought to nothing, and that "nothing" turning out to hold a pleasant and illicit polyandrous thought. There is no doubt, however, that the thought here eludes a censor, if there is one. It eludes, at least, the law and the Ten Commandments. It seems, moreover, to elude them furtively. Nobody has explicitly said: I would like to, or wouldn't it be fun if I should, or wouldn't it be nice if the world were so primitive that I casually could, commit adultery? Nobody has said that thing exactly. A form of words which was traveling with dignity in a quite different direction has got derailed, and landed where that illicit thing can and will be thought of. It looks as though disguising the idea in order to get it into consciousness might be the whole meat and purpose of the trick.

But now let us hear a similar but slower-moving story. My friend Judge Rainey down in Oklahoma City—I call him my friend because he supported me through the hours following the most frowned-upon and frostbitten humor lecture I ever delivered in my life—told me that the following incident caused uproarious laughter in his court. An Italian who was intelligent but knew little English had applied for American citizenship, and in trying to wrestle through the questions put to him by the clerk became a good deal excited and discouraged. At the question "Do you believe in polygamy?" he threw up his hands altogether.

"I no understan'!" he said. "I no understan' not'ing!"

"Well," the clerk said, "I'll put it this way: Do you believe in plural marriage?"

That was still worse.

"No capisco. I no understan' not'ing. I no Americano!" he shouted, and picked up his hat as though to walk out.

But Judge Rainey leaned forward helpfully:

"Let me ask this question. Benito, what do you think of the idea of having two or three, or perhaps four wives?"

Benito's face relaxed in a most comprehending smile.

"I tink pretty good, Judge. What you tink?"

Here a similar illicit idea is introduced, and it is introduced in the very face and august presence of "the censor," and it causes uproarious laughter. And yet there is no "eluding" of the censor, no disguise, no indirectness of statement, no "sense in nonsense" no "substitution," "modification," "change of order," "double meaning"—nothing whatever of what Freud describes as the indispensable technique of wit. The reason why none of these things is present is that the trick is not played upon our expectation as to what a word will mean, but upon a more general attitude of expectancy. There was nothing in Judge Rainey's question to imply that the Italian would make one answer rather than another, but the situation as a whole implied it. Every person in the room was awaiting in some tensity the completion, not of the meaning-pattern of a sentence, but of the behavior-pattern of a customary dialogue. That grosser pattern of behavior was collapsed and brought to nothing by the Italian's answer exactly as the meaning-pattern was in Heine's joke, and in its place was found almost the same illicit thought. Everything essential was indeed the same, except that the joke was not furtive, and it contained no trace of any of those intricate mechanisms which Freud describes as the "technique of wit."

Mark Twain frequently plays tricks like this upon his reader, fooling him as to the destination of a discourse rather than the meaning of a word.

When his Yankee in King Arthur's Court learned that he had been elected for the privilege of rescuing forty-four princesses from a castle guarded by giants, he said:

> On my side, I could have cursed the kindness that conferred upon me this benediction, but I kept my vexation under the surface for policy's sake, and did what I could to let on to be glad. Indeed I *said* I was glad. And in a way it was true; I was as glad as a person is when he is scalped.

Try to find a place for that among Freud's techniques of wit. Or this, from the story of his piloting lesson in *Life on the Mississippi:*

> Presently Mr. Bixby turned on me and said: "What is the name of the first point above New Orleans?"
>
> I was gratified to be able to answer promptly and I did. I said I didn't know.

CHAPTER IX

The Furtive Snicker and the Rabelaisian Laugh

THERE IS NO GETTING AWAY from the fact that what makes wit comic is the trick it plays upon the mind. What makes it rich, riotous or exciting is another question. You have to distinguish the atom from the molecule. You can never explain any pointed joke without that distinction. Humor is an element; the atom of humor is a playful unpleasantness or frustration. A joke is a compound; the jocular molecule contains an atom of humor mixed with an atom or atoms of no matter what other kinds of value. With apologies to both chemistry and brain physiology, we may lay that down—until "science" means more, because it knows more, than it does now—as a scientific fact and no metaphor.

Freud recognizes this compound character of witty jokes; his book from first to last is an ingenious demonstration of it. But in place of the comic atom, the instinctive pleasure of both infants and adults in having a trick played upon them, he puts an adult wish to escape from rationality and babble humorless nonsense. There is no such adult wish, outside of hospitals and Gertrude Stein. And if there were, it would have no magic force to overcome the inhibitions of our culture and unlock still deeper pleasure sources. Why should a pleasure in talking childish nonsense succeed, where pleasures such as eloquence and poetry and convincing logic fail to unlock these prisoned values? Freud no more explains that than he explains why these values when unlocked are funny.

I believe that the explanation will look as simple to a true science as it does to an unreflecting mind. It succeeds because it is not doing this seriously, but in fun. Tricks played upon the mind in fun tickle, and evoke a special feeling that is pleasant. This pleasant feeling gives such tricks an adult value-status which helps them to negotiate the release of repressed serious pleasures. It also gives these pleasures when released a comic color.

> A woman got on the train with nine children, and when the conductor came for her tickets she said: "Now these three are thirteen years old and pay full fare, but those three over there are only six, and these three here four and a half." The conductor looked at her in astonishment.
>
> "Do you mean to say you get three every time?" he asked.
>
> "Oh no," she said. "Sometimes we don't get any at all."

Is it not clear that the tripping of your mind in what it starts to make of the phrase "every time" is the jocular element here, and that the improper allusion to the sexual act is merely protected by this element, and rendered admissible to your polite speech? And is it not equally clear that whether your speech is polite and in the habit of repressing such allusions or not, will make no difference to the witty value of the joke? If you have that habit, you will enjoy it with a somewhat smirking giggle, if not, you will enjoy it with a jovial laugh.

The reason why it is important to our art of pleasure to get this thing right is that the latter kind of enjoyment is more natural and better fills the nerves. That is why we said in the previous chapter that Freud sins against humor in making it all furtive. He renders it impossible to distinguish the naughty snicker of the hothouse-bred modern from the merry outdoor laughter of the olden times. People do hide behind play-nonsense, just as they hide behind the barn, or behind a beautiful symbol by James Branch Cabell, to peep at things that are forbidden. Wit is not a disguise, but in its manner of letting on to mean one thing and then meaning another, it is *like* a disguise, and can fulfill this function for those who dare not speak their minds. It thus arises that two things as different as the dirty-minded smirk of the Victorians and the hearty sexual laughter of the Elizabethans are confounded and dismissed together as "obscene."

Mark Twain declared, you remember, that the stories told in King Arthur's court were so "indelicate" that they would make a Comanche blush. I do not know about the Comanches, but I know that they never made Mark Twain blush, and that in fact he cherished a quite different opinion both about delicacy and about those stories. In a letter to William Dean Howells, he said:

> Delicacy—a sad, sad false delicacy—robs literature of the best two things among its belongings. Family circle narrative and obscene stories. But no matter; in that better world which I trust we are all going to I have the hope and belief that they will not be denied us.

These two seemingly opposed attitudes to "obscene stories"—that they were unfit for a Comanche and that they were fit for the angels in paradise—are not deeply opposed. They only show that Mark Twain sensed the difference I am talking about between the prurient snicker and the robust laugh. The conflict in his feelings is evident where his Connecticut Yankee encounters a troop of Canterbury pilgrims, "pious, happy, merry and full of unconscious coarseness and innocent indecencies," and describes with such loving imagination the progress of a jest along their loitering line.

> Practical jokes worthy of the English wits of the first quarter of the far-off nineteenth century were sprung here and there and yonder along the line, and compelled the delightedest applause; and sometimes when a bright remark was made at one end of the procession and started on its travels toward the other, you could note its progress all the way by the sparkling spray of laughter it threw off from its bows as it plowed along; and also by the blushes of the mules in its wake.

I think we in America are going to have to take our stand either with the mules or the Canterbury pilgrims. For both our humorous literature and our comic theater are tiring of the steam-and-machinery repressions, and bent on reviving in an age of water power and electricity the outdoor right of comic free speech.

Tragic free speech was revived some time ago in America, and its rights—so far as sex goes—are fairly well established. With the exception of Boston and a few other back ends of the country, it is now generally conceded that if a man has to do it for serious purposes, whether of art or science, he is entitled to mention any physiological function and any portion of the anatomy that he finds necessary. To mention our hushed-up parts and proceedings playfully is a very different matter. Every humorist and every magazine editor knows this. Our comic papers still have on their taboo-list expressions which have become the everyday vocabulary of solemn fiction. Even a good round mouth-filling oath is not permitted in a joke. You can take the name of the Lord in vain, but you can not take it in comic vein. And as for the names of Priapus, to breathe these publicly with laughter continues to be a crime against our nineteenth century *mores*.

The task we have before us, in short, is not to "elude the censor," but to lift him into the ether from the backside with a broad plank. And Freud's nineteenth-century-sired, hysteria-damed, hospital-born and clinic-bred idea that the comic *consists of* eluding a censor, stands as a first small theoretic hindrance on the road.

CHAPTER X

Why Truth Is Humorous

Aristophanes boasted of old that he was "the only poet who had the nerve to tell the truth to the Athenians." Charlie Chaplin in modern times described his art of making people laugh as "telling them the plain truth of things." Will Rogers, commenting on his own "rustic" humor, said: "I guess I wouldn't be very humorous if it wasn't for the government. I don't make jokes, I just watch the government and report the facts." And E. B. White, at the other pole of the comic universe, discussing the "civilized" humor of *The New Yorker*—"awful damn civilized" was what he called it—said: "Humor at its best is a kind of heightened truth—a super-truth."

To these authorities I want to add that of David Freedman, who probably knows more about humor in a commercial way, and also in the way of having it fall out of his own mouth without premeditation, than anybody else in the country. Freedman has only forty thousand jokes catalogued where Harold Horne has upwards of a million. But Freedman's jokes, besides being catalogued, are "clocked," and you can find out on its card both the duration and the size—A, B, C, and D—of the laughter which properly belongs to each. Moreover Freedman has been personally through his forty thousand jokes in the last five years, preparing scenarios for radio comedians, and has some hundreds of thousands more in books and papers on his shelves to go through. He tells me that, aside from the legitimate commerce, there is a bootleg trade in "gags," a business of stealing them from burlesque houses and vaudeville comedians, and selling them to men in the radio-joke industry, that runs into the hundreds of thousands of dollars a year, the price of a good gag on the curb being anything from ten to fifty dollars. His contribution to our discussion of the predominant topics of laughter—substantially in his own words—was this.

> There are six kinds of jokes that if they are any good at all will draw the belly laugh, the Yokchadebokcha, from any human audience.
>
> One. Insults—and particularly any remark implying that a man is an animal. The animals, however, have different laugh-ratings: jackass first, skunk next, hog, monkey, dog. That's their status in the humor hierarchy.
>
> Two. Anatomical references—and by that I mean references to a certain part of the anatomy, and it is not the head. We call them rear-end gags. There is a fire, and a fat woman starts to back out of the window: "Men, get your axes, the walls are bulging!"
>
> Three. Kissing. I call it kissing, because that is as far as we can go on the air. "Can you do it with kissing?" is a part of the regular jargon of the air-joke industry. The greatest liberty so far taken on the air was to say that Admiral Byrd's dog went crazy looking for the south pole.
>
> Four. Matrimony. This is just the opposite of the kissing gag. It has nothing to do with love. It's a hate joke. "I came home the other night and kissed my wife. She slapped me in the face and said: 'The gas is turned off, the baby's sick, the butcher refused to deliver the meat, and now you come home drunk!' "
>
> Five. The dumb joke—and particularly dumb dames.
>
> "Gee, did I fool that fellow. Imagine trying to make me pay him $5,000 for a fur coat."
>
> "But I saw you sign the check."
>
> "I know, but he'll never be able to cash it."
>
> "Why not?"
>
> "I didn't fill in the amount!" *
>
> Six. Children's mistakes—the naïve or unintentional gag.
>
> "Willie, why do you pinch the baby?"
>
> "We're playing automobile, and baby is the horn."
>
> Any one of those six gags, if it is good at all, will get a big laugh. Those are the sure things.

Mr. Freedman reflected a moment and then added:

> There is one more, too, and that is any true portrayal of what happens to you in your own life. W. C. Fields decides to commit suicide by drinking iodine, and keeps his face going away at the same distance from the bottle all the way back. You love it because

* In both Mr. Horne's and Mr. Freedman's collections there are more jokes filed under "Dumb Dames" than any other topic.

> you recognize it. Ninety per cent of what Fields does is nothing but true life, and Fields is our greatest comedian. It's a beautiful kind of humor because you put yourself in the guy's place. It is really great humor. Great humor is still truth.

In short, we laugh almost as often with a sense of *sudden reality* as of "sudden glory," or sudden sexuality or cruelty. For some reason

TRUTH COMES TO FLEET STREET

Thomas Derrick

this kind of joke has acquired no special name, but everybody knows it to exist. The fact is but a generalization of what we have been saying about sex and aggression, cowardice and lack of sex. Our lives in all departments consist so largely of the cultivation of insubstantial pretenses and amenities, the feeding of thin glamours—of posturing and pretending, sometimes honorably, sometimes with self-contempt—that almost any perfectly candid speech about anything contains an element of release. Everything that we deeply know and are has need of the play-license to get out at times and get a breath of air. That is how it happens that the word truth itself, or candor, or reality—no less general term—belongs with insults and with "kissing" among the everlasting play-topics of the race.

It is not truth as such, of course, that is a joke. The joke is to have some other trend of expectation, one perhaps belonging to our cultural or stucco selves, go playfully to smash, and in the wreckage find this deeper satisfaction to our sense of what is real. The face of truth is a strange face, at which when it obtrudes suddenly we can not help but smile, and yet it is also an intimately familiar face, and notwithstanding our perpetual flight from it, well loved. That is why it falls so neatly in with the operation of a joke. It disappoints a superficial expectation but satisfies an underlying trend.

In explaining to me what he meant by "telling them the plain truth of things," Charlie Chaplin came very near to stating this:

"When I walk right up and slap a grand lady because she gave me a contemptuous look, it is really right. They won't admit it, but it's right, and that is why they laugh. I make them conscious of the reality of life. 'You think this is it, don't you?' I say. 'Well, it isn't, but this is —see?' And then they laugh."

The satisfaction in recurring to reality is so distinct a state of mind to me, that I identify the humor that belongs under this head as I would salt or sugar in the dark, by its immediate flavor. Almost all the humor in Clarence Day's book, *Life with Father*, belongs here. It too is "true life." He overhears his father praying: "Have mercy! I say have mercy, damn it!" That seems remote enough from Chico Marx's line in *A Night at the Opera:* "I'd give you my seat but I'm sitting here"; from Don Herold's imperturbable octogenarian: "If there is such a thing as evolution, there hasn't been any too much of it to suit me"; from Ring Lardner's: "Whatever else may have been my imperfections, I never lied save to shield a woman or myself"; from Joe Cook's political eloquence: "I can in all sincerity state that I owe my success to the fact that fear of the law has kept me on the straight if narrow path, and that if I am elected to the office on which I have had my eye for so many years—the presidency of these United States—I will see that old Joe Cook is well taken care of"; from the violinist in the orchestra who made such faces during the playing of a Brahms symphony that the conductor stopped and asked him: "Don't you like it?" "It isn't that," he said, "I just don't like music"; from Denys Wortman's wistful job-hunter in the accompanying picture. They are different enough, and yet in them all, commingled with a laugh, I taste the flavor of a truth. Even when Josh Billings said: "The one-legged hens, I know, are the last apt to scratch up a garden," my inward laughter ended in a kind of sigh: "Well, after all, it's absolutely true!" And the colored man who, when asked whether he would rather really have a woman or just dream about it, said: "I'd rather dream about it, I think ya gits a better class o' women that way," gave me the satisfaction of acknowledging a man of judgment. In my opinion anyone who tasted satire, smut, aggression, ridicule, or any other thing but truth and pathos, underneath the drollness of that speech, would be defective in the sense of life if not of humor.

To me, indeed, even when jokes are rankly sexual or sadistic, they frequently convey a pleasure in reality frankly spoken, rather than a specifically sexual or cruel pleasure. It happened so when I read of the harsh death of Reginald in Artemus Ward's *Mormon Romance.*

> "And so farewell!" cried Reginald. "Come to my arms, my own!" he said; "that is, as many of you as can do it conveniently at once, for I must away."
>
> He folded several of them to his throbbing breast, and drove sadly away.
>
> But he had not gone far when the trace of the off-hind mule became unhitched. Dismounting he essayed to adjust the trace; but ere he had fairly commenced the task, the mule, a singularly refractory animal, snorted wildly, and kicked Reginald frightfully in the stomach. He arose with difficulty, and tottered feebly towards his mother's house, which was near by, falling dead in her yard, with the remark, "Dear mother, I've come home to die."
>
> "So I see," she said; "where's the mules?"

I do not ask the reader to agree with me that this is a charmingly candid mother. He may find her horribly delicious. If so, the story will illustrate the various ways in which the point and pattern of a joke may be perceived—and that is the only proper ending for this section of our book.

Science can not, and does not pretend to, exhaust the qualities of individual things. Every experience, every element of being, might for

"Say, here's a swell job for us in the help wanted column, Duke—but it's all right because this is last week's paper."

all science can ever tell us be unique. It is not things, but classes of things, that are defined. And if this is true of such things as atoms and electrons, how much more true it is of those compound and intricate explosives we call jokes. They may contain all kinds of attitudes, perceptions, thoughts and feelings, and these may differ vastly in the different individuals who laugh at them. The finest edge of any flavor can not be described, but only tasted. The virtue of our definition is that it is the only one general enough to include all flavors of laughter and all kinds of individuals who laugh. It asserts merely that comic laughter is not serious, which is obvious; and it explains this laughter by reference to attributes no less common in experience than pleasant and unpleasant.

Look yourself in the face—are you honest?

Part Eight

HOW TO TELL GOOD JOKES FROM BAD

CHAPTER I

To Diagram a Joke

Groucho Marx told me that if with my analysis of humor I could provide a test by which a good joke could be distinguished from a bad one without trying them out on the public, I would soon be the richest man in Hollywood. He also confided that he thought I would probably die poor. It is a good deal beyond my ambition to educate the jokers of Hollywood. All I had in mind was to teach the public how to enjoy their jokes when possible. Our pleasure in any art grows with the refinement of our perceptions, and a mental grasp of what it is we are trying to perceive is a help in this process. That mental grasp, and that increase in the quantity of enjoyment has been the purpose of this book. It is a handbook in the art of taking comic pleasure.

However, I do not think it would hurt the jokers of Hollywood to know a little more than they do about what they are doing. I notice that the two of them who discuss most thoughtfully what "gags" are and how they accomplish their effect—Charlie Chaplin and W. C. Fields—are far from the bottom in the scale of eminence. Art at its best is spontaneous in origin but deliberate in perpetration, and I doubt if even the playful arts escape this rule. At any rate I am going to try to say a few things here which might conceivably be of use to a humorist or a comedian. They will at least be of use to the critics of humor. And they will be of use to my advanced students in pleasure, for in humor as in every other art, the best way to learn its fine enjoyment is to try to make a little of it.

The first thing to do, then, is to draw a diagram of a joke. A joke, remember, is not a thing but a process; and it is not an atom, but a molecule. An atom of humor is an unpleasantness or a frustration taken playfully. A witty joke is made by combining this unpleasantness or frustration with some idea or attitude-of-feeling in which one can find momentary satisfaction. To diagram a joke, therefore, we must have three signs, one each for the two kinds of humor-atoms, one for the satisfaction.

We may represent the unpleasant thing or image taken playfully, the atom of perceptual or poetic humor, by a scrawl. Thus:

A scrawl is, as a matter of fact, a little bit funny. It is something that your brain can not organize into a pattern. You can not make a "thing" of it, as you can for instance of the eight triangles in the accompanying figure, which when you fix your eyes on them become a cross.

You can readily imagine that if you were extremely hilarious, and perhaps a little bit insanely so—if you were on a hashish jag—you would find the scrawl funny long before you would begin to laugh at the triangles. I got the idea of my scrawl from Koffka's *Gestalt Psychology,* where he illustrates the unpleasantness of forms which the brain can not "organize." Being unpleasant to a serious brain, it is naturally a good symbol of what is comic to a frivolous one.

A frustration taken playfully gives you an atom of wit or practical humor, and we may represent this by a broken line—also a sad thing if taken seriously. Thus:

Besides these two signs for the playfully unpleasant, or comic, part of a joke, we must have a sign for the pleasant part—the point, or positive satisfaction in which, if it has a point, it comes to rest. For this purpose nothing could be more appropriate than the above eight triangles, which the mind so easily perceives as a neat and satisfying object—almost a badge, or medal, or Victoria Cross. In fact if you examine those triangles again, you will find that they form two crosses, and that the two compete with each other for a place in your attention. That makes them an especially good symbol for the point of a joke, because, as we have seen, jokes vary greatly in what they seriously mean to different people and at different times.

For example, one of our lush-voiced radio performers after completing a bedtime story for the kiddies, turned away with the remark: "There, I guess that'll hold the little bastards!" The microphone had not been switched off, and he found himself next day without a job.

Our reciprocating crosses will indicate the different ways in which you might feel pleased to hear it.

With these three symbols, then, let us proceed to represent the different fundamental forms of jokes.

1. A mere ludicrous word or image—like calling dishwashers "pearl divers," or saying "Jesus H. Christ," or "Parm me—my garter just stung me" (Winchell), or a picture like Peter Arno's "Oh, Redskin!" or even a whole story like that of the trombone player who made a toot at the wrong time, and when the conductor objected, said,

"I beg your pardon, I played a fly!"—would be represented by a scrawl with nothing but a stem to hold it up:

2. A ludicrous phrase or image which, besides being funny, conveys a thought or feeling-attitude of positive interest, will be represented by a scrawl that has with it a Victoria Cross. Thus:

Ogden Nash's poem:

> Philo Vance
> Needs a kick in the pance,

may serve as an example. In a similar although so different way, Walter Winchell's phrase "Moom pitcher" is not purely ludicrous—it is phonetically true and therefore satisfying.

George Chappell, in *The Younger Set,* describing a character who was always in arrears at the Club, but for such large sums that they couldn't afford to fire him, writes: "Luther Pritchett, our treasurer . . . has been trying to get Bert to sign an insurance policy in favor of the

Club, and then let nature take its course, but Bert says he is too nervous to look at a dotted line." A woman sneaking out of a hotel writing room with a bundle of stationery under her arm explained: "I was just gathering material for my next novel." There is a resourcefulness in these characters, a success that crowns their funniness and satisfies the mind. Their values are indicated by this diagram.

I think Cobb's story belongs here too, about the colored soldier who was told to zigzag as he crossed No Man's Land, and when he reached a dressing-station with a sniper's bullet in his sacro-iliac said: "De trouble wuz I musta zigged when I shoulda been zaggin'." To me, at least, there is an accuracy in his inference that requires notation.

3. A sentence which is funny because it sets up a plausible pretense to meaning, and collapses into nonsense, will be represented simply by a lengthening of our broken line:

Mary E. Wilkins Freeman's verse about the ostrich,

> He often runs so very fast
> He leaves himself behind,

may serve as an example here. Also any of the typical remarks of Stoopnagle and Budd on the radio:

> People have more fun than anybody.
>
> Noise is louder than anything.

If you feel a little shy about your taste for such pure foolishness, it will interest you to know that President Hutchins of the University of Chicago said in a commencement address—or was so reported:

"I understand that Harvard University is making its diplomas larger or smaller. I have forgotten which. This is a step in the right direction."

It will also interest you that in an experimental study made at Vassar College, an appreciation of "nonsense jokes" was found to increase with an increase of "mental ability as represented chiefly by academic standing." *

4. A witty joke, or such a piece of nonsense turning out after all to mean something, will be represented by a broken line recovering and arriving at the Victoria Cross. Thus:

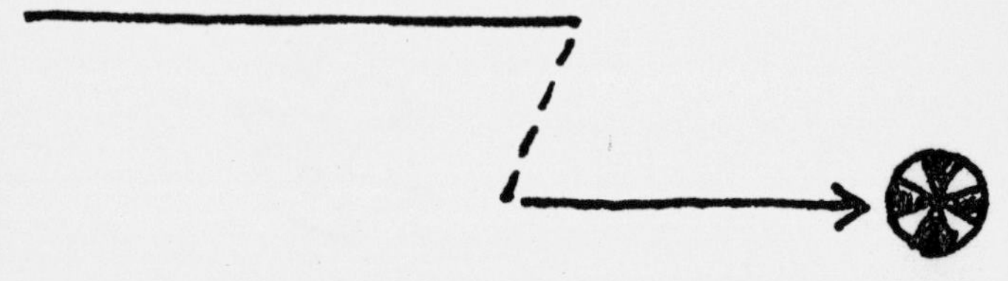

An example would be the complaint of the modern child, "Mamma, do I have to do what I want to all day long?" if regarded as a comment on present trends in education. Another would be the Irish bull, "One man's as good as another—yes, and by gorry, better!" if regarded as summarizing the history of democracy. Bill Arp's answer when asked how many Yankees he killed in the war, comes to mind here too: "I don't want to boast, but I killed as many of them as they did of me." Also Petroleum V. Nasby's summing up of the case for women's rights: "As it is now arranged, man and wife are one, and the man is the one." However, all "witty" remarks follow this pattern, and I choose these examples merely as revealing the relevance of the pattern clearly.

Naïve humor follows this pattern too, sometimes. The man who solemnly declared: "I have renounced the errors of the Church of Rome and embraced those of the Church of England," receives, according to my system, a Victoria Cross for his "mistake."

5. A poetic absurdity, or a piece of nonsense which does not arrive

* "Individual Differences in the Sense of Humor" by P. Kambouropoulu, *American Journal of Psychology,* 1926, vol. 37, pp. 268-78.

at a meaning, but does evoke an image which is ludicrous, would be represented by a broken line decorated with a scrawl. Groucho Marx's remark, for example: "Did I ever tell you how I shot an elephant in my pyjamas? How he got into my pyjamas I don't know." Or Ring Lardner's account of how Lily Langtry "swept Broadway, and then was given a job sweeping the side streets."

6. A very rich joke, or a joke with a point which also contains ludicrous imagery, will be represented by all three signs—a broken line carrying a scrawl and yet arriving at the Victoria Cross. My favorite example is the story of the man who was picked up unconscious in the street and rushed to a hospital, and when they opened his coat they found a note pinned to his vest, reading: "To the house surgeon: This is just a plain case of fit, not appendicitis—my appendix has already been removed twice."

I decorate that joke with two splotches and two Victoria Crosses, because not only is the picture of an unconscious patient telling the doctor in crisp language what is the matter with him ludicrous, but the phrase "plain case of fit," funny in any circumstances, is extremely funny here, and because after the doctor is completely knocked out and has taken the count, and the bell has rung, and the fight is called, and the doctor starts to get up, the mute patient takes a final swing at him in that word "twice," which lays him cold once more. Nothing less than two Victoria Crosses can symbolize the triumph of patients, and almost of corpses, over doctors in which that story comes to rest. It is what comedians call "topping a gag."

Those six diagrams will suggest the different kinds of molecules that can be composed of our three humor atoms. Of course they are far from exhausting the variety of these molecules. The phrase "Dante, the famous Yale book-end," for example, would show two scrawls on but a single stem, for Dante as a Yale end is ludicrous and a Yale book-end is also ludicrous. There is a "topping" of imaginative humor here. Moreover this phrase contains an attitude toward Dante, or toward book-ends made out of his face, that must be rewarded with our winking cross.

The mistake of most psychologists in the past has been to imagine that the comic quality resides either in the end-term or the whole adult jocular pattern, and not in the infantile atom. I have a dread that our very modern psychologists, with their new sense of the importance of patterns (or *Gestalten*) in man's mental life, are going to perpetuate this error.* It will be natural for them to assume that every

* The pioneer in applying the Gestalt theory in experiments on jokes, Dr. M. A. Harrower, (*Smith College Studies in Psychology,* No. 4) did not attempt to generalize her joke patterns. She did, moreover, include among them the very story I adduced on page 65 as an example of an unrelieved absurdity—the one about the cakes that were baked in the form of the letter S. Her picture of it, too, accords with my conception.

That is anything but a closed pattern, and I find nothing in Dr. Harrower's report—which is not concerned, by the way, with comic theory, but with memory—to justify my fears as to what the Gestalt psychologists may do.

The source of those fears is the work of Richard N. Sears, developing ideas scrawl or broken line in our diagrams has to be somehow cleaned up or mended in order to be enjoyed. The contrary is true. In anything that is funny some element must remain scrawly, remain broken, unorganized into a pattern. The funny is the surd, the *ab*surd, the very thing you can not fit into a pattern. I do not know how the "Gestalt psychologists" will fit that into their pattern, but I know it is the fact.

Read, for instance, the following from Ring Lardner's account of his wedding with the Eskimo bride, Hugga Much:

> At this point I wish to correct an error that was made by the New York newspapers in their account of the wedding. I was repeatedly referred to as the groom, though I have had nothing to do with the care of a horse since I was twelve years old, and then only as a favor. The mistake probably was due to a misunderstanding by an Associated Press reporter, who, when my engagement was announced, called up Hugga's mother, Sitta Much, and asked if she was satisfied with me as a son-in-law. Mrs. Much replied: "I certainly am. He is a hustler." The reporter, no doubt, thought she said "hostler." The two words "hostler" and "hustler" sound a great deal alike, especially in Eskimo.

Unfortunately I can not quote the whole book, and so the reader will hardly know how humorous this is in its place. But he will know, I think, if he knows anything, that the most humorous thing in it is the phrase "especially in Eskimo." And that is humorous because, although plausible, it is pointless. It is absolutely pointless. It is unman-

---

suggested by Dr. Harrower's report. Mr. Sears' book—unfortunately not yet published, but very generously loaned to me in manuscript—rests upon the assumption that the "two line joke" is "truly representative of natural spontaneous humor." The author makes no attempt to prove this assertion, and I fear it places him with those other philosophers of the comic who have never seen a baby. He ought to take a look at babies, also at great apes, and he ought to read the lyrical obituary to the "two line joke" penned by Robert Benchley in his preface to the *Fourth New Yorker Album.* Science might go at least as far as art, it seems to me, in getting back to the early elements of things. And the early elements of the humor situation certainly do not contain that adult jocular pattern, "tension-shock-relief," which Mr. Sears derives from two line witticisms. The mirth response itself, the act of laughter, is adequate "relief" for people merrily at play, and no tension need precede a funny image or perception.

I have paid my respects elsewhere to some of Mr. Sears' contributions, and I append a hope that his thoughtful book may soon be published.

ageable. You can not "do anything with it." It is, to quote again the phrase of Charles Lamb—especially invented as a warning to Gestalt psychologists—"an utter and inextricable absurdity."

With that much warning against the temptation to identify the comic as such with any pattern, we may proceed to remark that most jocular folklore can, with a little practice and a good deal of analytical labor, be fitted into the fourth diagram above. Take this well-known proverb, for instance:

> It's a sure sign somebody has been thinking about you when you find a tack in your chair.

That seems at first glance almost a simple declarative sentence. There is no break in it, no place even for a comma. As a fact, however, two tendencies collapse and come to nothing there. The first is the meaning-tendency set up by the words "It's a sure sign"—a phrase which leads us to expect the communication of some abstruse, perhaps occult, at least not obvious connection between events—a connection *worth calling attention to.* There is "no sense" in using the word *sign* to call attention to so obvious a connection, and "no sense," as we have seen, is the next thing to nonsense. In that respect our simple declarative sentence is a flop, and in that respect it never will get up on its feet. But another thing has also failed of its goal—the feeling-attitude evoked by the words "somebody has been thinking about you," words which normally suggest a not unfriendly thought. That also comes to comic grief. But within that grief, and constituting the very body of it we find the colder joy of watching somebody sit on a tack. As a matter of fact, to see somebody sit on a tack is not only joyful, but also ludicrous. Therefore we shall have to end our diagram of this joke

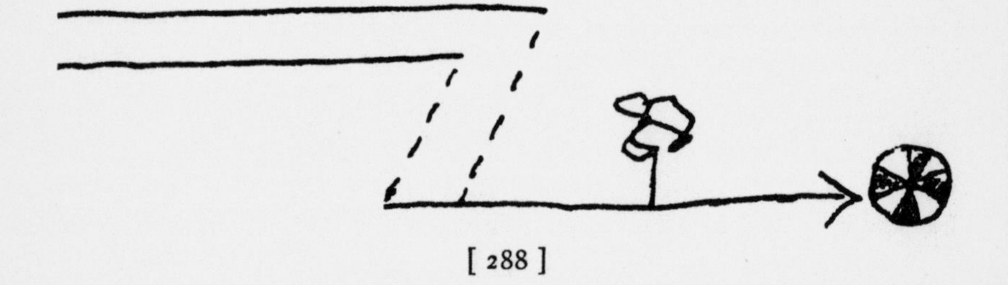

not only with a starry badge, but also with a scrawl. Two broken tendencies, a badge, and a scrawl will give its life history.

Since it takes that much apparatus, and that much worry, to diagram the simplest joke I could remember, you will be relieved to know that I am not going to diagram any more jokes. My purpose in introducing this idea was twofold. I wanted to show certain psychology professors that it is not so simple as they think. And I wanted to etch graphically into the minds of my own unstudious pupils the reality of these different delightful elements that I have been talking about—the comic unpleasantness, the comic frustration, and the end-satisfaction which gives point to a joke.

CHAPTER II

The Ten Commandments of the Comic Arts

IN MY BOOK on *The Sense of Humor,* I remarked that nobody in all the literature of this subject has ever discussed the points of difference between a good joke and a bad. And I endeavored to fill this gap by laying down the first eight laws of a code for serious joke-makers. I still remain the sole custodian, so far as I know, of this department of human morals. And moreover, I have received a further illumination and am now able to add the two missing commandments to the original eight. I would like to formulate them in a better order too, and illustrate them with some of our modern American sins and transgressions. The laws are, speaking briefly, these:

1. Be interesting.
2. Be unimpassioned.
3. Be effortless.
4. Remember the difference between cracking practical jokes and conveying ludicrous impressions.
5. Be plausible.
6. Be sudden.
7. Be neat.
8. Be right with your timing.
9. Give good measure of serious satisfaction.
10. Redeem all serious disappointments.

1. Be Interesting

This law is easy to understand. I do not pretend that any of them are easy to follow.

The fact that comic laughter is playful has been misjudged by many people—notably Henri Bergson—to mean that it is "intellectual." "The comic," says Bergson, "appeals to the intelligence pure and simple; laughter is incompatible with emotion." Since the comic *is* an emotion, since a comedy which did not appeal to the emotions would appeal to empty seats after the first five minutes, and since there is no such thing as "intelligence pure and simple," it is surprising how many sensible people go round repeating this unconsidered dictum. The fact is that if you do not arouse an emotional interest, your jokes, no matter how formally good, will be condemned as dull or cheap or tiresome or boresome, and yourself as "facetious," a wag, a witling, a smart-aleck, a mere wise-cracker.

There is nothing the matter formally with Groucho's answer in *Duck Soup,* when somebody suggests that he ought to organize a standing army. "Good," he says, "then I won't have to buy chairs." As it stands, however, that joke is about as dull as it could be, and the audience makes this clear. But if there had previously existed a problem about chairs, if the acquisition of furniture had entered even by one minute fiber into the suspense-tension of the plot, so that when the word *standing* dropped its original meaning and picked up another, the other would have tapped an *existing interest,* then a roar of laughter would have followed.

Let me illustrate this with a far worse joke, one of the worst puns, formally considered, that was ever dragged out of a hard-working brain and conscientiously put on the boards, but one that brought down a torrent of laughter because of the interest it satisfied.

An elevator boy was flirting with an office girl after business hours, and another irrelevant male was hanging around trying to pry in and be social, making one affable suggestion after another. The audience was as eager to get that extra male out of the way as the elevator boy was. After trying several ways to get rid of him politely, the boy said:

"What do you say we play the new game, Building and Loan?"

"Why, how do you play it?"

"Get the hell out of the building and leave us alone!"

Of course this problem of tuning up an interest can be obviated by making your jokes appeal to an interest that is always present and always wide-awake. That is what most jokes do, and that is why we have been able to arrange under four or five heads the prevailing topics of laughter.

Ring Lardner, in his *Story of a Wonder Man,* describes a facetious conversation between himself and a laundress named Mrs. Stevens.

> "Mrs. Stevens, I once had a sister who was quite fond of one of her gowns, but she would wear it only in the front yard."
> "Why?" This from Mrs. Stevens.
> "She said it was her laundress."

That does indeed appeal to "the intelligence pure and simple"—or simple at least, if not pure. And how fatuous it is! But rebuild it so that it appeals to a simple, if not pure, emotion. Have Mrs. Stevens say:

"I haven't any lawn dress, I can't wear this to the party."

And the author: "You're a laundress yourself, why wear anything?"

It becomes at least a fairly happy jest. It reminds me, indeed, of the first risqué joke that ever entered my young life.

> A man went to see a girl, and she called down from upstairs that she was not dressed. "Can't you slip on something and come down?" he called. So she slipped on the top step and came down.

Strange that a Frenchman should be the one to invent the legend that "the comic appeals to the intelligence pure and simple." I wonder if Bergson would think the *poilu's* interpretation of the letters *Y.M.C.A.* on the uniforms of American war nurses—*y a moyenne de coucher avec*—made no appeal to the emotions! If you examine jokes with your mind on jokes, and not on proving a system of philosophy, you find that they appeal frequently, as we saw, not only to one emotional interest but two. They appeal either to two interests, or to one interest that can travel in two directions. Our interest in nakedness travels normally in two directions. We are interested in keeping our clothes on and keeping other people's clothes on. We are so intensely interested that we pass laws against taking them off. A law recently passed by the New York legislature would make it a crime, I am told, for a doctor and a female nurse to be together in the same room with a naked baby. But we would not pass these silly laws if we were not also interested in taking our clothes and other people's off. It is this ambivalence, this facing both ways, of our emotional attitude toward nakedness which makes it a perennial joke topic. Any normal person will join heartily in a girl's impulse to put a dress on before coming down to receive a caller, and most normal persons will be capable of a secret wish that she wouldn't. The initial feeling-tendency set going by the words "slip on something and come down," is adequately strong, therefore, and is universal. But the satisfaction substituted when the verb *slip on* cracks up, is also universal, also strong.

We might then reformulate this law to read: When your jokes do not tap a stream from the eternal glee-reservoirs, try to dam up in advance a little puddle of specific interest in the thing or meaning upon which, after the breakdown, they are to come to rest. No comedian understands this better than Charlie Chaplin. I have in memory a picture of him arguing in a restaurant with a chance acquaintance who has generously offered to pay his bill. He being absolutely penniless, but wishing to appear polite, adopts an "Oh, by no means, let me pay it!" attitude. There is a conflict of courtesy, first one and then the other yielding. Charlie carries it just a hair's breadth too far, and the friend suddenly says "Oh well, since you insist," and reluctantly puts in the waiter's plate the money for his own bill. The waiter goes out for the change and Charlie sits there, downcast and desperate, but still trying gallantly to keep up an animated conversation with his new-found friend. The waiter comes back, and the friend picks up his change. He holds it in his hand a moment, and the waiter turns away. Then he puts down half a dollar as a tip. Charlie gazes at that half dollar with a yearning that has by this time become almost unbearable. And so does the audience. Then he takes his own bill, which is a small one, slips it under the half dollar, and hands them to the waiter with an inimitable gesture of munificence. The gesture is funny enough under the circumstances, but backed up with the billow of relief and joy that has been so carefully prepared, the effect is stupendous.

I will conclude this sermon on the first commandment by giving an infallible recipe for evoking a laugh from any human audience:

Arouse in them a tense, but not too tense, desire to hear something said, keep it unsatisfied a while, and when they think you are saying something else that is less interesting, suddenly—by any trick of speech or meaning you command—put in their ears the very thing they wanted to hear. If you can learn to do that right along, you will soon be the richest man in Hollywood. You also will probably die poor, however, for it can not be done by merely understanding it.

2. Be Unimpassioned

This commandment of course needs immediate qualification. What it means is that, while you must arouse feelings, you must not arouse feelings that are too strong and deep. Remember that humorous laughter is inseparable from the mood of play, and you will not try to crack jokes on subjects about which people feel too intensely to be playful. Violations of this law constitute the crimes known as inept or untimely jokes, jokes that are malapropos, sex jokes that are "too broad," and hostile jokes that are "carried too far."

Here again it is necessary to correct M. Bergson. "Depict some fault," he says, "in such a way as to arouse sympathy, fear or pity . . . the mischief is done, it is impossible for us to laugh."

Nobody who set out from the observation of laughter, and much less from the generation of it, could possibly make such a statement. It would rule out all those tense comminglings of humor with pathos, laughter with tears, which are among the most exquisite achievements of modern literature. It would rule out the subtlest of Chaplin, and the mellowest of W. C. Fields. It was this sentence, in fact, that I quoted to Fields, when he exclaimed: "Oh no, they laugh often with tears in their eyes!" (See page 336.) And he illustrated what he meant by recalling a passage from his own great stage success, *Poppy*.

"I had stolen a horse, and was trying to get it over the border into Canada. I said an affectionate farewell to my daughter, and disap-

1.
A.M.
2.
3.
4.
5.
6.
7.
8.
O. SOGLOW

peared into the wings, but came back in a few seconds, handcuffed and in the custody of a policeman. My daughter uttered the single word 'Pop!' She spoke this with heartfelt dismay, and there was not a sound or motion in the audience. They were liking us and caring what happened to us. I said: 'Fortunes of war, my dear! I never did think much of that horse, and he dropped dead right in front of the police station!' It was one of the big laughs of the piece, but there was warm feeling in it."

Everybody who has studied laughter with a need to understand it will agree with the comedian here, and not the philosopher. And yet there is a ground for the philosopher's mistake. If Bergson had said: "Depict some fault in such a way as to arouse *too much* sympathy, fear or pity . . . it is impossible for us to laugh"—that would have been a true statement. It would have been true not because comic laughter is intellectual, but because it is playful.

I can illustrate this in my own case with the story-without-words by Otto Soglow reproduced on page 295, a story which looked so sad to me that I could not even see the point for a day, and when it did dawn on me I could not feel its humor.

People differ so much in what they will and will not take playfully that obedience to this law is largely a matter of momentary intuition. I have confessed my inability to laugh at a dead bird, but not with any pride about it. In justice I should feel the same way about a worm, but I don't. And since jokes have to happen suddenly in order to happen at all, I can not do anything about this. I am at the mercy of my first reaction. That is why these laws are so important. There is no use of Mr. Soglow's getting up on a high horse and going out on a crusade to defend the right of his joke to be laughed at. I concede the right. I surrender unconditionally. But the joke is dead now that we have argued about it, and buried with it is the irrevocable fact that I did not laugh.*

*Here is another joke that I do not think funny, although Jack Goodman and Albert Rice like it so much that they offer it as an "acid test" of the reader's sense of humor.

It is the simple recital—to quote their words—of a young man's victory in a rough-and-tumble battle, as described by himself. It goes something like this:

Fields told me that the author of his play, *Poppy,* insisted that people would not laugh if he spoke the words "dropped dead" even about a horse. "It will make them think about mother's ailing kidneys, the little daughter that got run over, Uncle John's heart trouble—no, you can't say things like that in comedy." Fields put up an argument, but finally gave in and agreed to a compromise. He would say: "The mare succumbed in front of the police station." That, the author thought, would be fine. He did say it, too, all through the rehearsals, but on the first night he spoke his own line and brought down the house. When he saw the author in the wings, he threw up his hands. "I *am* so sorry! I got excited and forgot all about our little agreement!" "It's all right," she said graciously. "I'll forgive you!"

Another thing Fields will tell you is this: "If you are going to smash anything in comedy—an automobile for instance—don't take a new one. It isn't funny to smash a new car. They'll think: 'Well, what a shame, why didn't he give it to me?' If you are going to smash it, batter it up a little before you come on, so it doesn't matter so much."

And that, like all the other rules of comic action, applies with little change to spoken humor. Do not jest about things that *matter too much.* There must be feelings, but they must be experienced in that light and inorganic way—as though you tasted them but did not drink them down—for which we have no word but *playful,* and of which we have as yet no better understanding than is contained in that word.

Walt Disney told me another thing that illustrates this law. We

"Thrusting my nose firmly between his teeth, I threw him heavily to the ground on top to me."

I think that is a poor joke even formally for two reasons. First, because biting a person's nose is so unusual a form of triumph in battle that the mind hesitates upon it—the victory is not *instantaneously* reversed. And second, because biting a person's nose is a rather unpleasant procedure, almost as unpleasant to the biter as the bitee, and therefore the victory is not distinct. I should describe the joke on those two counts as both lame and flat. But aside from that, I find the idea of one person's putting his nose between another's teeth so unpleasant that I can not, at least upon the inducement here offered, enjoy it playfully. Instead of being funny it is disagreeable. And that shift back to the serious evaluations is, of course, what this second commandment aims to forestall.

were speaking of the artificial standards of virtue and propriety that have to be lived up to in the moving pictures.

"You remember the little potty-chair in *Lullaby Land,*" he said. "That didn't cause any trouble here, but we're beginning to get squawks about it from New Zealand. And do you know why? They still use 'em over there—it's too real!"

3. Be Effortless

This law also flows from the fact that the sense of humor is a play-instinct. It not only flows from this fact, but proves it. There is nothing more mysteriously awful in nature than the sudden death and wraithlike fading from the landscape of humorous emotion at the mere suggestion that somebody has done, or is doing, or is going to do, some work. The phenomenon is inexplicable until you know that playfulness is a state-of-being and humor inherent in it. When you know that, you will have only your conscience to wrestle with in applying this commandment.

It is designed to protect us against labored jokes, like Dorothy Parker's "Nearer my garter thee," when discussing her feelings on the occasion of a fallen garter at a party; against dragged in jokes, including any and every one ever introduced by the remark, "I am reminded by the subject of the evening . . ." or "by our little gathering this evening . . ." a sure proof that the speaker has been reminded of nothing whatever, but has searched through a joke book until he found something with some sort of associational loose end which he could with a stupendous intellectual effort *attach* to the subject of the evening; against all carefully memorized and loyally preserved jokes which are brought out on festive occasions by people concerned to prove that they are good fellows and do not take life too seriously; against the original jokes that certain eminent wits carry around in their heads and lead the conversation up to with such faithful toil and persistence; and against elaborate jokes like George Chappell's *Adventures in the Alimentary Canal*—for you can not conceal *labor* from the comic instinct by surrounding it with an *e* and an *a-t-e*. There exists, in short, such a thing as an odor of industry, and like the odor of sanctity in the nostrils of a demon, it drives laughter blenched and horror-stricken from the scene.

I will illustrate this fact with a transgression by Robert Benchley, who ought to know better. He is telling us in his usually gay and expertly unindustrious style about the pernicious effects of ocean travel, all of which, he thinks, result from the exercise one feels obliged to take.

> I sit at home—he says—for ten months of the year, right on one chair, getting no more exercise than is involved in thumbing a cigarette-lighter and turning the pages of a newspaper. . . . And my health during those ten months is simply elegant. If I were any healthier I would smell of pine needles. And I wouldn't take a walk around the reservoir if Greta Garbo were to offer to go along with me. I wouldn't take a walk around the reservoir even if I could be assured of being alone.
>
> But once on shipboard I feel that I must take exercise. I listen to people who say: "Of course if you don't get exercise on board ship you will get logy." Logy. Boy, if I were to get any logier than I am during the winter months they could prop me up in Wanamaker's window and hang dress goods on me. But somehow this never occurs to me at sea. . . .
>
> At five o'clock sharp each afternoon . . . I don a strange costume which I feel, in a way, is rather dashing and athletic-looking, but which really is made up of such unimpressive articles as an undershirt, a pair of trousers, and bed-slippers. Then it is up to the gymnasium, two steps at a time, and onto the first piece of apparatus which is vacant. This usually is an electric horse, which has a gait something between a trot and a canter, with just a suspicion of lope thrown in. I haven't been on a real horse since I discovered that horse hair gave me hay fever (and what a relief that was, *to know that I had a good excuse for not riding!*) but that does not deter me from letting myself be jounced up and down, with occasional attempts at posting, until my lower grinders are firmly imbedded in my upper ones and my head a throbbing mass of temples.

To my mind there is enough of the odor of industry in that phrase, "to know that I had a good excuse for not riding," to spread devastation, forward and back, over about fifteen lines of witty writing. It is a serious phrase, a painstaking phrase, an anxious phrase, an earnest and successful effort to make things clear—a task, in short, intruding on the mood of play. I doubt if it was ever there in the original at all. I can hear some conscientiously comic editor saying: "Look here, Benchley, they won't get you here at all. I didn't myself. You must remember the average magazine reader has a mental age of less than fourteen years. An ordinary person won't have the slightest idea why hay fever should give you a feeling of relief. I think you'll have to clear that up, Benchley, for our readers. Remember we're not a highbrow magazine."

These sins of industry are rare in Benchley, whose fault is that he is too facile. He not only leaves no thumbprints of hard work on his finished product; he does not always do the work. He does not always trim down and prune his writings to give a rich as well as lively flow of funny qualities. In the above quotation I drew the superfluous liquor off three pages of Benchley's piece on "Exercise for Those at Sea," and greatly enjoyed the favor I was doing him. Benchley, although he lacks what big tremendously rough fellows like Hemingway and me call "guts," is so truthfully and spontaneously charming that he could make an almost immortal book out of his dozen or so by drawing off unnecessary words and sentences.

Which will suffice, I hope, to make clear that when I say "Be effortless," I am not advocating a utopia in which anything good can be done without trying to do it. With a few exceptions like James Thurber's drawings, which usually turn out funnier the faster his hand moves, that is not true, I believe, of any human art. Least of all is it true of oratory, where our countrymen are most prone to believe it. Mark Twain, if humor can be great, was a great orator—remember that when calculating his celestial magnitude—and Mark Twain wrote all his speeches out and learned them by heart as conscientiously as Demosthenes did, or Cicero, or any intelligent schoolboy.

"I was so jaded and worn at the Taylor dinner," he says in one of his letters, "that I found I could not remember three sentences of the speech I had memorized, and therefore got up and said so and excused myself from speaking."

No, it is not trying to do it well that this third commandment inveighs against. To be effortless may require twenty-five years of effort. That is none of the lawgiver's business. His business is with the style of the finished product. And the style must never be arduous even in a good sense. It must never be, though laden with riches, heavy-laden.

The style of Shakespeare carries far too much weight of idea and imagination to be suitable for humor. The gloriously groaning and thundering language of Carlyle is fundamentally hostile to a laugh. It is not a question here of making humor good; it is a question of permitting it to exist. You can not feel at the same time that something is funny and that it is made so by an effort. Every comedian knows this instinctively, or soon finds it out. "Humor," as Josh Billings said, "must fall out of a man's mouth like music out of a bobolink."

Notwithstanding this early wisdom, there is a vast amount of labor in American humorous literature. The landscape, you may say, is littered with the corpses of jokes which have died by the sweat of their brow. There grew up after the time of Artemus Ward and Josh Billings and Petroleum V. Nasby—and Abe Lincoln who adored them—a sort of conscious cult, half business and half religion, of *being humorous.* You see it at the worst in Eli Perkins, who wrote a book called *Thirty Years of Wit,* but which might be called *The Thirty Years' War on Wit,* so ghastly is the scene it depicts, and so awful the stale breath of the professional joke collector hanging over it.

There is one jest in that book, contributed by a mysterious stranger never elsewhere known or spoken of, which deserves a place in history. He sat silent night after night in the smoking room of an ocean liner where a group of these story-swappers were at work—Evarts, Depew and others of "the Union League Club fellows." Finally in exasperation they called on him for a story. He protested at first that he did not know any, but under pressure at last conceded that he could perhaps produce one conundrum. The conundrum was: "What is the difference between me and a turkey?" And the answer: "They generally stuff a turkey with chestnuts after death. I am alive!"

It is important to observe that Mark Twain did not escape contamination from this rather green and provincial humor cult. There are many pieces of his writing in which he was evidently thinking of himself rather as a small-town wit or "cracker-box philosopher," than as a man of humorous mind and vision. Even *Huckleberry Finn,* which Andrew Lang described fifty years ago as "the great American novel" —and which still is so in part—contains that laboriously manufactured parody, or potpourri, of Shakespeare which must stand there, dead and dreadful in this living masterpiece, to the day of doom. There is truth in the charge of "mechanical fun-making" which J. B. Priestley brings against "Mark Twain and other Americans" in his incredibly humorless book about English humor. Mark Twain sinned often against our third commandment, and only a big job of surgery would cleanse his works of the resulting dead spots.

The reason why it is important to say this, is that Mark Twain, when in full flight of thought and imagination, excelled the greatest jesters of the world exactly in the spontaneity and naturalness, the simple inevitability, of his humor. It is this that has given him his place among the Titans of literature. Although he is known throughout the world as a humorist, not one of his great books is comic either in form or conception. That to me is the unique thing about Mark Twain, and the very American thing. He did not as an author "undertake" to be humorous. He asks no similar undertaking of the reader. He *was* humorous. He could not see, or think, or argue, or remember, or exist, for very long, in other terms. Therefore the humor in his greatest books, and in his speeches and his letters, exemplifies the meaning of this law—be effortless—as very little classic literary humor does.

Mark Twain was keenly aware, too, of the difference between the business of journalism and the art of literature, a difference which grows more sharp with every year that passes. "You will be surprised," he says in a letter to Howells, "that I was willing to do so much magazine writing—a thing I have always been chary about. . . ." And in a letter to Jeanette Gilder he made these statements, which I commend to the attention of some of our modern superintendents of humor factories:

> I have been accused of "rushing into print" prematurely, moved thereto by greediness for money; but in truth I have never done that. Do you care for trifles of information? Well then, *Tom Sawyer* and *The Prince and the Pauper* were each on the stocks sixteen years; another seventeen. This latter book could have been finished in a day, at any time during the past five years. . . .
>
> Long, long ago money-*necessity* furnished that impulse once, *(Following the Equator)*, but mere desire for money has never furnished it, so far as I remember. Not even money-necessity was

> able to overcome me on a couple of occasions when perhaps I ought to have allowed it to succeed. While I was a bankrupt and in debt two offers were made me for weekly literary contributions to continue during a year, and they would have made a debtless man of me, but I declined them, with my wife's full approval, for I had known of no instance where a man had pumped himself out once a week and failed to run "emptyings" before the year was finished.

Artemus Ward also declined a handsome offer for a *weekly* column.

> I needed the money badly—he remarked—and the offer was tempting, but I wasn't fool enough to accept it. To try to grind out an Artemus Ward column each week would have resulted in the dreariest drivel and would have ruined forever what little reputation I had made.

I bring these quotations to the support of Ernest Hemingway, whose resistance to that arty-looking but pecuniary ambition which constitutes the real drive behind most contemporary American writing, seems to me genuinely wise and courageous. In a dispute with Westbrook Pegler about the literary value of "dirty" words—where I also agree with Hemingway provided the words are used *as* dirty, and not with a noble resolution to use them until they grow clean—he says:

> I do not know how Mr. Pegler really feels because Mr. Pegler has to be funny once a day, or make it six days a week, the year around and when anyone has to do that it is often difficult to know how he feels exactly about anything, except getting his piece done.

4. Remember the Difference Between Cracking Practical Jokes and Conveying Ludicrous Impressions

This difference has been talked about enough in previous chapters. I will only remind the reader that by a practical joke I do not mean setting a can of water on the upper edge of a door and then calling someone in the next room—although that is a practical joke and a good one, especially if the person does not come, and you forget what you wanted him for and get up and go after him yourself. By a practical joke I mean a joke whose humor hinges upon a frustrated action, whether of your own or somebody else's, whether of the mind or body, and whether it signifies or "comes to" anything or not. By "conveying ludicrous impressions" I mean conveying ludicrous impressions.

The reason it is important for a practicing comedian to bear this difference in mind is that the two kinds of humor work differently. The previous three laws apply to them both, but the next four apply with full force only to practical jokes. Practical jokes, for instance, as we shall see in a minute, have to start off *plausibly* and collapse *suddenly*. A ludicrous impression can be preposterous right from the start, if the comedian has your interested attention; and suddenness, although it may add a charm, is wholly unessential to it. "Neatness," so almost absolute a law for practical jokes, would be the strangulation of poetic humor. And "timing," although it has a value in all arts, is not the crucial thing in painting funny pictures that it is in making witty cracks.

"You're a Liar!"

Artemus Ward's first lecture in New York is remembered by the tribute he paid to his absent pianist, who, he said, "always wore mittens when playing the piano." Plausibility and suddenness have nothing to do with the humor of a remark like that. There is nothing in it that could be "neat," and little that could be regulated as to timing.

Mark Twain anticipated this law in explaining how to tell what he called a "humorous," as opposed to a "witty" or a "comic," story. He meant by a humorous story what we mean by poetic humor; he meant conveying ludicrous impressions. And he described the difference thus:

> The humorous story may be spun out to great length, and may wander around as much as it pleases, and arrive nowhere in particular; but the comic and witty story must be brief and end with a point. The humorous story bubbles gently along, the others burst.

All versatile story-tellers are aware of this difference, however they describe it. Stephen Leacock says:

> "Of funny stories there are, in point of construction, two kinds. In one kind all the fun, all the joke, turns on the dénouement, the end—what sometimes is called the 'nub'. . . . There is no fun, no amusement in the story until the end is reached. The listener must wait for it." In "the other class, the far smaller class . . . the story is amusing all through. . . . We laugh as we listen. . . . In the case of the *nub* story the listener agonizes and then explodes. With the other kind he comes to a boil and stays there."

"Aw—Shut up! This is a Free Country!"

Both Mark Twain and Leacock seem to prefer the poetically humorous story to the one that waits entirely for the "nub" or point, but Mark Twain's preference is violent.

> "The humorous story"—he says—"is strictly a work of art—high and delicate art—and only an artist can tell it; but no art is necessary in telling the comic and witty story; anybody can do it."

Another difference in their opinions is that Leacock thinks the "nub" class comprises "ninety-nine per cent of all stories told in America"—which would seem to imply that in other countries a better proportion might prevail. Mark Twain, on the contrary, asserts that "the art of telling a humorous story—understand, I mean by word of mouth, not print—was created in America, and has remained at home. . . . To string incongruities and absurdities together in a wandering and sometimes purposeless way, and seem innocently unaware that they are absurdities, is the basis of the American art, if my position is correct."

To me his position seems correct, and seems but an incident in the general theme of our digression—that a fuller cultivation of poetic humor is what distinguishes the American art.

In that phrase "string incongruities and absurdities together in a wandering and sometimes purposeless way," Mark Twain has, at any rate, distinguished the technique of poetic humor from that of practical jokes in strict accord with our theory. Poetic humor being, broadly speaking, the playful enjoyment of a mess, the messier it is, within the limits of patience, the better. The loose, rambling, fantastically inconsequential monologues of Ed Wynn—the old and great Ed Wynn of the vaudeville stage, I mean—are a modern example. They did contain jokes and witticisms, as did those of Artemus Ward, and to these our further laws apply. But whatever such incidental values they may carry, a total want of any structure to carry them upon is their essential charm. They mull around and get mixed up and meander. Their technique, if they have any, is to add the charm of logical inconsequence and slow progress, or no progress at all, or progress backwards, to the other qualities and combinations of qualities, unendurable to a serious mind, with which they delight the feelers of a mind at play.

"An' you mean to tell me that that dog ain't got no fleas?"

5. Be Plausible

By plausibility I mean successfully leading a person on. And that this is necessary if you are going to fool him is obvious. Indeed this law derives so directly from our definition of wit, and of comic action in its practical form, as to need no special elaboration. When a comedian, going somewhere in great haste, jumps into the side car of a motor-cycle, and the motor starts and the driver and the two wheels rush away without him, it is very important that his hurried intention and expectation should seem real. His acting at that point must be perfect. He must take the audience with him wherever he *purports* to be going.

The words in a jocular sentence or dialogue must behave in the same way. They must take the reader along. The first joke Art Young ever had published—way back in 1887—was a picture of a boy dragging a dog by the neck, and an irate old gentleman exclaiming, "Why, this is an ignominy!" "Naw, 'taint," the boy said. "It's nuthin' but an ordinary pup." It is ludicrous to call a breed of dog ignominy, a name better suited I think to a species of lizard, but still there is a condescension in our giggle at this joke. It is because we know that an old man under those circumstances would not say, "Why, this is an ignominy!" We balk right there, and suspect a trick, and refuse to go along with our whole minds and hearts. The joke lacks plausibility.

Compare for contrast Joe Penner's best line in *Collegiate.* He has lost his memory and is going around trying to find out who he is. He meets a sympathetic girl who says:

"I don't know who I am either. I was left on a doorstep."

"Maybe you're a bottle of milk."

That too finds its chief value in a ludicrous suggestion, but it is also perfect as a trick. What the girl said was exactly what she would say, and what you wanted her to say. She carried you along. Moreover she was the kind of a girl you like to have carry you along.

Fred Allen made this announcement the other day over the radio:

> Next Sunday the Reverend Dr. Jones will preach on "Skiing on the Sabbath" or "Are Our Young Women Backsliding on Their Week-Ends?"

He placed a barely perceptible, but helpful, accent on the word *ends.* A joke which plays as complicated a trick as that, and yet retains a flawless plausibility, is entitled to praise. I quote it because I hate to disfigure this page with one of the daily thousands of radio jokes that, for lack of plausibility, are entitled to contempt. Suffice it to say that the air is full of artificial and faked-up jokes, jokes in whose take-off the listener can not honestly participate, and which therefore play no genuine trick upon his mind.

In private life many excellent jokes fail of plausibility because of the faltering or diffident manner in which they are told. It is hard for a shy person to make people laugh except at shyness. He may carry them with him logically, but emotionally they will drop off. By the same token the one trait indispensable to a comedian is confidence. As Mark Twain said when discussing his famous flop when trying to have fun with the literary divinities of New England: "If I showed doubt, that can account for it, for you can't be successfully funny if you show that you are afraid of it." What accounted for his failure was the dearth of plausibility and overplus of hard labor in the speech itself, but what he says there about "showing that you are afraid of it," is true and absolute. The law of plausibility applies to feeling-attitude as well as meaning.

6. Be Sudden

This law is designed to protect the public against five crimes on the part of story-tellers. First, giving away the point in advance; second, turning a joke into a conundrum; third, merely alluding to the possibility of a joke instead of cracking it; fourth, telling stale jokes; and fifth, repeating the "nub" of a joke after everybody has got through laughing at it.

As we saw on page 43, a witty joke, being a trick upon the laugher's mind, has to be kept up the sleeve and then "sprung" or "cracked" suddenly. This necessity for suddenness has been the inner and insoluble mystery in all books on laughter and the comic, but for us there is no mystery. If you give the victim of a trick a hint what is coming, permitting him to accommodate himself in advance, there is no trick. To go back to that all-clarifying baby again: If Miss Washburn, instead of swinging him out toward the arms of the mother and "rapidly withdrawing him," had started him tentatively in a maternal direction, at the same time giving him a slight impulse toward the father, and then finally, passing the mother, had carried him to his father's arms, he might have been interested, but he would not, certainly, have gurgled and crowed.

The same thing holds of the thought-process of an adult. You are fairly likely to laugh if I tell you that a physician after examining a patient said: "Why, there is nothing the matter with you—you need a little change—take a night off and go see Al Jolson," and the man replied: "I am Al Jolson!" But if I say: "Al Jolson consulted a physician, and the physician, not knowing he was Al Jolson, said to him: 'Why, there's nothing the matter with you—you need a little change—take a night off and go see Al Jolson,' and he replied, 'I am Al Jolson!' " you may find the fact interesting, but you will hardly shake down the ceiling with gurgles and crows. Yet nothing is changed here either between Al Jolson and the physician, or between either one of them and you. All the incongruities and absurdities—also the superiorities and degradations—are exactly as they were. The sole thing lost is the suddenness with which a train of thought moving through *your* mind has been wrecked.

That is what is called giving away the point—or in more modern parlance, telegraphing your shots. A still worse crime is turning jokes around and backing them into the mind in such a way that they have no point. A conundrum is a pun in reverse. "Why is an old white horse like a stick of candy?" we ask. And instead of begetting an attitude of expectancy upon which a genuine trick can be played, we have begotten the one thing upon which a trick can not be played—an attitude of inquiry. All we can do now is to give the listener exactly what he is expecting, the answer to our question. If the answer contains a gleam of ludicrous imagery, as it happens to in this case—"The harder you lick it the faster it goes"—the performance is not wholly humorless. And moreover, if the answer is remote and astonishing enough to transcend the scope, or transgress the tentative trend, of the inquiry, so that it is felt as collapsing instead of completing it, there can be some witty humor too. Just as far as it can, however, the conundrum technique, whatever other interests it may satisfy, destroys the humor of a witty joke.

Let us take a witty joke and turn it into a conundrum, and see how ghastly true this is. Mark Twain in his speech at a banquet given by the Army of the Tennessee to General Grant in 1879 made these remarks:

> Among the three or four million cradles now rocking in the land are some which this nation would preserve for ages as sacred things, if we could know which ones they are. In one of these cradles the unconscious Farragut of the future is at this moment teething—think of it!—and putting in a world of dead earnest, unarticulated, but perfectly justifiable profanity over it, too. In another the future renowned astronomer is blinking at the shining Milky Way with but a languid interest—poor little chap!—and wondering what has become of that other one they call the wet nurse. In another the future great historian is lying—and doubtless will continue to lie until his earthly mission is ended.

Suppose, instead of that crack at the historian, so rich in suddenness, Mark Twain had said:

> Gentlemen, let me now ask you a conundrum. Why is our infant historian in his cradle like our future historian at his desk? Give it up? Because they both lie there.

Every witty pun in the world could be turned into a conundrum in this same sickening fashion. Let us flee from the subject.

Another crime against this law is the habit of merely alluding to the possibility of a joke and imagining you have made one. I believe that this crime, so commonly committed by punsters, accounts for the too sweeping disfavor in which puns are held. Take this for instance, from Josh Billings:

> I am no gourmand, for I kan eat bread and milk five days out ov seven, and smak mi lips after I git thru, but if I am asked to eat briled quail by a friend, with judishious accompanyments, I blush at fust, then bow mi hed, and then smile sweet acquience—in other words, I always quail before such a request.

That last is the kind of joke—is it not?—which we instinctively greet with a groan, and a groan that means business. We greet it that way for the very good reason that it is not a joke at all. It does not lead us along in a certain direction depending upon the name of a bird, and allow us suddenly to discover that we are somewhere else by virtue of the similar name of a movement. Nothing of the kind takes place. A bird has been mentioned, and the joker, having thought of a movement bearing the same name, has contrived to mention it; and that is all. And after that he looks up at us and grins—or looks absent and does not grin, whichever his technique—in expectation of a tribute to his ingenuity. It happens, however, that we do not laugh at ingenuity, even though far more impressive than that, but at a joke.

"The invading visiting boat," says Ring Lardner, "was nicknamed *Shamrock,* but they was no sham about the rocking on our little destroyer."

With all respect to the immortal author, that also is not a joke. Perhaps it was when it was born. Perhaps somebody on the destroyer said: "That's the *Shamrock,* isn't it, over there?" and Lardner replied with more than earnestness: "Well, this right here is the real thing."

It is going to be necessary, if American humor is to flourish in the future, to build up a sales resistance to the flood of cheap, flat, silly, and perfunctory and unplayful wise-cracks that are poured out daily upon a long-suffering public—first, by the fruity-throated voices that accompany newsreel pictures with their useless gab, and second, by tired-out comedians working overtime reading other people's skits over the radio. The former evil is the more appalling, because you can not do anything to stop it except not see the pictures. The latter perhaps has arrived, after long wanderings, in just the right place—where you can turn it off. It might be one short step toward abating these nuisances if it were generally understood that a joke is a mental process having a certain sequence, and that merely indicating the existence of the raw materials is not making a joke, and is not funny.

Another crime that this law is designed to protect us from is that of repeating jokes that are already familiar. As everybody knows, there is nothing quite so stale as a stale joke. Other salts do slowly lose their savor, but it is the unique property of wit to be incapable of one entirely effective repetition. We encore a song and dance; we beg for the repetition of a serious story; we buy the pictures we like best and hang them on our own walls until we can not see them; we send notes up to the orchestra asking for the repetition of a favorite dance; and still more strangely, go and get the same girl, if we can, to dance it with us. There is no other pleasure in the world that we would not ask to have repeated before we had forgotten it. But we consider it an act of mercy to stop a man before he tells us a joke we have enjoyed, no matter how delightedly, before. This proves, of course, the crucial relevance of "suddenness," and reveals the reason for it. When somebody proposes to tell a "funny story," we set ourselves to have a trick played upon our mind and take it playfully.* And we can not do this if we know the story. Hence the ancient maxim: Do not spring old jokes. And hence the modern corollary, born of the researches of the air-joke industry: An old joke is anywhere from

*Remember that I am speaking here of stories that trick the mind, not those that amuse the ear or the imagination. Stories of the latter kind, the kind that Mark Twain called "humorous," do of course grow stale, but they lose their humor much more slowly than the "witty" kind. This was proven statistically by H. L. Hollingsworth in the psychological laboratory at Columbia University.

one to fifteen years of age; older than that, they all, potentially, are young again.

And one more minor rule derived from this same law: After you have made people laugh by playing a trick on their minds, do not try to do it right over again by repeating the quintessence of the trick! Try to understand that when you have once said it, it is gone forever—or gone at least for fifteen years.

To ignore this is the common crime of males against the art of humor, an indication that self-complacence and not humor is the emotion that is being enjoyed. The prevailing female crime of giving away the point is an evidence, it seems to me, that nothing is being enjoyed. They both, at any rate, fall under this sixth law, and the penalty for both, when I become the dictator, is death.

7. Be Neat

This law does not mean that a humorist should go round with his shirt-tail tucked in. Nor does it mean that he should speak concisely or write a good prose style. Ed Wynn's bubbly utterance is essential to his humor. Stephen Leacock has no style at all—perhaps that is why he can parody all styles so brilliantly—and Robert Benchley has a style that is weak and lies down frequently to rest. Yet they are all three skilled jokers, and their jokes are usually, in the sense of this commandment, "neat."

Neatness is an attribute of the "points" of jokes. A joke with a point consists, as we have seen, of an original tendency, the break or wrecking of this tendency, the discovery within the wreckage of something else, whether meaning or attitude of feeling, that is satisfactory. And what we call a "neat" joke is one in which the substituted satisfaction lies right *in* the wreckage, or grows immediately out of it. It is a joke which requires no stretching, or patching, or inferential bridgework, or laying down of special rails, to get the train of thought over on the new track.

I will illustrate this quality of neatness with a joke which sins against it flagrantly. When Artemus Ward arrived in San Francisco for his much advertised lecture tour, a leading citizen was on hand at the hotel to invite him to dinner. His trunk, however, had not come up from the steamer, and he was worried about his clothes.

His host said: "Never mind, it doesn't matter what you wear in California."

He answered: "That's fortunate. I never *was* much."

That, I think, is a fair example of a lame, or forced, or far-fetched joke. The words *wear* and *were,* not being identical, either in spelling or sound, have to be fetched into position and spliced together before the joke can walk at all. "*Were* is sometimes pronounced *wear,*" we have to say to ourselves, "and maybe it was on that occasion, and at any rate we must think so for the sake of the joke."

This business of far-fetching and splicing belongs in the category of skilled labor, and therefore, unless redeemed in some way, kills the playful humor of a jest. The fact that Artemus Ward never was *anything at all* in California, having that moment arrived, made this joke not only a lame pun but also a playful understatement, and that, although you may not think so at first glance, went a long way toward redeeming it. Remember that two humor sources welded together yield more humor than the sum of their two separate yields.*

Another fact which greatly braced that joke was, that although far-fetched it was fetched so quickly as to seem a miracle of wit to those who were awaiting one. Admiration for ingenuity often takes the place of comic pleasure in impromptu jokes. Moreover, in humor as in other arts, the master is above all laws.

It is not only against lame, forced, or far-fetched jokes that this seventh law is designed to protect us, but also against jokes which are oversubtle. There is hardly a phrase more often heard in the office of a comic paper, or the studio where a comedy is being concocted, than "That's too subtle—they won't get it." It means that while the joke may be neat for those who are in touch with the subject matter and variously alive to it, it will not flash instantly in the minds of those who are supposed to laugh. It will have to be explained to them,

* "From the harmonious confluence of two pleasure-sources which of themselves amount to little, there arises a greater, often a much greater pleasure-result than . . . can be explained as the sum of their separate action."
(Th. Fechner, *Introduction to Aesthetics.*)

or they will have to explain it to themselves, and that again is labor and destroys the jest.

Our diagrams have shown what neatness is, and can show in general terms what constitutes a violation of it.

The straying line represents an act of sober reflection, an inquiry addressed to the joker, or perhaps even a consultation of the dictionary or the encyclopedia. It represents a serious effort interrupting the free play of the mind.

I want to remark here that there are several different kinds of not-seeing-the-point, and they are not all due to a failure of the sense of humor. There is, in the first place, emotional disinclination to see it, sometimes unconscious as in my stupidity about Soglow's early bird, sometimes half-conscious as in the woman who said: "Well, if it's what I think it is, then I don't see it!" Another kind of not-seeing is due to unfamiliarity with the subject matter. One of my cleverest friends failed to get the line quoted on page 282, "I beg your pardon, I played a fly," merely because, not being musically trained, she is unaccustomed to think of music as being read from a score.

Another kind of not-seeing is due to mental inertia or inflexibility. Some people's brains seem to be so ponderous that a train of thought once it gets started won't stop even for a wreck, to say nothing of getting over on a new track and starting again. My own brains are sometimes, although I think not always, in this condition. At least I am able to illustrate this kind of not-seeing without hurting anybody's feelings but my own. I was in a situation where I particularly desired to appear bright too, being surrounded, after a dinner in my honor, by a "corpse of experts" in English literature. One of them told a story about a man who came to London from Germany and called up a friend on the telephone; the friend was out and he tried to leave his German name, which was Siegmann, with the maid. He spelled it out: S as in sugar, I as in Indian, E as in elephant. . . . "E as in what?" the maid asked, and he laughed so hard that he finally hung up the telephone and gave it up.

Every one of those experts laughed loudly, but I, after giggling and then sitting some time in a duncelike stupor, confessed I could not see why he laughed, or why they laughed either. Can you?

And if you can't, would you have been as noble as I was, and candidly said so, or would you have laughed the hollow laugh—of all hollow things the hardest to make sound as if it contained anything? It is always better, I think, when you fail to see the point, to say so. And then you can restore your pride afterwards by explaining, as I am here, that you are not lacking in the sense of humor, but merely stupid.

Moreover, do not be afraid to say you did not see the point because you gave a titter without seeing it. That was natural and childlike, and if your state was mirthful, quite inevitable. You tittered because you were going somewhere and found yourself nowhere at all, and that is fundamentally what we all laugh at.

The only kind of not-seeing-the-point which is really desperate is the kind exemplified in the Scotchman whom Eli Perkins met on board ship, and who told him that he had heard Artemus Ward in London and could not see any fun in him.

"He is so illogical and says such impossible things."

"What is one illogical thing that Mr. Ward has said?"

"Why, he said he was bound to live within his means if he had to borrow money to do it. Why, he wouldn't be living within his means if he borrowed money. Impossible! How absurd!"

That is not a failure to see—the seeing is accurate—but a failure to see playfully. And that means lack of the sense of humor—another phenomenon which tends to prove our thesis that the sense of humor is a native emotional endowment like anger and fear. As Josh Billings says: "One of the meanest things in the comik lektring employment that a man haz to do, iz tew try and make that large class ov hiz aujience laff whom the Lord never intended should laff." It is a class of people very similar to those who "don't know how to get mad"—or those who "don't know what fear is," as Mark Twain remarked of Clive, Nelson, Putnam and the flea.

I am often asked whether a sense of humor can be learned. It can not be learned in so far as it is a native response. But a great deal can be done to limber its action in people who have been foolishly brought up to associate all real merit with seriousness. Bechterev discovered that the reflex centers of laughter and weeping, "more even than other reflex centers of the same region . . . can show symptoms of excitation through the mere absence of inhibition from the cerebral cortex." * The cerebral cortex is where the conscious self, if any, resides, and if Bechterev is right, there ought to be some hope for those whom the Lord never intended should laugh. You can not, I suppose, teach them to feel the comic feeling, but you can teach them to allow their reflex centers a little free play!

8. Be Right with Your Timing

It is hard to write about this law, because it applies primarily to spoken or acted humor, and its specific application in every case has to be felt. Almost any comedian, if you bring up the subject of his technique, will tell you that "timing is all there is to it." A tennis player will make the same remark about tennis, however, and you may safely remind him that it is also a vital question where you send the ball.

If timing is more important in joking than in any other art except dancing, it is because jokes have to be sprung. They have to come as a pleasantly unpleasant surprise to a mind that is on the way to something else. Therefore, not only must the mind be genuinely on the way (plausibility), and the not-getting-there a genuine surprise (suddenness), but the surprise must come at the instant when the on-the-wayness is most complete, and the surprise most unexpected.

That oversimplification will serve to indicate in general terms the meaning of this law. The best way to see its meaning—and to see in

* Georges Dumas, *Traité de Psychologie,* Vol. I, 694-5.

fact what a joke is, when stripped down to its naked essence—is to watch Bill Robinson dance. Bill Robinson makes jokes out of time itself. He starts a simple tapping rhythm and gets the audience going with him in that rhythm, and just when they are "going good," with a most dexterous suddenness he stops and leaves them in the air. And they laugh. That is what a joke is—getting somebody going and then leaving him in the air. And even when the going is toward a meaning and the progress decorated with words and images, this naked element of time is there, and it has to be handled much as Bill Robinson handles it.

Mae West has a time sense like a dancer. Her droll humor of understatement is often meatier in rhythm than in content. Her Chinese captor, threatening to kill a suspected lover, says: "There are two good men: one is dead and one unborn." She does not answer snappily. She leaves him alone a second with his eloquence; she allows a feeling to gather in the atmosphere. Then she precipitates it with an otherwise not brilliant line: "Which one are you?" To use her own expression in discussing it, she "times her punches like a fighter."

The tendency of American comedy since George M. Cohan has been to obviate this problem of timing by having everything happen *too* fast. The whole performance thus becomes a boisterous exaggeration, and the audience, if they go with you at all, get into a state of semi-hysterical hilarity, in which it does not much matter what you do or when, so long as it is quick and not sensible. The "slow burn," so often employed on the screen by Laurel and Hardy, is more appropriate to understatement, more subtle, infinitely more precarious. Artemus Ward was a master of the "slow burn." If you will imagine yourself doing what he did on the opening night of his momentous lecture course in London, and imagine getting the timing wrong, you will appreciate the importance of getting it right. I quote from an account of the event by J. E. Preston-Murdock:

> The opening night of the show Hingston introduced him in a neat little speech, and claimed the indulgence of those present for any nervousness the entertainer might display on this his first public appearance in London. He said it was a critical moment for Ward, and his fate trembled in the balance. Then Ward rose, came

down to the footlights, and stood silent, casting his deep-set, brilliant eyes over the vast audience, and twiddling his thumbs in the most unconcerned way. A minute or two passed; under such circumstances it seemed much longer. The audience became fidgety. I heard one gentleman sitting near me exclaim to a lady at his side: "What a fool! Why doesn't he say something?" Once more a silence fell upon the assembly, but the imperturbable man stood twiddling his thumbs. A murmur of disapproval swept like a wave over the audience, then a little more clapping, a little more stamping, followed by a silence during which a pin might almost have been heard to fall. At last, in his inimitable drawl, Ward spoke:

"Ladies—and—gentlemen. When—you—have—finished this—unseemly interruption, I guess I'll begin my discourse."

It was as if an electric shock had passed through the people. They saw the humor of the situation. They rose to it. And seldom has a showman received such an ovation. The audience almost raised the roof with their cheers and applause, and it was fully five minutes before he could proceed. From that moment he became the idol of London. (Quoted by Don Seitz in his life of Artemus Ward.)

9. Give Good Measure of Serious Satisfaction

This law, like Einstein's theory of relativity, has both a general and a specific application. In general, a jocular person can carry his audience with him and keep them longer, if he does not totally ignore the value-standards of serious life. And in particular, a joke, if it was something of an enterprise to get its initial tendency started and produce a wreck, requires good value in the substituted satisfaction, if anybody is to enjoy it very much.

The General Law

Certain people are born with a hair-trigger sense of the comic, just as others are born with a quick temper, a short-fused sexuality, or a self-starting sense of fright—one of the proofs, by the way, that humorous laughter is an emotional reaction of the same sort as these others. Such people often acquire a habit of cracking jokes or little negligible jocules all day long, and doubling the production at night by paralyzing their inhibitions with alcohol. Their talk is more like a mental disease than a social contribution. It does, in fact, sometimes turn out to be a disease—another indication that playful humor has some separate identity in the nervous system. Drs. Binet and Raymond described the case of a woman to whom "everything around her seemed ridiculous" and who kept on making wise-cracks and laughing intermittently for a period of four months. I have known people in whom the attack lasted, with occasional intermissions for a funeral, or a shipwreck, or an Ashtabula horror, as long as seventy years. It is the most terrible disease in the world, because its victims are not those who get it, but everybody else.

I flatter these patients, however, when I attribute their condition to a quick hereditary sense of humor. It may start with that, but what confirms it is the discovery that they can center the attention on themselves by cracking jokes, and the erroneous inference that this attention is always a delighted one. The disease is, in short, usually an inflammation of the ego rather than the sense of humor. A passion for real humor, or a still living sense of it, would put an end to their apelike chatter as quickly as anything else except a club.

Jokes with no point at all can be funny in an absurd way, as we have seen, but only if their plausibility is deftly managed, their subject matter colorful, and if surrounded with a good magnetic field of humor. The witless day-by-day pouring out of quips and cracks that have no drawing-power in the character of the speaker, no color in themselves, and either no point or a point that is so weak as to be a mockery of something to say, is as far away from humorous absurdity as it is possible to go. To the victims of this habit of facetiousness our seventh commandment says: Remember that even babies require some "social stimulation" before they can enjoy being tickled, and then they can be tickled only by a friend. Remember, also, that we are not babies, but grown-up people accustomed to getting something for the expenditure of our attention. Or in other words it says: "Get the hell out of the building and leave us alone!"

A very different misfortune from this fixed habit of wise-cracking, and yet sometimes similar in result, is the unrestrained fit of foolishness. It does no harm if people get foolish together. On the contrary, the foolisher, the better. I at least have only pity for those who never rolled on the floor in laughter at a most utter nothing, and staggered up at last, praying with aching cheeks and chest for mercy, and yet refreshed and comforted, and proud, if anyone should raise the question, that they could be carried away by so beneficent a passion. I find no grain of sense in the dictum of Plato that "persons of worth should not be represented as overcome by laughter." That is of a piece with his banishment of poetry from the ideal republic, a self-punitive rather than a moral crusade—a big bluff in other words, a Spartan bluff on the part of one who knew too well that he was incorrigibly Athenian. Gorky tells how Lenin loved to laugh, and "laugh till the tears came, till he choked with laughter," and remarks that "to laugh like that one must have the soundest and healthiest of minds." Lenin was, in my opinion, the nearest this world has come to Plato's idea of the "Guardian," the philosopher without self-interested ambition who should rule an ideal state. Moreover, I have never seen a man to match him in completely stable equilibrium, mental, physical and emotional. Gorky may be right in associating with this the gift of being "overcome by laughter." He is far more right than Plato was.

However, if it happens to a joker to be overcome by laughter, and does not happen to his audience, that is a disaster. He may be laughing with inalienable right at *nothing,* but they meanwhile are sitting there longing to join him, but devoutly yearning for a tiny *something* to help them start. It would be better to give them something—give them, I mean, a taste of serious satisfaction. I notice that Frank Sullivan, the first and only man to carry the humor of the laughing fit into literature, rarely leaves a piece of nonsense absolutely pure for long. Take his piece on "Celebrity Bumping," for instance. Here is a section of it:

> The recent bumping of the Hon. Winston Churchill by an automobile on Fifth Avenue interested me very much, as I am quite a celebrity-bumper myself. When I read of the bumping I was curious to know whether it was an accident or whether the young man who did the bumping shared my hobby; i.e., did it *pour le sport*. Later I learned that it *was* an accident; that the young man was not a professional celebrity-bumper and that on the contrary he was stricken with remorse at having bumped a gentleman of such eminence.

> As a matter of fact, I had quietly suspected he was not a professional. In the first place, the bumpee was knocked down. I never knock them down. I am all for painless bumping. I graze my celebrities lightly and pass on. . . .
>
> In any case, I should never bump Mr. Churchill. I should never bump any British statesman. British statesmen have enough troubles as it is, and anyhow I learned long ago that as bumpees they are veritable pushovers. It is really no fun to run them down. This is partly because our strange traffic system bewilders them, and partly because they are British statesmen. . . .
>
> I once did bump a Winston Churchill, by the way, but he was not a British statesman. He was an American author who had written a book called *The Inside of Will Cuppy*. . . .

You see how that vicious and real crack at British statesmen—that solid and noble gratification to the insulting instinct—bucks us up and gives us a fresh enthusiasm for the ensuing nonsense? That is what I mean by saying that *in general* a humorist, even so contagiously hilarious a one as Frank Sullivan, must have a thought for serious satisfactions.

The Specific Law

Our first commandment was that humor ought to appeal to some interest, and we saw subsequently that a joke, properly so called, appeals to two interests—or a two-way-traveling interest—one of which is disappointed, the other satisfied. What this commandment has to add is, that if you make a considerable fuss about engineering the disappointment—if your joke is something of a perpetration—and then the satisfaction turns out to be trivial and perfunctory, your wit will be condemned as flat. The process called "twisting" or "switching" is a cure for this. You keep the form and mode of operation of the old joke, but apply it to a livelier matter.

The story is told by Cicero about a man who came weeping to his friend and said that his wife had just hanged herself on a fig tree in his garden. The friend, also a married man, said: "I wonder if I might procure some slips of that same tree to plant in my garden?"

King George II, when some enemies of General Wolfe told him that the general was mad, said: "I wish you could persuade him to bite some of my other generals."

Abraham Lincoln, when some temperance cranks came complaining of General Grant's drinking so much whisky, said: "I wonder if you could get me a few barrels of that same whisky for my other generals."

Those three jokes illustrate the process of twisting, and how far it can go. W. E. Woodward, who is writing a lively history of the United States, tells me that Lincoln himself denied that he ever made that remark. "Lincoln was too good a politician," he added. But if Lincoln was a politician, we still do not know whether he made the remark or not.

At any rate he ought to have made it. And you will see how far from a flat joke it was, if you will go back and imagine the situation in which it was attributed to him: the doubtfulness of Grant's early tactics around Vicksburg, the recent criticisms of this, the whispering campaign against Grant's morals, the downright fact that he drank heavily and got drunk, his victory at Vicksburg offsetting that, a widespread liking for good liquor also offsetting it, a widespread distaste for temperance cranks (especially among those who love to laugh), a tense anxiety and a terrific doubt. Go back and imagine that, and imagine, if you can, a genuine humorist in the White House, the first and last one that ever got in there, and the whole situation precipitated, the national sky cleared, with a joke—you will see what our law means, in the specific sense, by saying: Give good measure of serious satisfaction.

10. Redeem All Serious Disappointments

Our second commandment declared that the feeling-attitudes aroused by a humorist, especially those to be tricked and disappointed, must not be too strong and deep. They must be feelings whose frustration can be taken playfully. This tenth commandment is a modification of that one. You can disappoint a pretty strong feeling, it declares, if your joke finds its point in a strong satisfaction.

I illustrated the second commandment with the effect upon me of Otto Soglow's story of an early bird—the lyric enthusiasm with which

I joined that bird in his flight across the morning sky, and how his sudden death so wrenched my heartstrings that I could not find the humor of the joke. I blamed this upon the frailty of my heartstrings. But there was another factor too. That was that I have no grudge against early birds, nor against proverbs which celebrate their virtues. I am not a late riser. I do not know how to snooze. I regard the morning as the best part of the day, and everything after the noon meal, other things being equal, as a fading out of colors. Thus the satisfaction which gives this tale so sharp a point for many people, that of successful and complete revolt against the entire doctrine of the early bird, hardly has existence in my breast. For me, therefore, the bird's untimely end was not only sad, but *unredeemed*.

Perhaps all that I am proving here is that the application of these humor laws is largely individual. There is a truth in Groucho Marx' thought that comedy is more difficult to write than tragedy because men laugh at wholly different things. A joke, at least, is not a simple entity like good or bad news. A joke is a compound, a procedure, a thing made up of delicately adjusted elements. That is the reason why, besides the eight laws which control its total operation, there are these two laws relating to the equilibrium to be kept up between its parts. Let us sum up these last two laws once more.

9. If the arousing and frustrating of the initial tendency is an *extensive* operation, then the substituted satisfaction must stand up visibly in the wreckage, or the joke will be condemned as flat.

10. If the arousing and frustrating is an *intensive* operation—if the matter carries a strong feeling, so that the disappointment tends to be serious—then the satisfaction too must be intense. Otherwise the joke will be condemned as unsensitive or vulgar, flip or flippant, or whatever term for violated feelings lies at hand.

It is largely an individual matter, but there is also such a thing as knowing your audience. There is such a thing as calculating the degree and kind of satisfaction necessary to redeem a violated feeling, and turn a shocking flippancy into a jovial and immortal joke. This may be seen in the remark with which Mark Twain brought to an electric climax that famous banquet of welcome to General Grant of which I have already spoken. I quote the story from Mark Twain's autobiography.

> My own speech was granted the perilous distinction of the place of honor. It was the last speech on the list, an honor which no person, probably, has ever sought. It was not reached until two o'clock in the morning. . . . There was only one thing in it that I had fears about, and that one thing stood where it could not be removed in case of disaster.
>
> It was the last sentence in the speech.
>
> I had been picturing the America of fifty years hence, with a population of two hundred million souls, and was saying that the future President, admiral, and so forth, of that great coming time were now lying in their various cradles, scattered abroad over the vast expanse of this country, and then said "and now in his cradle somewhere under the flag the future illustrious commander-in-chief of the American armies is so little burdened with his approaching grandeur and responsibilities as to be giving his whole strategic mind at this moment to trying to find some way to get his big toe into his mouth—something, meaning no disrespect to the illustrious guest of this evening, which he turned his entire attention to some fifty-six years ago——"
>
> And here, as I had expected, the laughter ceased and a sort of shuddering silence took its place—for this was apparently carrying the matter too far.
>
> I waited a moment or two to let this silence sink well home, then, turning toward the general, I added:
>
> "And if the child is but the father of the man there are mighty few who will doubt that he succeeded."

The effect of that act of redemption was described at the time in one of Mark Twain's boyishly exuberant letters home to "Livy":

> When I closed with "And if the child is but the prophecy of the man, there are mighty few who will doubt that he succeeded," I say it who oughtn't to say it, the house came down with a crash. For two hours and a half, now, I've been shaking hands and listening to congratulations. Gen. Sherman said, "Lord bless you, my boy, I don't know how you do it—it's a secret that's beyond me—but it was great—give me your hand again."
>
> And do you know, Gen. Grant sat through fourteen speeches like a graven image, but I fetched him! I broke him up, utterly! He told me he laughed till the tears came and every bone in his body ached. (And do you know, the biggest part of the success of

the speech lay in the fact that the audience *saw* that for once in his life he had been knocked out of his iron serenity.)

In that carefully calculated practical joke upon the minds and feeling-attitudes of an audience, you see, again as though in a slow-movie, exactly what the mechanism of all wit is. In the unpleasant image playfully presented of the military hero and ex-president of the republic in an infantile contortion, you see what poetic humor is. In the concluding tribute to the hero, you see how the comic enjoyment of both these unpleasantnesses can be sanctioned and certified in the mind of an adult by inserting into the heart of them a serious satisfaction. It is a good place to stop, for it summarizes our subject. It also summarizes our digression—for I do not know any other people in history who would have given their humorist the place of honor at such a banquet, or whose humorist would have fulfilled his function with just that deed of wit and ludicrous imagination.

Supplementary

SUPPLEMENTARY

Some Humorists on Humor

IN VIEW OF THE CLOSE RELATION of humor to play, and of play to infancy, I have based my argument in this book very largely on babies. Grown-up people are amateurs in laughter; babies are the real thing. If there is any exception to this rule, it is the professional humorists and comedians—people so exceptionally endowed with comic feeling and perception that they keep on laughing or causing laughter a good deal of the time all their lives. Their testimony, if you can find any common element in it, might be almost as valuable as that of the babies. For this reason I have, whenever the occasion offered, discussed the problem of laughter and the comic with men and women of this profession, and I list their answers here.

The question I found most provocative, when a mere raising of the general problem was not enough, was this: "What do you think of the idea that there is hostility, or a feeling of superiority, in all laughter—or, to put it in another way, that all jokes are 'on' somebody, and that all laughter is at bottom ridicule?" In one or two cases I quoted a sentence from Bergson as illustrating an eminent authority who takes that view.

The answers are necessarily fragmentary, and they are—except where I quote from a letter or a printed statement—obviously not reasoned opinions in defense of which the authors are prepared to face the firing squad. For this reason I omit the quotation marks. But they were immediately and carefully written down, and their offhand character makes them, from my point of view, all the more valuable. I preface them with a few quotations from men famous for their wit and humor in the past.

"Laughter always arises from a gaiety of disposition, absolutely incompatible with contempt and indignation."

VOLTAIRE.

"If I laugh at any mortal thing,
'Tis that I may not weep."

BYRON.

"And when the heart in the body is torn,
Torn and bleeding and broken,
We still have laughter beautiful and shrill."

HEINE.

"The jest has no other purpose but its own being—the poetic bloom of its nettle does not sting, and one can scarcely feel the blow of its flowering switch full of leaves. . . . Laughers are good-natured and place themselves often in rank-and-file with those they laugh at; children and women laugh most; the proud self-comparer the least; and the harlequin who holds himself worthless laughs over everything, and the proud Mussulman over nothing. No one is ashamed of having laughed, but we should be ashamed of such a gross elevation of ourselves as Hobbes describes. And finally, no laugher takes it badly, but right well, if a hundred thousand others laugh with him, and thus a hundred thousand self-elevations surround his; which would be impossible if Hobbes were right."

JEAN PAUL RICHTER.

"Jests which slap the face are not good jests."

CERVANTES.

"Anatomically considered, laughing iz the sensation of feeling good all over, and showing it principally in one spot. . . .

"Laughing iz just as natural to come to the surface as a rat is to come out of his hole when he wants to.

"You can't keep it back by swallowing any more than you can the hiccups.

"If a man *can't* laugh there is some mistake made in putting him together, and if he *won't* laugh he wants as much keeping away from as a bear-trap when it is set. . . .

"Genuine laughing is the vent of the soul, the nostrils of the heart, and it is just as necessary for health and happiness as spring water is for a trout. . . .

"I say laugh every good chance you can git, but don't laugh unless you feel like it, for there ain't nothing in this world more hearty than a good honest laugh, nor nothing more hollow than a heartless one.

"When you do laugh open your mouth wide enough for the noise to get out without squealing, throw your head back as though you was going to be shaved, hold on to your false hair with both hands and then laugh till your soul gets thoroughly rested."

JOSH BILLINGS.

"I laugh because I must not cry—that's all, that's all."

ABRAHAM LINCOLN.

"Everything human is pathetic. The secret source of humor itself is not joy but sorrow. There is no humor in heaven."

MARK TWAIN.

* * *

I don't think that superiority idea is true at all. The funny people you like best are the ones you laugh *with*. There's Benchley, for instance. You live through his troubles with him—they are your own troubles—and that is why you enjoy them so particularly. A humorist, I think, is just balancing on the edge of the dumps.

DOROTHY PARKER.

Of course they are often sympathetic with me while they laugh! Playful pain—as you say—that is what humor is. The minute a thing is overtragic it is funny.

CHARLIE CHAPLIN.

To get a belly laugh you have to destroy something, either in the object or in the person who appreciates the joke. But humor has to have a background of sympathy too. You laugh at somebody and then you go up and give him a dime. . . . If you think you're better than he is, it's no good.

RUBE GOLDBERG.

"I must say that, in writing, my feelings about my characters and the harassing activities in which they get involved are not at all those of superiority or hostility but something very like compassion. I sense the sadness in all their triumphs and the 'jokes' in their catastrophes. I never feel superior when a hero or a villain stubs his toe and falls on his fanny—I only hark back in memory to times when I have done the identical thing and my laughter is philosophical, slightly shamefaced and pretty close to tears.

"It seems to me that this is the basis of reactions to figures like Chaplin, Mickey Mouse, and Donald Duck and that the audience is not sitting in superior amusement but is rather translating its own activities into those of the futile little souls on the screen and laughing at them with brotherly understanding and sympathy. In my own case, every pie that hit Chaplin has also hit me. This certainly is not superiority."

ANITA LOOS.

Humor is based on defeat. It overcomes defeat by disparaging the goal. My own humor is the product of inferiority. The first manifestation came when as a boy I was persecuted—called duck-lip by the other boys. I found out that I could kid. I began calling myself duck-lip before they could get to it, and then I turned the kidding on them too. My comic hero would be a man who overcame death, not by religion, but by humor, a man who could laugh at the electric chair as he walks to it.

DONALD OGDEN STEWART.

Franklin P. Adams agrees with me that humor is an elementary emotion, and his further contribution to the discussion is described on page 90.

It seems to me that the common denominator of humor is the contact of incongruous ideas. This mixture causes a series of little explosions as in an internal combustion engine. More often than not the joke is at somebody's expense but sometimes it pays its own way.

Jests, I observe, can be reactionary as well as radical. There is a school of humor, popular in newspapers and magazines, which holds that anything which is different from what it used to be, has high risibility.

HOWARD BRUBAKER.

I don't know what humor is, but I always know in advance whether a thing is going to be funny. In a piece with two hundred and fifty laughs in it, not more than one or two will be unexpected. If I say to a man: "Here's a nickel—drop down to the corner and get me a cigar," and he drops through a trapdoor and disappears, I know that the total surprise will make everybody laugh, but I can't tell you why.

JOE COOK.

"Humor is the coward's livery, and there is great wisdom in the popular challenge 'Laugh that off.' For generally we laugh at the things which we are afraid to face and fight. If the story of Peter in the high priest's house were more detailed, we should probably find that some funny remark accompanied his denial of association with Christ.

"Humor is grit in the evolutionary process. 'Does it matter?' is the underlying mood in almost every expression of humor. And, of course, it does matter.

"'Oh, he takes himself too seriously,' is the standardized set-up to tangle the feet of all marching men.

"The heart's breath which is needed to keep on going when the taste of blood is in the mouth can easily be dissipated in a laugh. Of course, there are situations in which humor eases tension. People can and do forget their troubles when the clowns perform. But I can't see that this is signal service. Troubles are not solved by the simple process of forgetting them. I've never seen one laid except by those who had the nerve to keep on boring in and swinging, and the man

The Timid Soul

said to be worth while who can smile when everything goes dead wrong is a quitter who is just about ready to heave in the sponge and make a jest of all his tribulations.

"When the sense of humor is very strongly developed something else must be atrophied. People who laugh a great deal are not truly quick but are actually unimaginative. No man who uses his eyes to observe all the things which lie within his range of vision can possibly avoid the conclusion, 'What is there to laugh at?' . . .

"Of course, this is too sweeping."

HEYWOOD BROUN.

"I suspect that Bergson was nearly right when he said that all laughter at the expense of someone else is really founded on a 'feeling of superiority,' on the part of the amused person over the victim of the incident which arouses the laughter . . . However, it may often happen that laughter will be aroused by the statement of an obvious or well-known fact in an entirely new way."

GEORGE ADE.

People often write in and ask me to use them in a comic strip, but how can I use them? I have to ridicule people. . . .

Yes, you've got to make fun of somebody. People laugh when they see somebody fall down. That's the typical laugh. But if he doesn't get up, they stop laughing.

GEORGE MACMANUS.

Laughter can be sympathetic too. The really great humorists laugh at themselves. Look at Chaplin, for instance, the greatest of them all.

MILT GROSS.

I myself feel sympathetic—definitely so.

H. T. WEBSTER (speaking of *The Timid Soul*).

A humorist is a man who feels bad but who feels good about it. The nearer humor is to pain, the longer it is apt to last.

DON HEROLD.

There are all kinds of humor. Some is derisive, some sympathetic, and some merely whimsical. That is just what makes comedy so much harder to create than serious drama; people laugh in many different ways, and they cry only in one.

GROUCHO MARX.

An audience doesn't laugh without contrast, and the contrast must be abrupt enough to amount to a shock. If you let an action hang fire long enough to give them a chance to detect what's coming and digest it, they won't laugh at all. Moreover the line of action that surprises them must rise naturally out of the situation. No matter how funny it is intrinsically, they won't laugh if it isn't something that might have been done or stated seriously.

To my mind the person who sees the humor of a situation is often more sympathetic than the person who doesn't. There is a sentence in *Tom Sawyer Abroad,* a very bad book most of it, which illustrates the kind of humor I like best. Their balloon landed in a desert somewhere and some lions came after them. They just barely got in and got away in time, and Tom looked back down at the disappointed lions. "I couldn't help seeing their side of it," he said.

THOMAS MITCHELL.

I never saw anything funny that wasn't terrible. If it causes pain, it's funny; if it doesn't, it isn't. I try to pretend that it isn't painful. I try to hide the pain with embarrassment, and the more I do that, the better they like it. But that doesn't mean they are unsympathetic. Oh no, they laugh often with tears in their eyes. Only of course it mustn't be *too* painful. I never would try to make love funny, for instance. I was in love once myself, and that's too painful—that's too painful!

W. C. FIELDS.

When people laugh at a play or a picture, that means they really like it. They like it, I think, because laughing is doing something. The kind of art most people don't really like, although they pretend to, is the kind you just contemplate without doing anything yourself.

DENYS WORTMAN.

There is superiority in most of the humor that is popular now—the *New Yorker* style of humor. But it isn't true of my humor. I describe what I call humor this way—I don't know whether this will mean anything or not—I call it "the possible impossible," or "the practical impractical." I mean you think it is going to work all right, but it won't.

AL FRUEH.

I pondered that question of the social attitude of the humorist endlessly when I started out to write. Mark Twain was my model and I studied his method. I concluded that what Mark Twain was saying to mankind as a humorist was this: "Look what fools we are, and I at the head of the procession!" I concluded that a man who can't laugh and doesn't laugh—fundamentally—at himself, is not a humorist in the full sense.

IRVIN S. COBB.

"The savage who cracked his enemy over the head with a tomahawk and shouted 'Ha! Ha!' was the first humorist. Here began, so to speak, 'the merry ha! ha!' the oldest and most primitive form of humor. It seems odd to think that even today when we give our acquaintances the 'merry ha! ha!' over their minor discomfitures, we are reproducing true to type, the original form of humor. . . .

"But . . . humor, in its highest form, no longer excites our laughter, no longer appeals to our comic sense, no longer depends upon the aid of wit.

"We have recalled the picture of little Huckleberry Finn floating down the Mississippi on his raft or discussing with his Nigger Jim the mysteries of the Universe. We have seen the poor debtors of Dickens' debtors' prison, with their broken lives, their pots of porter, their tawdry merriment, their pitiable dignity and their unutterable despair. Such pictures as these call forth a saddened smile of compassion for our human lot; it all seems so long past, so far in retrospect, that the pain is gone.

"Such is the highest humor. It represents an outlook upon life, a retrospect as it were, in which the fever and fret of our earthly lot is contrasted with its shortcomings, its lost illusions and its inevitable end. The fiercest anger cools; the bitterest of hate sleeps in the churchyard; and over it all spread Time's ivy and Time's roses, preserving nothing but what is fair to look upon."

STEPHEN LEACOCK.

I don't know what humor is. Anything that's funny—tragedy or anything, it don't make no difference, so you happen to hit it just right. But there's one thing I'm proud of—I ain't got it in for anybody. I don't like to make jokes that hurt anybody.

WILL ROGERS.

Humor is a very high form of intelligence. If people weren't too dumb to see it, it would blow them into smithereens. I can't imagine myself hitting anybody even in a dream, but I want the world to be what I want it to be, and if I didn't I wouldn't write. Humor is meant to blow up evil and make fun of the follies of life.

WILL CUPPY.

Ridicule is just one phase of humor and is not always the basis for a laugh, although it's a sure-fire short cut. In ridicule, too, all those who laugh are not necessarily amused. Sympathy may be aroused for the poor fellow who is the object of ridicule.

MAE WEST.

Why we laugh is generally because we have seen or heard something that is at variance with custom. Customarily a man stands upright on his two feet. If he falls down it is considered funny. I see no reason why we should be amused at his fall, except on the theory that he is supposed to keep his balance like everybody else. . . . Analyze most jokes, and you will find that the reason that they are jokes is because they depart from the accepted standard of conduct or of things. Dialect, side whiskers, new theories, new styles will always be subjects for jesting until they become customary. Of course to enlightened imaginative people a sheeplike acceptance of custom is sometimes funnier than a departure from it, but enlightened, imaginative people are a small minority.

ART YOUNG.

"Humor is the art of adapting oneself to another temperament. . . . We fancy that the cave man, some primitive brute who argued with a stone ax and disposed of ideas in an adversary by dashing out his brains, might get on well without a sense of humor, provided that his own skull remained uncracked; if once, however, you acknowledge the right of all your fellows to survive, even though they disagree with you, you must learn how to bend to their peculiarities without surrendering your own pet queernesses. It's a great art."

JOHN ERSKINE.

I think that there are several varieties of the Comic, each of which produces laughter or amusement, just as there are several varieties of the Poetic. But it seems to me there are two main divisions.

The first source of comedy is found in the well-known theory of Frustrated Expectation. I explain it this way. Our minds have associated ideas connected by thought-tracks much like the network of a railroad system. Procedure along these tracks gives ideas that are logical, or at least natural or normal. In the comic, however, there is a frustration of this logical process, much as if a train jumped the track, arriving at an unexpected terminus. In the Comic of this sort there is always a gap which must be filled by reasoning and the difficulty, or shock, we feel as comic. Why it should be pleasant, amusing, or funny, is hard to say.

But the second grand division, and undoubtedly the first cause, in psychological development, is the sense of Superiority and Cruelty. Just try this experiment. Tell to several persons the story of an accident you had. I have found that 90% of the hearers laugh. This may sound amazing, but I have seen it tested many times. Especially when you tell of the accident to a group of persons (when you have a sort of mob psychology, reducing the common intelligence). If they see the accident and it is grave, then laughter is inhibited. But the mention of it is, somehow, comic, even when it hasn't the downfall-of-the-pompous element.

GELETT BURGESS.

You ask what is the cause of laughter. Frankly, I don't know. Some people laugh at things that appear to me to have not the slightest vestige of humor, and vice versa. However, to cover it broadly I should say that the cause of laughter is the complete disengagement of the subject from all broader problems by means of humorous words or actions.

The theory that there is hostility, or a feeling of superiority in all laughter, that all jokes are "on" somebody and that all laughter is ridicule, I believe to be a mistaken idea. This is not to say that at some time or other laughter does not assume the form of ridicule.

Therein, I think, lies the difference between satire and humor. Satire is barbed and malicious, and likely to hurt, whereas, the genuine quality of humor is founded on tenderness and gentleness. It is my belief, and I speak from twenty-five years' experience of hearing it, that the most pleasant type of laughter is rarely evoked by touching upon human follies or deformities.

EDDIE CANTOR.

"I have been trying to think of an answer to your query, What is humor? but every time a definition seems within my grasp it flips out like a cake of wet soap, and skids off. I am tempted to the belief that humor is a will o' the wisp, and eludes definition. I am tempted even more to the belief that if I tried to put down a definition of humor, it would seem to me to be inadequate, inaccurate and incomplete; and would remind me of Harry Watson, the comedian. In a scene in a musical comedy he was called upon to eat a plate of soup, and the head waiter asked him how he liked it. Harry's answer was pensive. 'I'm kind o' sorry I stirred it,' he said. Maybe humor is refusing to take yourself, or anyone else, or anything else, too seriously. But if you don't take things too seriously the psychologists tell you that you are engaged in a Flight from Reality. Well, not such a bad idea, I sometimes think, particularly in these troubled times. The difficulty is obvious. One man's humor is another man's poison. A humorist may think he has been writing humor all his life, but somebody else may think he has only been writing prose. What seemed humorous fifty years ago, or ten, may not seem funny now. Trite but true. I am sure of one thing, however. All humor, all laughter, is not based on ridicule; is not due to the feeling of superiority the fellow who has not slipped on the banana peel has for the fellow who has slipped on one. There is humor that is warming, and tender, and friendly. I don't mean whimsy, either. But the humor that has for its object the puncturing of some pretentious balloon, or some pompous stuffed shirt, should be based on ridicule, and good whacking ridicule, too. I am sure of something else, and that is that whenever anyone says to me, 'Oh, you'll like So-and-So. He has such a wonderful sense of humor, he always sees the funny side of things,' I never do like So-and-so. Why is that? In conclusion, if you will allow me to be reminded again, I will be reminded of something a friend of mine, who was what we call 'in his cups,' at the time, once said to Bob Benchley: 'Now, Bob, I don't want you to think I'm not incoherent.'"

FRANK SULLIVAN.

It seems to me people are often sympathetic when they laugh. Take this dog we're working on. He has swallowed a magnet, and he gets in an awful predicament. All the kitchen knives jump out of the drawer when he comes by and go after him. People laugh, but I think they sympathize with the dog. They are glad, not sorry, when he gets out of his trouble. Sometimes little children sympathize too much, and have to shut their eyes during a cruel scene.

WALT DISNEY.

Are all jokes derisive? Definitely no! That philosophy was invented by people who are vicious without laughing and call it humor. Humor has nothing to do with being mean, or not being mean. If a lion laughs he will still eat you. If he's a skunk, it doesn't matter whether he laughs or cries, he smells just as bad.

DAVID FREEDMAN.

You have to enjoy humorous writing while you're doing it. Anybody who says he doesn't is lying (he may, of course, not like to start). You've got to be enjoying it. You can't be mad, or bitter, or irate. If you are it will be no good. . . . The things we laugh at are awful while they are going on, but get funny when we look back. And other people laugh because they've been through it too. The closest thing to humor is tragedy.

My English teacher at Ohio State, Herman A. Miller, told me of something he saw which illustrates this.

One gray and snowy Sunday morning, about 10 o'clock, a smallish husband leading a little fluffy dog on a leash went into a delicatessen store to buy food. Herman said he looked like the cartoon of the Common People in the conventional political caricature. Well, his wife had given him a formidable list of things to buy, so that when he came out of the store both arms were laden with butter, bread, eggs, oranges, etc. It was a problem to handle the dog and the bundles both. Finally, the dog made a lunge and broke away. The man stood there juggling his bundles, dropping one, picking it up, dropping another, calling "Here doggie, here doggie" all the time; then finally setting out onto the icy street, gingerly, in pursuit of the dog. Before he got to it a car rounded a corner and struck the dog and killed it. The little man just stood there blinking, holding his bundles. That was the highest point of sadness in the scene, all right. But then, still bewildered, always the husband who had to get the groceries home, he tried to pick the dog up and still hold the bundles. After dropping the butter and bread he had to drop the dog again to pick them up. In this amazing moment there was that almost crazy laugh, for here so closely joined as to be almost incredible, was pathos and slapstick. Herman used to relate that story to his class and ask their opinion of whether it was funny, sad, horrible, or what. And why.

I think humor is the best that lies closest to the familiar, to that part of the familiar which is humiliating, distressing, even tragic. Humor is a kind of emotional chaos told about calmly and quietly in retrospect. There is always a laugh in the utterly familiar. If a play is going on on the stage, a love scene, say, and from the wings a Scotty should wander on, with muddy paws, having got away from its owner's dressing room, and if the Scotty should jump up on the best sofa and lie down, it would be funnier than if a kangaroo popped in. There'd be a laugh at the kangaroo, too. The laughers would think "that poor sap!" (of the man in the love scene). There you'd have your sense of superiority in a laugh. In the case of the Scotty, however, the laughers would say, "just what Rowdy did when the Smiths called that time." This is my way, anyway, I think. People can laugh out of a kind of mellowed self-pity as well as out of superiority.

Human dignity, the humorist believes, is not only silly but a little sad. So are dreams and conventions and illusions. The fine brave fragile stuff that men live by. They look so swell, and go to pieces so easily.

You know that hysterical laugh that people sometimes get in the face of the Awful. Maybe it's the rockbottom of humor. Anyway it exists.

JAMES THURBER.

Humor is a final emotion like breaking out into tears. A thing gets so bad and you feel so terrible that at last you go to pieces and it's funny. Laughter does just what tears do for you. My life as a humorist began in a Child's restaurant when a waitress spilled buttermilk down my neck. That great smear of white wet coming down over a blue serge suit, and her words, "Jesus Christ!" were the turning point in my career.

E. B. WHITE.

Two things, it seems to me, stand out in your mind after reading these quotations. First, the preponderance of testimony in favor of a genial as opposed to a derisive view of instinctive laughter, and second the frequent recurrence of the idea that humor is closely associated with pain. I regard them, in their general drift, as evidence tending to corroborate my theory.

Notes

IT WAS MY INTENTION to avoid technical argumentation in this book; but a few thoughts about the literature and laboratory reports that have been published since I wrote *The Sense of Humor* so beg for utterance that I am going to offer them a little space in these concluding pages. One is that a number of writers have more or less explicitly conceded that the comic is objectively identical with the unpleasant, but instead of regarding our laughter and our pleasant feeling when we take an unpleasantness playfully as an innate response, subject to the same kind of explanation as tears and a feeling of pain, they have tried to think up some way of making the enjoyment of an unpleasant thing seem *reasonable.*

Freud, for instance, in his addendum on "Humor" (*International Journal of Psychoanalysis,* January 1928) describes humor as the assertion by the ego of its invulnerability, and says that its meaning is: "Look here! this is all that this seemingly dangerous world amounts to. Child's play—the very thing to jest about!" And he tries to explain this achievement on the part of the ego as due to the super-ego's telling him, as it were, to run and play. To me, with all my respect for the author, this sounds almost like the mythological anticipation of a scientific explanation of comic laughter on the basis of innate response. And it is not made a bit more scientific to my ears when expressed in this way: "The subject suddenly effects a cathexis of the super-ego, which in its turn alters the reactions of the ego."

E. F. Carritt ("A Theory of the Ludicrous," *Hibbert Journal,* Vol. XXI, 563) defining the comic as the ugly, tries to justify our pleasure in it by saying that laughter "expresses" our dissatisfaction. He does not explain why we do not experience comic pleasure when we happen to express our dissatisfaction with serious words or brickbats.

Herbert Barry ("The Role of Individual Differences in the Sense of Humor," *Journal of Genetic Psychology,* 1928, Vol. 35, 112-127) after experimenting upon two persons with jokes and association tests, concluded that "topics which are capable of evoking a humorous reaction in an individual seem to be frequently loaded for that individual with an unpleasant emotional effect," and added: "It seems probable that the humor is due to a change of affective tone of the original perception from unpleasant to neutral or pleasant." He tried to make this change seem reasonable by attributing it to a "perception of the unreality" of the unpleasantness when it occurs in humorous narration. I think he would find that his two subjects laugh at the same kind of thing when it really happens, provided their relation to it is such that they do not have to take it seriously.

Norman R. F. Maier in an article which he calls, with some exaggeration, "A Gestalt Theory of Humor" (*British Journal of Psychology,* 1932, Vol. 123, p. 69) tries to make the unreality of the ridiculous the very reason why we do not take it seriously—again as though we never laughed at anything but what is not true, or "only momentarily true."

Donald Hayworth's idea ("The Social Origin and Function of Laughter," *Psychological Review,* 1928, Vol. 35, 367) that laughter, as a mode of communication preceding speech, was *"a vocal signal to other members of the group that they might relax with safety,"* is also an implicit acknowledgment that laughter occurs when something seems to be the matter, and yet is not to be taken seriously.

Laughter no doubt fulfilled this function—and also that of informing parents that all is well among their young, and calling others to share a satisfaction (H. C. McComas, *Psychological Review,* Vol. XXX, 45). But that the play function as I have described it is the primary one, at least of comic laughter, seems to me proven, not only by the example of tickling, but by the illumination that is shed all over the subject of wit and humor the moment you take a firm hold of the distinction between "being serious" and "being in fun." It is not an accident, I think, that my theory alone has produced, or even suggested, the formulation of laws for making good jokes, or at least distinguishing them from bad. When theory is really on the right track, some impulse toward practical application follows as a matter of course.

Page 23: Dr. George W. Crile, a brilliant surgeon whose scientific theories are also brilliant even when not convincing, is the latest to recur to what I call the "mechanical" method of explaining laughter, or rather explaining away laughter. He says that "every one of the causes of laughter, when analyzed, resolves itself into a stimulation to motor activity of some kind." (Which shows that he has never spent five minutes analyzing the causes of laughter.) The laughter, he thinks, results when the stimulated motor activity is for some reason checked, and its value to man as an "adaptive mechanism" is that of a "gymnastic exercise" which "clarifies the body," just as the appropriate motor activity would have, had it not been checked. (*Man An Adaptive Mechanism* by George W. Crile.)

The one example of a cause of laughter which Dr. Crile presents shows just how unrealistic it is thus to ignore the comic emotion, and explain laughter away as an incidental mechanical result of the play of other impulses. He describes a muzzled fox terrier rushing upon a rabbit, and how his muzzle glanced off at each attempt. "These actions were witnessed at various times," he says, "by various scientific visitors, and in every instance the sight provoked laughter. The laughter was undoubtedly due to the fact that in the mind of each onlooker the spectacle of the savage terrier rushing upon the helpless rabbit as if to mangle it aroused a strong desire to exert a muscular act to prevent cruelty. This integration caused a conversion of potential into kinetic energy in the brain cells, and a discharge of activating secretions into the blood stream, for the purpose of producing muscular action. When the danger was unexpectedly averted, the preparation for muscular activity was appropriated by the neutral muscular reaction of laughter."

Now, I believe that if Dr. Crile would forget his theory, and allow himself one moment of realistic introspection, he would know that neither the impulse to exert a muscular act to prevent cruelty, accompanied as it is with a feeling akin to alarm, nor the checking of that impulse, accompanied in the given case with a feeling of relief, has anything whatever to do with the feeling that the situation is comic and the impulse to laugh. But if he is not inclined to introspection, he can prove it by a very simple experiment. There are plenty of people in the world, and some surely in the medical profession, who are not disturbed but gratified to see dogs pounce upon rabbits. Substitute a badger for the rabbit and you have one of the most ancient diversions of the Anglo-Saxon tribe. Will Dr. Crile maintain that all those people who are not moved to rescue the rabbit will also not be moved to laughter, and will fail to feel the comic feeling? Will he maintain that in others the degree of the laughter will be in any way proportional to the strength of the kindly impulse toward the rabbit? Of course not. An impulse to protect a rabbit and an impulse to laugh at a funny situation are two emotional impulses that stand parallel and are subject to the same *kind* of explanation, whatever the explanation may in the long run prove to be. The only reason why Dr. Crile, and so many earnest investigators before him, have sought to explain laughter away as a by-product of the other impulses is that the laugh impulse and its emotion are *not serious*. That is the fact upon which our theory rests, and whether it explains laughter or not, at least it explains these attempts of serious minds to explain it away!

Another recent attempt of this kind is that of J. C. Gregory (*The Nature of Laughter*, 1924) who manages, with a difficulty frankly acknowledged, to achieve the belief that all laughter and all jokes can be subsumed under the concept of "relief."

"A survey of the occasions of laughter," he says, "discovers always, sometimes clearly, sometimes less distinctly and sometimes, perhaps, with difficulty, but discovers always, the common element of"—if he had only said "playfulness," how true it would be!—"relief."

If Mr. Gregory has actually made that "survey of the occasions of laughter," he is one of the few people with a catchword theory of humor who has. He gives, moreover, but a single hint of it in his book, and the hint he gives reveals a deductive approach and a total lack of introspective realism. Here is his illustration of the fact that "relief . . . is evident in a survey of the comic and the humorous":

> A workman engaged in blasting operations dallied too long and went up with the charge. As the unfortunate man went upwards, the foreman drew out his notebook. When the workman received his week's pay a sum corresponding to the time he had spent in the

air was deducted from his wage. The beginning of this story makes a big call on sympathy and the end makes a small one. It is distressing to have even sixpence deducted from one's wage, but it is much more distressing to be dashed into pieces. The sympathies rapidly collected for the major distress are suddenly required only for the minor, and relief clearly pervades the laughter that greets the story.

Now as a matter of simple fact, when Mr. Gregory, after announcing that he was going to tell me a comic or humorous story, proceeded to describe how a workman engaged in blasting operations "went up with the charge," he made not only no "big call," but no call at all upon my sympathy, nor did I find it either a little distressing, or distressing at all, that the man had sixpence deducted from his wage. He might have told the story in such a way that these feelings would be aroused, and the story might still have made me smile, although with a very different flavor of humorous feeling. But he did not do so, and still I found the story funny. Moreover, the story would be funny to people without sympathy either for injured workmen, or for workmen who get their pay docked for no reason. It would be funny to sadistic people who like to see men who get blown up come down dead, and who like to think about workmen starving to death. Therefore it is obvious that all this manipulation of little and big sympathy, even when it occurs, is—like Dr. Crile's impulse of mercy toward the fox terrier—entirely aside from the *humor* of the joke. It is deduced from Mr. Gregory's notion about laughter, and not arrived at through a "survey," to say nothing of an examination, of even this one actual example of the comic.

In other ways Mr. Gregory overworks his catchword beyond the bounds of mercy, being compelled to regard scorn, for instance, as a relief from the fear of a menace, and the smile with which we greet a friend as a relief from the social tension which *would have* existed if he *had been* a stranger. He even forgets at times that relief has to be a relief *from* something. And he forgets always that laughter is itself a thing from which we frequently beg for relief.

"O, enough, Patroclus,
Or give me ribs of steel!"

The best answer to Mr. Gregory, as to all those who try to explain laughter away as an accidental by-product of more serious concerns, is to call attention to the existence of "fits of laughter." Stephen Leacock (*Humor, Its Theory and Technique,* 1935) has described one of these fits admirably. It is the best beginning of a book on humor that I have seen, although the book itself profits little by it, or by anything else that is known about this subject. (Mr. Leacock actually seems to think he is a pioneer in the psychology of humor.)

"Everybody," he says, "has often witnessed the spectacle of a man in an armchair bending over toward another man in another armchair and telling him a funny story. We know it is a funny story because of what happens. The face of the man who is listening begins to be visibly affected. There is a tightening of the maxillary muscles together with a relaxation of the muscles of the lips and tongue. The areas of the east and the west sides of the eyes become puckered in a peculiar way, and in extreme cases (very, very funny stories) there is a distinct wobbling of the ears. In other words the man is smiling. Presently, as the culmination of the story is reached, the listener goes into a form of convulsion, emitting his breath in hurried gasps as if about to shout. His condition reacts upon the story-teller, who now sits back, expands his stomach and goes into a similar convulsion. If we were not absolutely habituated to this, we should be alarmed and think the men were ill. But we know that they are only laughing."

When such a convulsion lasts five or ten or fifteen minutes, and leaves both victims limp in their chairs, exhausted and in pain and crying for mercy, the inappropriateness of describing what they have been doing as "relief" is all too obvious. It can only be described as a seizure of passion. That the passion is not serious, and does not result in any action designed to affect the environment, does not alter this obvious fact. It only helps to explain why the inward feeling attending such convulsions is unique.

Page 33: Mr. Ludovici asserts that if instead of the word "laugh" we always use the words "show teeth," we shall find that this "explains everything." He then proceeds to remark that "animals show teeth, that is to say, they make a deliberate display of teeth, only when they wish to warn a fellow, a foe, or man, of the danger of pursuing certain tactics too far." This he calls an expression of "superior adaptation"—although the fact is that animals unflesh their fangs most often when they are brought into a corner by a power that they fear is superior. A world in which even the animals went around snarling whenever they felt good would be a snarly world indeed. But at any rate, from this lopsided assumption about animals Mr. Ludovici reasons that human beings also show their teeth in a somewhat "volatilized, spiritualized" manner in all those situations in which they "find or feel themselves superiorly adapted . . ." When you realize that Mr. Ludovici is compelled in support of this theory to explain the smile with which we greet a friend as a volatilized snarl due to the fact that "every friend means an access of support, strength and good adaptation," you will see what a fantastic theory it is. Animals snarl at their enemies because they feel *better* adapted than they, and we snarl at our friends because the very support and strength which they bring us makes us feel *well* adapted!

The phrase "superior adaptation" is of course so vague—especially when it can be changed at will to "good adaptation"—that it applies to almost any person at any time who is not sick or in some sort of distress. Therefore it is possible for Mr. Ludovici, with only an average amount of casuistry, to show that this condition is present in a majority of the occasions when laughter occurs. It is indeed usually present when play occurs. He neglects to remark that it is also present in the most normal occasions when laughter does not occur. Which of course makes his argument, if it can be called an argument, entirely valueless, even were it not founded on the false assumption that animals snarl only when they feel superior.

That Aldous Huxley permits himself to be quoted on Mr. Ludovici's jacket to the effect that his is "the best hypothesis" must be put down as one more evidence of the irresponsibility of the literary mind.

* * *

The more rabid advocates of the derision theory are usually, I think, people not interested in general knowledge, but biased by strong hatreds suppressed in themselves, or some unsatisfied craving for place that flows out into every channel of fun.

Mr. Henry A. Murray, describing some experiments made by him at Harvard (*Journal of Abnormal and Social Psychology,* April 1934) corroborates this view.

"The result indicates," he says, "that the enjoyment of derisive humor is associated with the possession of egocentric, individualistic, aggressive and world-derogatory sentiments. Further confirmation of a more decisive sort was obtained from subjective reports and unsolicited autobiographical contributions." And again: "An intense enjoyment of crudely disparaging jokes was chiefly an indication of repressed malice, that is, of an unconscious need for destruction."

Another type inclined to favor the derision theory is the person not himself richly endowed with humorous perception, and for that reason on the whole more laughed against than laughing. He judges all laughter, instinctively, from the point of view of the victim of ridicule.

In *The Sense of Humor,* I explained how, since the comic is the unpleasant taken playfully, the person who causes comic laughter is, if he takes himself seriously, in a humiliating position, no matter how friendly and how free from scorn those may be who enjoy the laughter. It is an inferiority feeling in the person laughed at, not a superiority feeling in the laugher, that is strong and constant enough to give this theory the hold it has upon men's minds.

(This reasoning was beyond Mr. Ludovici, who dismissed my book on the ground of it as "muddle-headed," but I think it can be grasped by the attentive reader.)

The *unaggressiveness* of the human race, its lazy puny-hearted cowardice when compared to other meat-eating animals, is perhaps another thing that makes it preserve so stubbornly this fighting-glory theory of laughter. Men would like to think that when they laugh they are ferocious gorillas, gnashing their teeth and thumping their chests and exulting over a broken foe. They are so certainly not these gorillas at any other time. I am sure I have detected this mood in certain conversational advocates of the derision theory.

It is really the fact that we are social-minded *as well as* spiteful, which makes it so easy to crack derisive jokes. It is easy, I mean, to set our minds going *with* a person we observe or hear about, and thus give ourselves the pleasure of being frustrated as well as delighted, when this person suddenly "gets it in the neck."

Page 174: Albert Nock, in his preface to a recent book of selections from Artemus Ward, takes an opposite view to mine of his significance. He asks why Artemus Ward still lives when so many contemporary jokers are forgotten, and like most Anglo-Saxon essayists he finds a moral reason. I do not know why people who spend half their free time enjoying experiences for their own sake, and the other half talking about them, should, when they come to write essays, have to pretend that every worth-while thing in human life has some moral purpose. But so it is. And it is only this inherent necessity of essay writers for bluffing themselves, I am sure, that explains Mr. Nock's belief that Artemus Ward survives because of his criticisms of American life. He was, to be sure, a sweet, faithful, generous and upright man. And moreover, he expressed a number of opinions—more subtle opinions, considerably, than were expressed by Josh Billings, for example, or Will Rogers, although fewer of them. But so many of his opinions were a mere unimaginative standing pat on the *status quo* that they would obtrude like sandbags and bunkers if quoted in the flight of Mr. Nock's moral eloquence.

His attitude toward the Mormons was Philistine. Upon the subject of woman's rights he was an ordinary male bigot. His one perfectly nonsensical remark on that subject—"The femaile woman is one of the greatest institooshuns of whitch this land can boste"—is worth everything else he said. His attitude toward the welcoming of Negroes in Oberlin College—about which, by the way, he made the same joke that Will Rogers did about the village of Muskogee, Oklahoma, finding it so dark you couldn't make your way around without a light—was, to say the least, unhandsome. Politically he was vague. Like Mark Twain he had no interest in the Civil War—unless having the audacity to say that "it is better to be a coward than a corpse," is having an interest in it. There is nothing in his writings which now appears remarkably farseeing, as does for example Petroleum V. Nasby's satirical lecture on Woman Suffrage. I do not see how anybody who has felt the charm of Artemus Ward's humor, and who sees it in historical perspective, can think that it needs buttressing up with any large or general imputation of moral values. He himself told the whole truth when he said: "I have only drifted with the current, which has carried me gaily on of its own accord. As I am frank enough to say this, I hope I have a right to say that I have always meant the creatures of my burlesques should stab Error and give Right a friendly push." A friendly push! Of course, and who has not? But his place in American and English humor, if not the humor of the world, is unique. He made pure absurdity funny as it had never been before.

Page 276: Merrel D. Clubb (in *The University of California Chronicle*, July 1932) made a "Plea for an Eclectic Theory of Humor," the gist of which was this:

"The work of men like Aristotle, Hobbes, Schopenhauer, Richter, Darwin, Spencer, Lipps, Sully, Bergson, Freud, Dumas, Eastman and Fabre is all too useful to be waved aside. The only way to overcome the defects which are present in the writings of all of them is to attempt that which none of them tried to do, namely to build a harmony out of the surprisingly large number of true statements which have been made regarding the nature of humor. . . . The result would be a new theory, but one new in a really novel way. Moreover, it would inevitably produce a new generalized formula, but the newness would be that of a new combination rather than that of a new word or ingenious phrase. One could not reconcile [these statements] without constructing some sort of higher generalization . . ."

That sounds very wise, and I feel honored to see my name mentioned in such a row of dignitaries, but I must protest that my theory is not the proposal of "a new word or ingenious phrase," but is an attempt to make that higher generalization for which Mr. Clubb so rightly yearns. Laughter, according to my view, may be a response to any pleasant stimulus, and to any unpleasant one that can be taken playfully. Since there is no unpleasant thing which can not in some circumstances, or by somebody, be taken playfully, all experiences whatever, except those to which we are indifferent, may become the occasions of laughter. It would be difficult to invent a higher generalization than that. Even R. S. Woodworth's noncommittal statement (*Psychology. A Study of Mental Life*) that "while laughing is a native response, we learn what to laugh at, for the most part, just as we learn what to fear," does not leave the field any wider open than I do. My idea of progress in this sphere would be to make precise, through an experimental study, the distinction between the laughter of pleasure and the comic laugh, to determine just what is the state called playfulness or being-in-fun, and what are its conditions, and so gradually, in an empirical and verifiable manner, to narrow this generalization, which as it stands is about as wide and high as the universe.

Index

Adams, Franklin P. ("F. P. A."), illustrates essence of humor, 90-91, 332; cited, 95-96
Ade, George,
  supports Bergson's "superiority" theory, 335
adults,
  conception of fun, 3, 10-11;
  their laughter analyzed, 37-39
Adventures in the Alimentary Canal (Chappell), 298, 299
Aeschylus,
  use of tragic irony, 204
Aesop,
  on braggarts, 194-195
Alden, William L.,
  use of satire, 236-237
Alice in Wonderland, 261
  nonsense in, cited, 64
Allen, Fred, 121, 308;
  use of exaggeration, 151-152
Allport, F. H.,
  on child laughter, 37
American humor, 167, 169-178;
  imagination supreme in, 99;
  horseplay vs. verbal tricks in, 122;
  its uniqueness, 165;
  essence of, 165-166;
  rooted in native myth, 167-168, 169;
  exaggeration in, 169-170;
  irony in, 193-194;
  effortlessness of best, 302
American Humor (Rourke), cited, 151, 166-167, 168-169
American Language, The (Mencken), cited, 171
animals,
  play of, 16;
  possible comic sense of, 34-36
Anything Goes, 37
apes,
  their "laughter," 34-35, 36
Aristophanes, 221, 247, 270; his faded jokes, 217-218
Aristotle, 140; definition of the comic, 9, 10, 49, 51
Arno, Peter, 76, 281;
  his style analyzed, 73;
  Robert Benchley eulogizes, 74
Arp, Bill, 284
Asquith, Margot, 206

babies, and their idea of fun, 3, 9-10, 27-28, 49;
  reaction to tickling, 18-19;
  reaction to dissatisfaction, 28-29;
  do not support the "derision" theory, 30-32;
  their sense of humor, 36
Bacon, Peggy, 161
Baer, Bugs, 111, 140
Bain, Alexander,
  on puns, 128
Balzac, Honoré de,
  on child laughter, 37
Barns, Cornelia, 72
Barry, Herbert,
  experiments with jokes, 345-346
Baudelaire, Charles,
  enjoyment of pain in, 100
Bechterev,
  on laughter reflexes, 317
Beerbohm, Max, 161
Bellows, George,
  not essentially a comic artist, 72
"Bells, The" (Poe), 142;
  a serious or comic poem?, 141
Benchley, Robert, 234, 287, 331, 341;
  on the illustrated joke, 73-74;
  on Thurber's drawing, 87;
  puns in, 118;
  use of anticlimax, 139-140;
  rarely labors a point, 299-300, 313
Bergson, Henri, 38;
  theory of "hostility" in laughter, 30, 68, 329, 335;
  refutes own theory by quoting Twain, 66;
  on the "intellectual" appeal of the comic, 291, 292, 294
Bible, 82
Biglow Papers, The (Lowell),
  word distortions in, 132
Billings, Josh, 111, 273, 353;
  as a practical joker, 53;
  a typical gag, 55, 60;
  on twins, 57-58, 59;
  on the poor, 61;

Billings—*Continued*
a "funny picture" by, 76;
poetic vision of, 85;
on "superiority" and laughter, 128;
dialect in, 135;
exemplifies American blend of humor, 174-175;
understatement in, 183;
on lecture strategy, 190;
dated at times, 215-216;
on effortlessness, 301;
makes a sickly pun, 311;
on laughter, 330-331
Biography of a Baby (Shinn),
cited on infantile laughter, 28
Bonaparte, Napoleon,
tragic irony in life of, 209
"Bridge of Sighs, The" (Hood), 140
Bright, John,
on Artemus Ward, 26
Brooks, Van Wyck,
on Mark Twain, 153
Broun, Heywood, 333-335
Brubaker, Howard,
on humor, 333
bullfighting,
funny or not, 26-27
Burdette, Robert J.,
quoted, 139, 234
Burgess, Gelett,
his purple cow, 102;
on varieties of the comic, 339
burlesque,
function of, 159-161
Butterworth, Charles,
his style analyzed, 69
Byron, Lord, 144, 145, 170;
on laughter, 330

Cabell, James Branch, 267
Cagney, James,
on "superiority" theory of laughter, 235
Cantor, Eddie,
his auction-block joke, 42-44;
his autobiography, 50;
in *Kid Millions,* 63-64;
puns in, 126-127;
repartee in, 227;
on laughter, 340
"Care of House Plants, The" (Nye), quoted, 117
caricature,
more creative than parody, 161-162
Carlyle, Thomas, 301
Carritt, E. F.,
on the comic, 345
Carroll, Lewis, 255, 261
cartoons,
as a medium of imaginative humor, 72-74;
defined, 103;
dual appeal of, 105, 107
Century Dictionary, The,
defines irony, 197, 205
Cervantes,
on jests, 330
Chaplin, Charlie, xi, 179, 263, 270, 279, 332;
his style analyzed, 70-71, 90;
on modern humor, 107-108;
on "hostility" in humor, 263;
on truth in humor, 273;
"universal" quality of his humor, 293-294;
defines humor, 331
Chappell, George, 282-283, 298
Charcot, Jean,
finds that Eskimos laugh, 130-131
Chase, Salmon P., 214
Chekhov, Anton,
poetic condensation in, 85
Chesterton, G. K.,
on the origins of nonsense, 174
children,
reaction to the comic, 36-37, 254, 255, 258
Cicero, 322
Clarke, Creston, 111
clowns, 245;
fuse wit and the ludicrous, 50-51
Clubb, Merrel D.,
pleads for an eclectic theory of humor, 354
Cobb, Irvin S., 283;
on funny food, 68;
a simile by, 83;
poetic humor of, 97-98;
gibes at Will Rogers, 226-227;
on the humorous point of view, 337
Cohan, George M., 318
Columbus, Christopher, 177
comic,
defined, 9, 10;
analyzed, 9, 10;
etymology of, 15;
infant reaction to, 36-37;
and pain, 70-71
comic art, ten commandments of, 290-326
comic strips, 93
Connecticut Yankee at King Arthur's Court, A (Twain), quoted, 121, 206, 260-261, 265, 268
conundrums, 310-311
Conway, Jack,
brilliant synecdoche by, 82

Conway, Moncure D., 173
Cook, Joe, 90, 219, 273;
  as a practical joker, 53, 59, 60;
  use of nonsense, 256, 258;
  on surprise as an element in humor, 333
Coolidge, Calvin, 194;
  use of irony, 193
Cornwallis, Marquess, 99
Covarrubias, Miguel, 161;
  exaggeration in, 162
Coward, Noel,
  use of exaggeration, 152
Craven, Frank,
  a pun by, 121, 127
creative evolution,
  function of laughter in, 30
Crile, George W., 349;
  theory of laughter, 23, 345-347
Crockett, Davy, 192;
  evolution of his legend, 166-167
Cuppy, Will,
  a simile by, 83;
  puns in, 116, 117, 126;
  on humor, 338

Dante,
  understatement in, 179
Day, Clarence, Jr., 273;
  quoted, 105
Death in the Afternoon (Hemingway), 204; cited, 81-82
Depew, Chauncey, 301
"derision" theory (Bergson, Ludovici), 30, 33, 87, 263, 296, 329, 341, 350-351, 352;
  not supported by infant reactions, 30-32
  puns refute, 127-129
  not supported by humorists, 234-235
Dickens, Charles, 139, 170, 175, 185;
  poetic humor of, 96-97, 98, 99, 109
Ding, J. N.,
  defines the cartoon, 103
disappointment, as an element of humor, 3, 7-8;
  as element in infant pleasure, 28-29;
  redemption of, a law of comic art, 323-326
discrimination,
  a law of comic art, 303-306
Disney, Walt, xi, 255, 297-298;
  adduces evidence for children's feeling for the comic, 36;
  on laughter, 341
Dreiser, Theodore, 253
Dryden, John,
  on puns, 117
Duck Soup (Marx Brothers), 291
Dumas, Georges, 317;
  on duality of laughter, 38
Duncan, Isadora, 99
Dunne, Finley Peter,
  use of brogue, 133
Dupréel, E.,
  on duality of laughter, 38
Durante, Jimmy, 69, 255

Eastman, Max, 165;
  on annoyance value in comic experience, 51;
  furnished a code for joke-makers, 290;
  on the "superiority" theory, 352
enjoyment,
  conditioning limits, 26-27
Erskine, John,
  on humor, 339
Eskimos,
  excessive laughter of, 130-131
Euripides,
  use of tragic irony, 204
Evarts, W. M., 301
exaggeration,
  hyperbole defined, 150;
  types of humorous, 150-155;
  as a weapon, 156-162;
  in American humor, 169-170

"Facts, The" (Lardner), quoted, 139
Fechner, Theodor, 314
Fichte, Johann Gottlieb, 204
Field, Eugene,
  impersonates Oscar Wilde, 53;
  on an actor, 111;
  verse jingling in, 141;
  exaggeration in, 155
Fields, W. C., 69, 92, 150, 279;
  his most successful act, 91;
  on the psychology of enjoyment, 93-94;
  humanity of his humor, 294-296, 297;
  on pain in humor, 336
figures of speech,
  comic use of, 81-89
First Year, The (Craven), 121
Foch, Ferdinand,
  an artist in words, 81
Folkways (Sumner), cited, 260
Ford, Corey,
  a pun by, 129-130
Forts (Ward),
  cited, 65
Fourth New Yorker Album, cited, 73-74, 287
Franklin, Benjamin,
  on poets, 164
Fratellini, the,
  gruesome humor of, 26

Freedman, David,
on Ed Wynn, 69;
nomenclature of laughs, 182;
on the "gag" business, 270-272;
on humor, 341
Freeman, Mary E. Wilkins, 283
Freud, Sigmund, Part Seven, Chapters VI, VII, and VIII, *passim;*
his "psychic economy" theory of comic pleasure, 23, 61, 250, 251, 253, 260, 262, 263, 269;
on children's lack of feeling for the comic, 36, 254, 258;
on adult inhibition, 37, 249-250, 260;
differentiates between jests and wit, 58, 59
on technique of wit, 60, 265;
inadequate analysis of nonsense, 62, 254, 255
describes humor, 345
Frueh, Al,
his style analyzed, 73, 161-162;
and by himself, 337
funny, meaning of, 15
furtiveness, 267, 268, 269;
key to Freud's theory of enjoyment, 254

Gary, Sid, 255
Gentlemen Prefer Blondes (Loos), quoted, 137
George II of England, 322-323
Gestalt psychology,
pioneering in jocular pattern, 280, 286-287
Gestalt Psychology (Koffka), 280
Goldberg, Rube,
victimized by insurance men, 80;
his cartoons analyzed, 103-105;
on humor, 332
Goldsmith, Oliver, 99
Goodman, Jack, 296;
use of repartee, 228
Gorky, Maxim,
on Lenin, 321
grammar, bad,
as a medium of fun, 138-145
Grant, U. S., 310, 323, 324
Great Apes, The (Yerkes),
cited on laughter, 34-35
Gregg, A.,
on child laughter vs. child feeling for the comic, 38
Gregg, J. Y. T.,
derives laughter from love, 30
Gregory, J. C.,
on "relief" vs. play, 23, 348-349, 350
Gropper, William,
a true comic artist, 72
Gross, Milt,
on Charlie Chaplin, 70-71, 335;
visual imagination of, 80;
effective use of dialect, 133-134
Grundlagen der Aesthetik (Külpe),
on duality of laughter, 38
Guiterman, Arthur,
on a cow, 103;
as a verse juggler, 142

Harris, Joel Chandler,
dialect in, 133
Harrower, A. M.,
and joke patterns, 286
Hays, Will, 226
Hayworth, Donald,
on laughter as relief, 346
Heine, Heinrich, 69, 263, 265;
on laughter, 330
Hemingway, Ernest, 300;
on bullfighting, 26, 27, 204;
poetic choice of, 81-82;
on journalistic urgency, 303
Heraclitus, 109
Herold, Don, 273;
on humor, 335
Herriman, George, 102
"High-Handed Outrage at Utica, The" (Ward), 214
Hilton, A. C.,
parody of Swinburne, 157
Hobbes, John, 330;
theory of "sudden glory," 44
Hollingsworth, H. L., 312
Hood, Thomas, 140
Horne, Harold,
as a joke fancier, 79-80, 112, 270, 271
Horse Feathers (Marx Brothers), 50
How to Tell Your Friends from the Apes (Cuppy), quoted, 116
Howells, W. D., 268;
on Twain, 238
Huckleberry Finn,
vitiated by labored fun, 301-302
humor, classification of kinds of, x;
nature of, xi, 340-341;
four laws of, 3, 21;
as disappointment, 7-8;
and play, 15-16;
pictorial, 72-74;
poetic (*see heading* poetic humor);
satire weapon of, 229-232;
some humorists on, 343
Humor: Its Theory and Technique (Leacock),
quoted, 130, 349-350

Hutchins, R. M.,
reputed use of nonsense, 283-284
Huxley, Aldous, 351
hyperbole, *see* exaggeration

I Wish I'd Said That (Goodman and Rice), cited, 228
ideology,
ironical evolution of the term, 209
imagination,
role in poetic humor, 77, 89
Immigrant, The (Chaplin), 263
"incongruity,"
meaning in the psychology of laughter, 51
"Individual Differences in the Sense of Humor" (Kambouropoulu), 284
Innocents Abroad, The (Twain), 252
instinct,
as an explanatory concept, 29
Instinct as an Explanatory Concept (King), 29
interest, holding the,
as a law of the comic art, 291-294
Introduction to Aesthetics (Fechner), 314
"Irish bulls," 63
irony, 192-201;
various meanings of, 192-193;
in American humor, 193-194;
Socrates' use of, 195-197;
further examples of, 197-201;
Greek development of tragic, 202-204;
of fate, or tragic irony, 202-210
Irony: An Historical Introduction (Thomson), cited, 192
Irwin, Wallace,
uses bad grammar humorously, 140
Is Sex Necessary? (Thurber and White), cited, 87, 256-258

James I of England,
gives the *cachet* to puns, 122
Jeffers, Robinson,
similes by, 83;
and metaphors, 84
Johnson, Alva,
on Charles Butterworth, 69
Johnson, Burgess,
on nonsense, 62
Johnson, Samuel,
theory of the "sudden and unexpected," 44
jokes,
nature of, 10-11, 44;
dual character of, 11;
etymology of, 15;
subject matter of, 25;
serious satisfaction in, 37-38, 102;
provokes two kinds of laughter, 39;
testing comic merit of, 41-42, 44, 246-247;
analysis of a specific joke, 42-44;
the importance of "suddenness" in, 44;
two kinds of, 51-52;
practical, 51-52, 54-61, 268, 306;
"Irish bulls," 63;
wit and the ludicrous fused in best, 109-112;
"degradation," 226-227;
risqué, 248-249, 250, 251, 252, 253;
telling good jokes from bad ones, Part Eight, *passim;*
diagrams of, 279-289;
fundamental forms of, 281-286
Jolson, Al, 309
Joslin,
on therapeutic value of laughter, 24
Journey's End (Sherriff),
understatement in, 188
Joyce, James,
literary tricks in, 100
"Jumping Frog of Calaveras County, The" (Twain),
popularity of, 213-214
Jung, Carl Gustav, 141

Kambouropoulu, P., 284
Kant, Immanuel, on the cause of laughter, 9, 10, 49, 51
on the nihility of laughter, 37
Kid Millions (Cantor), 63-64
kidding, 237
Kimmins, C. W.,
on infantile laughter, 28, 232;
on babies and bumps, 31;
on duality of child laughter, 38;
on ridicule content of laughter, 232
King, Lester S.,
on instinct, 29
Kober, Arthur,
use of dialect, 133
Koffka, K., 280
Kohts, 34
Krapp, George Philip,
on English vs. American slang, 171
Krazy Kat, 102
Külpe, Oswald,
on duality of laughter, 38

Lamb, Charles, 99, 288;
puns in, 116-117
Lamont, Robert, 152
Lang, Andrew, 301
Langtry, Lily,
tragic fate of, 285

Lardner, Ring, 202, 205, 273, 285, 292;
and the intellectual "practical joke," 56, 57, 59;
a metaphor by, 84;
puns in, 118-119, 127;
word distortion in, 135, 137;
humorous Latinity in, 139;
use of fantasy, 169;
understatement in, 182-183;
use of irony, 200-201;
use of sarcasm, 207-208;
on "consolation cup" for Lipton, 216-217;
on matrimony, 224-225;
use of repartee, 228, 230;
use of nonsense, 287-288;
muffs a pun, 311
Latinity, humorous, 139
laughter,
theories of, 9, 10, 22-23, 345-355;
therapeutic value of, 24;
as exercise, 24;
among apes, 34-35;
as an emotional instinct, 35;
analysis of adult, 37-39;
"incongruous" sources of, 51;
objects of, 67-68;
topics of, 213-225;
also see "derision theory"
Laughter: An Essay on the Meaning of the Comic (Bergson), 30
Laurel and Hardy, comic technique of, 318
Leacock, Stephen, 170, 175, 217, 313;
on puns, 130;
on "The Sweet Singer of Michigan," 144
exaggeration in, 155;
as a parodist, 158-159, 161;
on lecture strategy, 190-191;
an ephemeral masterpiece by, 218-219;
on conveying ludicrous impressions, 305, 306;
on the "highest humor," 337-338;
on "fits of laughter" and "relief," 349-350
Lear, Edward,
a nonsense verse, cited, 64
Lenin, V. I.,
fulfills Plato's "Guardian" concept, 321
Lewis, Sinclair,
caricatures of, 162
Life on the Mississippi (Twain), 252;
quoted, 199-200, 265
Life With Father (Day), 273
Lillie, Beatrice, 255;
her style analyzed, 69-70
Lincoln, Abraham, 135, 301, 323;
a simile by, 83;
and a metaphor, 84;
a representative American, 165;
understatement in, 181;
tells a two-track joke, 222;
on laughter, 331
Lipps, Theodor,
theory of laughter, 23, 61
Lipton, Sir Thomas,
a "consolation cup" for, 216-217
Little Book of Necessary Nonsense, The (Johnson), 62
Loos, Anita,
word distortion in, 137;
on compassion in humor, 332
Low, David, 161
Lowell, James Russell,
and verbal distortions, 132
ludicrous,
meaning of, 15, 49;
based on perception, 49-50;
imagination in, 70-71
Ludovici, Anthony M., 352;
theory of derision, 32, 33, 129;
on puns, 128;
theory of "superior adaptation," 350-351
Lullaby Land (Disney), 298

McComas, H. C., 346
McDougall, William,
on play, 16;
on laughter as an instinct, 35;
on laughter as an "antidote to sympathy," 51
McEvoy, J. P.,
on comic strips, 93
MacManus, George,
on comic-strip technique, 335
Man: An Adaptive Mechanism (Crile), cited, 346, 347
Martin, Abe,
on whiskers (ludicrous), 49;
on saving money (wit), 49;
fuses the comic with serious satisfaction, 101
Marx, Chico, 273
Marx, "Groucho," xi, 10, 109, 216, 279, 285, 291, 324;
his style analyzed, 69, 109-110;
on comic "business," 110;
on humor, 336
Marx, Harpo, 90
Marx, Karl,
borrows from Bonaparte, 209
Marx Brothers, 50

Masses, The,
illustrated jokes in, 72, 73, 74
matrimony,
as a topic of laughter, 223-225
Melville, Herman,
use of native myth, 169
Mencken, H. L.,
on English vs. American slang, 171
mental action,
main component of wit, 49-50
metaphors, 84
Mickey Mouse, 230, 332
miosis, *see* understatement
Mitchell, Thomas,
on the serious element in humor, 336
Moore, Julia ("The Sweet Singer of Michigan"), inspires Ogden Nash, 144;
her ingenuousness, 145
Moore, Victor, 37
Mormon Romance (Ward), cited, 274
Mormons,
Artemus Ward on, 26
Morrow, Dwight W., 234
Mr. Dooley (Dunne),
use of brogue in, 133
Mr. Noodle (McEvoy), cited, 93
Munchausen, Baron, 170
Murray, Henry A.,
rationalizes the "derision" theory, 351-352
My Financial Career (Leacock),
dated, 218-219
My Life and Hard Times (Thurber), quoted, 87-89
My Life Is in Your Hands (Cantor), 50

Nasby, Petroleum V., 284, 301, 353
Nash, Ogden, 282;
lines on a cow, 103;
puns in, 115, 120;
analysis of his style, 140, 143, 144, 145
Nathan, George Jean,
on outmoded humor, 219
Nature of Laughter, The (Gregory), cited, 348
neatness,
a law of comic art, 313-317
New Yorker, The, 207, 270;
illustrated jokes in, 74, 181-182
Night at the Opera, A (Marx Brothers), 273
Nock, Albert Jay,
on "moral values" in Ward, 383
nonsense,
two types of, 62;
plausible, 63-66, 262;
Freudian analysis of, 254, 255
exemplified, 256-260
Nonsense Novels (Leacock), quoted, 158-159
Nye, Bill,
a "funny picture" by, 76;
and a metaphor, 84;
puns in, 117-118;
dialect in, 135;
understatement in, 184-185

Œdipus, 203, 204
Of Thee I Sing (Kaufman and Ryskind), 219
Outline of Humor (Wells), cited, 246
"Ozymandias of Egypt" (Shelley), quoted, 78

pain,
as a component of the comic, 70-71
Paradox of the Ludicrous (Seward), cited, 255-256
Parker, Dorothy, 298;
a pun by, 118;
exaggeration in, 155;
use of sarcasm, 206-207, 242;
on the "superiority" theory, 331
parody,
a weapon, savage or mild, 156-157, 158-159;
function of burlesque in, 159-161
Pegler, Westbrook, 303
Penner, Joe, 308
perception,
main component of the ludicrous, 49-50;
refined into imagination, 67-71
Perkins, Eli, 301, 316
Perl, R. E.,
on shared vs. private appreciation of jokes, 68
Phelps, William Lyon, 206
Piaget, Jean,
on infant consciousness, 30-31;
on juvenile laughter, 232
Pickwick Papers, The (Dickens),
quoted, 96-97
pictorial humor, 72-74
Piddington, Ralph,
on the ludicrous, 102
Plato,
use of irony, 195-197;
on laughter, 321
plausibility,
importance of, in nonsense, 63-66;
a law of comic art, 307-309
play,
and humor, 15-16, 27;
of animals, 16

playthings of the moment,
as a topic of laughter, 213-221;
susceptibility to "dating," 217-219
pleasure sources, 59
Poe, Edgar Allan, 87, 140, 174;
possible comic intention in, 141
poetic choice,
defined and exemplified, 81-84
poetic humor, 51, 52, 78-80, 82, 85-87, 101-103, 306;
exemplified and defined, 76-77;
imagination and, 77;
poetry and, 95-96;
various media of, 95-100;
essence of, 100
Popeye the Sailor, 230
Poppy (W. C. Fields), 294-296, 297
pranks, 53-54
Preston-Murdock, J. E.,
on Ward's technique, 318-319
Preyer,
on duality of laughter, 38
Priestley, J. B., 302
Primitive Man As Philosopher (Radin), cited, 232-234
Prince and the Pauper, The (Twain), 238
Problème sociologique du rire, La (Dupréel), 38
"psychic economy" theory of comic pleasure (Lipps, Freud), 23, 61, 250, 251, 253, 260, 262; also read thoroughly Part Seven, Chapters VI, VII, and VIII
Psychology: A Study of Mental Life (Woodworth),
cited, 354-355
Psychology of Humor, The (Wolff and Smith), 59
Psychology of Laughter, The (Piddington), quoted, 102
Psychology of Laughter and the Comic, The (Gregg), 30
Puddinhead Wilson's Calendar, 60-61
Punch, quoted, 127
puns, 110, 111;
atrocious, 115-119;
attitude toward, 116;
defects of, 119;
witty, 120-122;
American resistance to, 122;
poetic, 126-130

Rabelais, François, 171;
compared to Joyce, 100;
exaggeration in, 153-155, 189
Rabelaisianism, 267, 268, 269
Radin, Paul,
on fear of ridicule, 232-234
Rainey, 264, 265
Randolph of Roanoke, John, 229
"Raven, The" (Poe), 141, 142; quoted, 140
Reade, Charles,
on Artemus Ward, 173, 190
repartee, 227-230
rhyme,
effectiveness of, in poetic humor, 95-96
Rice, Albert, 296;
use of repartee, 228
"Rich Man, The" ("F. P. A."), quoted, 95-96
Richter, Jean-Paul Friedrich,
on laughers and laughees, 330
ridicule, 338;
element of, in laughter, 232-235;
self-ridicule, 234
Robinson, Bill,
his style analyzed, 318
Robinson, Boardman, 162
Rogers, Will, 270, 353;
one of his stories quoted and analyzed, 122-125;
proposes "consolation cup" for Lipton, 216, 217;
timeliness of his humor, 219-221;
gibed at by Cobb, 226-227;
sympathetic content of his humor, 338
"Role of Individual Differences in the Sense of Humor, The" (Barry), cited, 345-346
"Romance of the Carpet" (Burdette), quoted, 139
Rourke, Constance, 151, 177;
on the evolution of Davy Crockett lore, 166-167;
on folklore in American literature, 168-169
Ruggles of Red Gap (Harry Leon Wilson), 230

sarcasm, 205-210;
related to tragic irony, 204
satire,
verbal distortion effective in, 137;
defined and exemplified as "humor as a weapon," 229-232;
biting, 236-243
Schlegel, Friedrich von,
identity of art with irony, 204-205
Seaman, Sir Owen,
on parody, 157
Sears, Richard N.,
tests the humor value of jokes, 44, 246, 247;

Sears—*Continued*
and the two-line joke, 286-287
Secret of Laughter, The (Ludovici), 33
Seldes, Gilbert,
on comic strips, 93
sense of humor,
instinctive, 26
Sense of Humor, The (Eastman), 51, 165, 345, 352;
furnished a code for joke-makers, 290
serious satisfaction,
provided by jokes, 37-38, 102, 273;
good measure of, a law of comic art, 319-323
sex,
as the main component of many jokes, 248-249, 250, 251, 252, 253
Shakespeare, William, 82, 170, 171, 301
Shelley, Percy Bysshe,
on transitory fame, 77-78, 79, 85
Shinn, M. W.,
on infantile laughter, 28
similes, 83-84
slapstick, 245-247
Smith, C. E.,
on reactions to jokes, 59
Smith, Sidney,
sums up his own life, 54
"Social Origin and Function of Laughter, The" (Hayworth), cited, 346
Social Psychology (Allport), cited on child laughter, 37
Social Psychology (McDougall),
cited on play, 16
Socrates, 202, 204, 205;
a mouthpiece for Platonic irony, 195-197, 201
Soglow, Otto,
a dubious joke by, 296, 315, 323-324
Sokolovsky, Alexander,
on a laughing gorilla, 35
Song of Solomon, The,
poetic hyperbole in, 150-151
Sophocles,
use of the irony of fate, 203
Spencer, Herbert,
theory of laughter, 23
Springs of Laughter, The (Kimmins), cited, 28
Stanton, Edwin McM., 214
Statistical Analysis of Crowd Laughter (Lange), 110
Stein, Gertrude, 266
Stewart, Donald Ogden, 177, 255;
on humor, 332
Story of a Wonder Man (Lardner), cited, 56, 292
Study of Laughter in Three Year Olds (A. Gregg), 38
Study of Laughter Situations among Young Children, A (Wilson), cited, 232
Study of the Smiling and Laughing of Infants, A (Washburn), cited, 19
subject matter of laughter, *see* topics of laughter
"suddenness,"
an important element in jokes, 44, 51;
a law of comic art, 309-313
Sullivan, Frank,
a simile by, 83;
on "card sharps," 91;
puns in, 118, 127, 136;
use of exaggeration, 149-150;
provides serious satisfaction, 321-322;
on various aspects of humor, 340-341
Sumner, W. G.,
on obscenity, 260;
and delicacy, 261
"Sweet Singer of Michigan, The," *see* Moore, Julia
Swift, Jonathan, 229
Swinburne, A. C.,
parodies himself, 156-157;
parodied by Hilton, 157
Symons, Arthur,
on parody, 157
synecdoche, 82

Tall Stories (Thomas), 166
Tarkington, Booth, 213
Taylor, Bert Leston ("B. L. T."),
paranomasia in, 110
textbooks, methods of writing, ix-x, xi
"Theory of the Ludicrous, A" (Carritt), 345
Thirty Years of Wit (Perkins), 301
Thomas, Lowell, 166
Thomson, J. A. K.,
cites 26 definitions of irony, 192
Thurber, James, xi, 223;
disproves Bergson's "hostility" theory, 87;
his style analyzed, 87, 89;
quoted, 87-89;
his comic drawings analyzed, 105-107, 300;
on funny lines, 120-121;
use of nonsense, 256-258;
on the best humor, 341-343
tickling,
and sex, 18;
psychology of, 18;
and babies, 18-19;

tickling—*Continued*
mental and physical, 20
timing, right,
a law of comic art, 317-319
topics of laughter, Part VII, *passim;*
playthings of the moment, 213-221;
matrimony, 223-225
Traité de Psychologie (Dumas), cited, 317;
on duality of laughter, 38
truth,
its humorous component, 270-276
Twain, Mark, 60-61, 99, 177, 202, 205, 310, 317;
on remembering repulsive things, 21-22;
on human malice, 32;
as a practical joker, 53;
an aphorism by, 56-57, 101;
effectively refutes Bergson's "hostility" theory, 66;
on transitory fame, 78, 79, 85;
a metaphor by, 84;
puns in, 121-122;
exaggeration in, 152-153, 155, 170;
a representative American, 165-166, 174;
understatement in, 180-181, 183-184;
use of irony, 199-200;
use of sarcasm, 206;
beginning of his fame, 213-214;
vast range of his satire, 237-240;
on obscenity, 260-261, 268;
tricks his readers, 265;
on delicacy, 268;
as an orator, 300, 324-326;
essential effortlessness of, 301-302;
on conveying ludicrous impressions, 305, 306, 312;
explains his flop, 308;
on humor, 331

Uncle Remus series (Harris),
dialect in, 133
understatement,
miosis defined, 150;
types of humorous, 179-191;
Wodehouse master of humorous, 185-190;
as a weapon, 192-201 (*also see* irony)
unimpassionedness,
a law of comic art, 298-303
"Unspoken War Prayer" (Twain), 240

Venus de Milo, 152
verbal distortion,
as a medium of fun, 132-137;
in satire, 137
versification, bad,
as a medium of fun, 140-145

Victoria, Queen, 8
Villa, Pancho,
Will Rogers on, 122-124
Virginian, The, 15-16, 19-20
Voltaire,
on laughter, 330

Walker, M. A.,
tests children's reactions to the comic, 36
Walsh, J. J.,
on laughter as exercise, 24
Ward, Artemus, 102, 138, 177, 274, 301, 303, 316;
John Bright on, 26;
on the Mormons, 26, 111;
as a practical joker, 53, 55-56, 59;
his *Forts* cited, 64;
defines the comic, 67-68;
use of dialect, 134-135;
a minstrel of laughter, 171-172;
essence of his style, 173-174, 306;
lecture style, 190, 304;
use of irony, 197-198, 199;
why some Ward jokes have faded, 214-215;
far-fetched, 313-314;
of the difficulties of lecturing, 316;
use of the "slow burn," 318-319
Washburn, Margaret Floy,
tests children's reactions to the comic, 36
Washburn, Ruth W., 54;
on infantile reaction to tickling, 19;
conducts experiments on infantile laughter, 27, 31, 39, 61
Webster, H. T., 335
Wells, Carolyn, 255;
on parody, 157
West, Mae, 179;
her sense of timing, 318;
on ridicule, 338
White, E. B., 223;
on Bergson's "hostility" theory, 68;
cited, 81, 87, 345;
use of nonsense, 256-258, 262;
on humor as truth, 270
Whitman, Walt, 99
Why I Will Not Imitate Four Hawaiians (Cook),
gags in, 55, 256
Wilde, Oscar,
impersonated by Eugene Field, 53
Wilson, Clara O.,
on juvenile laughter, 232
Wilson, Harry Leon,
use of repartee, 230
Wilson, Woodrow, 122; amused, 7-8

Winchell, Walter, 281, 282
Wister, Owen, 15, 19
wit,
essence of, 49;
based on mental action, 49-50;
expository definition of, 54-61;
Freudian view of the technique of, 60;
in puns, 120-125
Wodehouse, P. G.,
a "funny picture" by, 77;
poetic choice of, 82;
an Anglo-American reunionist, 99;
understatement in, 185-190, 201;
use of irony, 198-199;
repartee in, 227-228
Wolfe, James, 322-323
Wolff, H. A.,
on reactions to jokes, 59
Woodward, W. E., 323
Woodworth, R. S.,
on the psychology of laughter, 354-355
Wooster, Hon. Bertie, 82, 185-187
Wortman, Denys, 273;
on laughter, 336
Wynn, Ed,
his style analyzed, 69, 306, 313

Young, Art, 72;
essence of his caricatures, 161;
his first joke, 307;
on the psychology of jokes, 338-339
Young, Roland, 230
Younger Set, The (Chappell), cited, 282-283
"You're the Top," hyperbole in, 151

A Note on the Author

Max Eastman was born in Canandaigua, New York. His father and mother were both ministers. He was graduated from Williams College in 1905, studied and taught philosophy and psychology at Columbia University for four years, published his first and most famous book *Enjoyment of Poetry* in 1913, and at the same time became Editor of *The Masses,* a radical socialist magazine of art and literature. When *The Masses* was suppressed in 1917 for opposing America's entrance into the World War, he founded another magazine *The Liberator,* which he edited until 1922. He then went to Russia, where he spent two years learning the language and studying at first hand the soviet experiment, and the Marxian theories on which it was founded. His important book *Marx and Lenin, the Science of Revolution,* and several other studies resulted, including a biographical portrait of Leon Trotsky and the English translation of Leon Trotsky's *History of the Russian Revolution.* Max Eastman lives in New York, but is known throughout the country as a lecturer on literary, psychological and political subjects.

THE INNER SANCTUM *of*
SIMON *and* SCHUSTER
Publishers, 386 Fourth Avenue, *New York*